CHRIST, CHRISTIANITY, CHURCH

Noel Doyle, SSC

Christ, Christianity, Church

A Study Course for Groups and Individuals

the columba press

First published in 2012 by
the columba press
55A Spruce Avenue, Stillorgan Industrial Park,
Blackrock, Co. Dublin

Cover by Bill Bolger

Origination by The Columba Press
Printed in Ireland by SPRINT-print

ISBN 978 1 85607 791 0

How to use this book

A person can read these books on his/her own. In that case I would advise you to take them slowly and give yourself plenty of time to think about the material in them.

I always consider it is better to study in a group even if it is only three or four people. There is a better atmosphere and people will bring up all kinds of questions and opinions. If you do not have the answers just write down the question or point/problem as it may well come up later. At the end I will suggest a couple of books that you can refer to where you may find an answer, and I am always willing to answer any question sent to me by post. Common sense often provides a good answer and there are certain things we cannot answer, like what will heaven actually be like or can we fully comprehend the meaning of eternity?

It is always good to make notes on the books and emphasise points that appeal to you. A clean book is not the best kind!

I suggest that you start the meeting on time and have it last not longer than 90 minutes. Take holidays during the course at appropriate times when it suites the participants. Some people may feel like chatting afterwards and that is alright.

You will be using your Bible as you go along and like the books it is good to write on it with a pencil. I use the Jerusalem Bible as I like the notes in it and I have been using it for many years. Use whatever Bible you like!

Acknowledgements

First of all I would like to thank my fellow Columban priest, Fr Maurice Hogan STL, LSS, PhD, who was kind enough to read and correct this book for me and made many useful suggestions to me. We worked together in Japan and he then went on to be Professor of Scripture in Maynooth College, and also a member of the Pontifical Biblical Commission who are special advisers to the Pope on Biblical matters.

I also thank the many other Columban priests whom I worked with in Japan and the ideas that I got from them in various discussions we had about evangelisation methods, teaching catechism, Bible study etc.

After baptism, I usually did a year's course with the new Catholics, based on the Bible. I spent over forty years in Japan and this may give a slightly oriental flavour at times but the church is catholic or universal and that may make the books more interesting.

Finally I would like to thank all the Japanese people whom I met, both living and dead, Christian and non-Christian, who taught me so much when I was supposed to be teaching them.

Fr Noel Doyle,
St Columban's College,
Dalgan Park,
Navan,
Co. Meath

Contents

BOOK ONE

BOOK TWO

SESSION ONE

Jesus and His Background

Opening Prayer

This kind of prayer is to be found in Asia, and Jesus was from Asia, and is also found in the Orthodox Church.

I will introduce it in stages:

Sit up in your chair, close your eyes and try to relax. Leave your hands in your lap.

Now I want you to breathe from your stomach. Just forget about your lungs and breath from your stomach. Breath slowly and deeply. If you get distracted just go back to breathing deeply from your stomach. Let any thoughts just pass through your mind. Let them come and go. Do not try to get rid of them. It does not matter whether you breathe through your mouth or your nose. After about five minutes the Leader tells everybody to open their eyes. Stretch or yawn if you feel like it. This breathing technique can be used to help you relax if you are stuck in traffic or you are waiting to give a talk, do a reading etc. We will use it in prayer later.

Introduction

To go into all this we would need first of all to spend a year studying the Old Testament. For just a brief overview, the Old Testament was written under the inspiration of the Holy Spirit. It tells of the creation of the world and of human beings. God gave the world and its maintenance, its environment, and all the creatures that inhabit it into the care of human beings. The sources of the scripture would have been oral and experts come up with different sources. At least four sources are now commonly accepted for the first five books in the Old Testament. There are two accounts of creation at the beginning of Genesis. They follow one another and there is no attempt to combine them. The book of Genesis is usually divided into two parts. The first part before the Patriarchs until after the flood is called *primordial* (existing at or from the beginning) history and ends at the end of Chapter 11. The second part, from Chapter 12 to 50, deals with Patriarchal history and starts with Abram, later called Abraham. Abraham is always seen as the man of faith who believed God's promise to him and left his country to fulfill it.

All was good at the beginning of creation but then humans sinned and lost their happy situation. Yet, God promised them a deliverer. We read of the growth of sin in the world and how that led to all kinds of evil deeds and disasters. God chose Abraham and the people of Israel and made his Covenant with him and them. They were to be his people and he would be their God. He made a promise to them that he would lead them into their own land, and that from them would spring a great leader.

Why did God choose the people of Israel? The answer is a mystery of love. They were a small primitive nomadic people from near present day Baghdad. Abraham and his people arrived in Canaan (Israel) about 1850 BC. From a human point of view it would have been better for God to have chosen the Greeks who were a people of learning or the Romans who would control most of the known world at the time of the birth of Jesus.

Many times the Israelites forgot about God and wandered away on their own selfish paths. When some kind of disaster afflicted them they returned to God and he forgave them. They are unique in their belief in only *one* God. Some six hundred years after the original promise to Abraham they received the Ten Commandments through Moses at Mount Sinai after their escape from Egypt, in what is called the Exodus – sometime between 1250–1230 BC.

They wandered for forty years in the desert before re-entering Israel or Canaan. It was during this journey that they probably developed their identity as a nation; a unique one with a special purpose and a special relationship with the One True God.

1. They were first led by Abraham and his descendants. This is often called the era of the Patriarchs. Jacob, the grandson of Abraham, had twelve sons and from these came the twelve tribes of Israel. Eventually they ended up as slaves in Egypt.
2. Then they were led by Moses from Egypt during the Exodus, followed by Joshua.
3. They had Judges as leaders for some centuries after they entered Canaan and then they demanded a king from God.
3. They got Saul followed by David and Solomon and others. Solomon built the first Temple in Jerusalem. It was here that sacrifices were normally offered. The Temple was very important to the Jews as it was regarded as the dwelling place of God among his people.
4. Divisions in the Monarchy 931–587 BC. The country split in two with Israel in the north and Judah in the south. Israel lasted until 721 BC with the fall of Samaria, and Judah survived until AD 587 with the fall of Jerusalem and exile in Babylon.
5. Exile in Babylon 587–538 BC.
6. When they came back to Jerusalem, they rebuilt the Temple. They refused any help from the Samaritans, who had not gone into exile with the other Jews, and this led to bad relations of which we read about in the life of Jesus. From this time onwards they were under different foreign powers and at the time of the birth of Jesus it was the Romans. Then came the destruction

of Jerusalem and the Temple in AD 70, and in AD 135 after another rebellion had been put down Jews were forbidden to live in Jerusalem. They lost the Promised Land at the time of the Babylonian exile and then lost their spoken language from the time of their exile. Aramaic became the normal spoken language. It was only in 1948 that the State of Israel was once more established and Hebrew introduced as a common spoken language.

The Bible is not written as a modern historian would write it. It was not meant to be a strict history of the Jewish people but of God's plan of creation of the universe, of human beings, especially his Chosen People, of the entrance of evil into the world and of God's plan of salvation. Where we would be concerned in getting facts and then writing a story based on the facts, the scriptures will often tell us a story to give us facts. God made the universe but his exact method of doing that is not mentioned. Evolution is not in the scriptures and these simple nomadic people would not have understood such a concept as evolution. Evolution and the big bang theory start and continue with many questions marks but a scientist will only accept provable facts and the concept of God is not accessible to science. These theories are all right as far as they go, but where did it all come from originally?

Some people may be shocked at the cruelty manifested by the Israelis but such thinking and acting was the norm at that time. Are we any better? All we need to think of is the large numbers killed in modern warfare and the viciousness involved. In one air raid on Tokyo in early March 1945 about 130,000 people were burned to death in one night. Add to this the numbers who died in Stalin's gulag camps, the Nazi attempt to exterminate the Jewish people etc. Nobody is exempt, as we look at the murders and viciousness that happened in the North of Ireland. Old Testament history was written primarily to convey a religious message, not military history.

We also need to be careful when numbers are mentioned in the Old Testament. If there are a large number alleged to be killed in a battle then it was a way of saying that it was a great victory over evil. The number alleged to have been involved in the Exodus may be greatly exaggerated. Oral tradition could also be relied upon to add to numbers.

The Jewish people suffered much discrimination over the centuries but the Second Vatican Council condemned such actions and thinking. The Jewish nation was not responsible for the death of Jesus. They were and still are God's chosen people.

The Catechism of the Catholic Church sums up what is scattered in various Vatican II documents in Article 839:

The relationship of the Church with the Jewish People.
'When she delves into her own mystery, the Church, the People of God in the New Covenant, discovers her link with the Jewish people, the first to hear the word of God. The Jewish faith, unlike other non-Christian

religions, is already a response to God's revelation in the Old Covenant. To the Jews 'belong the sonship, the glory, the covenants, the giving of the law, the worship, and the promises; to them belong the patriarchs, and of their race, according to the flesh, is the Christ (Romans 9:4–5) for the gifts and the call of God are irrevocable.' (Romans 11:29)

Discussion
1. Discuss what you know about Jewish religion, customs, culture, history etc.
2. Anybody have or had a Jewish acquaintance? What is/was the person like?
3. I was once asked by a busy catechumen to recommend a few books from the Old Testament for him to read in order to get a feeling for it. I suggested Genesis, Exodus and Isaiah to him. What would you suggest?

Final Prayer
End with a short prayer like the Our Father and make sure you end on time.

Reflection Isaiah 53:1–9
Who would believe what we have heard,
and to whom has the power of Yahweh been revealed?
Like a sapling he grew up in front of us,
like a root in arid ground.
Without beauty, without majesty (we saw him)
no looks to attract our eyes;
a thing despised and rejected by men,
a man of sorrows and familiar with suffering;
a man to make people screen their faces;
he was despised and we took no account of him.

And yet ours were the sufferings he bore,
ours the sorrows he carried.
But we, we thought of him as somebody punished;
struck by God, and brought low.
Yet he was pierced for our faults,
crushed for our sins.
On him lies a punishment that brings us peace;
and through his wounds we are healed.

We had all gone astray like sheep,
each taking his own way,
and Yahweh burdened him
with the sins of all of us.
Harshly dealt with, he bore it humbly,
he never opened his mouth,
like a lamb that is led to the slaughterhouse;

like a sheep that is dumb before its shearers
never opening its mouth.
By force and by law he was taken;
would anyone plead his cause?
Yes, he was torn away from the land of the living;
for our faults struck down in death.
They gave him a grave with the wicked;
a tomb with the rich,
though he had done no wrong
and there had been no perjury in his mouth.

By his sufferings shall my servant justify many,
taking their faults on himself.

This was probably written around 550 BC.

Homework
Read the next chapter before the next Session and continue that practice in the future.

How We Got the New Testament

Opening Prayer

Sit up in your chair. Breathe from your stomach. Pause for a while.

Now we will start by relaxing different parts of the body. Today we will start with the upper body. Move the muscles of your face and then relax them ... Move and then relax the different parts ... Move the muscles of your face, eyes, neck in turn and then relax them ... Move your shoulders and then relax them ... Then move your hands and relax them ... Move your hands, arms, chest in turn and then relax them ... Gradually relax your upper body but if you are distracted in any way move back to breathing deeply from your stomach ... After about five minutes the Leader tells everybody to open their eyes; stretch and yawn if they like.

Introduction

The New Testament is the greatest source that we have in getting to know Jesus. The Old Testament is also important as it is the background source of the New Testament. So how did they come down to us in the form that we have today? What was the *actual* original script of any text of scripture that we have today? We do not have the original text and it was in a different language. Moreover there were many copies made over the centuries. All the work would have been done by hand and hence liable to mistakes. Jesus would have spoken mainly in Aramaic, but the gospels have been written in Greek, which was the common language of that time.

No manuscript actually written by the author or editor of any book of the Old Testament is extant. No Old Testament writing composed wholly or in part before the Babylonian Exile (587–538 BC) has come down to us or even a fragment written from that early period. According to biblical scholars, writings about the ancient period 250 BC–AD 135 approximately, we have about 190 manuscripts or fragments, and just over 100 of these came from Cave 4 at Qumran near the Dead Sea. The Essenes, who lived at Qumran were wiped out by the Romans in AD 68. Writing was on sheets of papyrus or the skins of animals. The skins were stitched together and much longer lasting. The strips of papyrus were glued together to form scrolls that could be unrolled and read aloud. We read of Jesus doing exactly that in Luke 4:18-23.

From the time of the Babylonian Exile the Jews got used to using Aramaic which was the common language of the Ancient Near East at that time, and later many Jews found Hebrew difficult to understand. Targums in Aramaic came into use. The word targum means a translation from Hebrew to Aramaic, and these came to be used in liturgical worship.

Hebrew and Aramaic are rather alike. They could be compared to Spanish and Italian. Hebrew and Aramaic were written with 22 consonants and no vowels. (If you wish to know the consonants you can look up the Book of Lamentations where they are used to separate the paragraphs.) By the time the Muslim Koran came into existence in the seventh century AD they had added symbols for the vowels. This seems to have started in Syria in the sixth century AD. Sometimes Yahweh is written as YHWH in English.

Another problem was that there was no such thing as footnotes, and hence a scribe copying scripture felt free to embody them in the text or add the result of his own private studies into the text. Along with this, there were no full stops or commas. There were also many manuscripts, limited in the amount that they could cover, that need to be reconciled by experts to find the original text. The experts have many ways to discover the original text, like the shorter version rather the longer one is probably the original, style of writing etc. Moreover to know the context and situation when a manuscript was written helps in deciding the original text. Again the Hebrew and Aramaic and Greek have changed as spoken languages over the centuries, just like the English of Chaucer or Shakespeare. Fundamental doctrines are not affected, and the New Testament is easier than the Old Testament.

The Septuagint or Greek version of the Old Testament came into existence in Alexandria from about 250 BC. Greek was the common language of the Roman empire and many Jews living there and in other places could not understand either Hebrew or Aramaic. (According to the fictitious letter of Aristeas 72 translators were sent from Jerusalem to Alexandria, 6 from each Jewish tribe, to do the translation and they did it in 70 days).

In addition to the fragment texts before AD 100 now available, there are approximately 1,800 extant Septuagint manuscripts of a later period. They are generally divided on the basis of the material used, papyrus or parchment, or the type of alphabet – the way or style it was written.

Papyrus, made in Egypt, came from a tall reed-like plant. The stem was sliced lengthwise into strips that were laid side by side to form a layer and layers were pressed together at right angles to form a sheet. After drying, papyrus made a good, inexpensive writing surface, however it became brittle with age. Papyrus sheets were glued together to form a scroll, which was wound around a stick and constituted a volume. Early in the second century and seemingly because of church use, and to avoid the trouble of unwinding a whole scroll to get at a part that was needed, a book-like format came into frequent use.

Even when they were no longer fit for regular use they were considered sacred and put away in a safe dry place, and hence in some cases have survived. The great discovery of many manuscripts at Qumran near the Dead Sea was only made in 1947 when a shepherd's dog chased a rabbit into a cave.

Parchment or vellum was a more durable, if more expensive, form of writing material. It consisted of a sheepskin scraped and made smooth. The parts were sown together to form a scroll. Its durability made it more important for books designed to be read over and over again, and so we find that the major biblical codices book-like forms, were written on parchment.

The Codex Vaticanus is one of the oldest and best. Even though it lacks a few parts of the scriptures it is in a class by itself and was written in the mid-fourth century. It bears witness to the earliest form of the Septuagint.

Latin Versions

All the early versions of the Old Testament were made from the Greek Septuagint. The exception was that of St Jerome at the end of the fourth and beginning of the fifth centuries. Jerome studied in Rome but spent most of his life living in Jerusalem. His translation is from the Hebrew, and is scholarly and very famous and known as the Latin Vulgate. (The New Testament was of course in Greek from the beginning.)

There were other translations made into other languages like Syrian, Coptic, Ethiopian and Egyptian. This shows how great is the ongoing work of scholars in deciphering these works. A biblical scholar would also need to be able to at least read English, German, French, Spanish and Italian.

Greek New Testament

The New Testament books accepted as canonical were compiled during the first centuries AD. However, the oldest copies available to scholars today are the Great Uncial Codices from the fourth and fifth centuries. (The name Uncial is from the style of writing.)

It is still possible that we may discover other papyrus or parchment fragments that will help us to discover more about the scriptures. Egypt was and still is a good source. The writings of the Fathers of the Church give us forms of the Greek text that they were familiar with and which they quote. They often commented on various texts. They wrote up to AD 700.

English Translations

There are many. The King James or Authorised Version was done in England and the work began in 1607, but much of the work can be traced to earlier editions including a Catholic version done at Rheims in 1582. There are earlier Protestant versions than the King James version but it is the most famous. The Revised Standard Version of 1946–52 in America, is considered to be the best and the most scholarly. It was approved by Cardinal Cushing of Boston and a Catholic edition of it was later released in England with a few minor changes. The Code of Canon Law of 1917 said that it was all right for Catholics to read Protestant versions.

The Catholic *Jerusalem Bible* 1948–54 appeared first in French and was pre-pared by Dominicans in Jerusalem. When the English version came out it was not just a translation from the French, but it was all checked against the original languages. The introductions and footnotes are recognised as very scholarly. It was revised and re-published in 1989. There are many more Catholic, Protestant and Jewish editions of the Bible.

Canon of Scripture
The Catholic canonical books of scripture were first recognised by two local church Councils in North Africa, at Hippo in AD 393 and Carthage in AD 419. St Augustine of Hippo (AD 354–430) had been a strong advocate of recognising these books as he said that 'they were in constant use in the church'. The Coun-cil of Trent (1545–1563) also dealt with the matter by saying that the present canonical books had to be in continuous use over the centuries, which really left the matter open to some extent. The problem here is that some churches like the Coptic Church have books that are not in use in the Latin Church. More-over, Trent went along with the books in the Latin Vulgate of St Jerome. Again they had a problem that took years to sort out, and that was what was the orig-inal version of the Latin Vulgate. At that time, with additions made over the centuries by various transcribers, there were different versions. It is important to remember the difficulties when you translate something into different lan-guages and also the effect of different cultures. (In Japan, we would talk about having 'a running nose' and translated into Japanese the equivalent expression is 'a water nose'.) In Exodus 3:13–15 we read about Moses asking God what is his personal name in order to tell the Israelites who had sent Moses to lead them to freedom. God tells him that his name is YHWH (Yahweh) or 'I am Who am'. As time went on the Israelites were reluctant to use this name and would often instead say the 'God of our fathers'. Also in Hebrew Adonai (Lord) was often used instead of YHWH. In Greek it became Kyrios and Kyrie (eleison) is familiar to us from the early part of the Latin Mass. Now in the English Mass it is Lord (have mercy on us). Lord equals YHWH or Yahweh.

With both Aramaic and Greek in common usage and with also a little Latin it was not unusual for somebody to have two names: Peter or Simon and Paul or Saul etc. The lack of the use of surnames also makes for difficulty in transla-tion and research, but surnames were not necessary for most people at that time. It was a slower moving society and based mainly on agriculture and fish-ing. Peter the carpenter or Peter the silversmith could also identify those limited number of people involved in special trades.

In Judaism, the Canon of Scripture of the Old Testament was not completed until possibly the rivalry spurred by Christian books caused it to be discussed at the Jewish council of Jamnia at the end of the first century, although it may have been towards the end of the second century AD before it was finally closed.

How the New testament was Actually Written

Most people are more interested in the New Testament and so we deal with how it came into existence. We need to split the actual development process into stages.

1. The public life of Jesus when people got to know him from his actions and also from his teachings. This ended around AD 30 with his death and resurrection.

2. The period of *oral* tradition or reporting. In Acts 1:15–26 we read of the election of Matthias to fill the place of Judas who had betrayed Jesus. Peter says: 'We must therefore choose someone who has been with us the whole time that the Lord Jesus was travelling around with us, someone who was with us right from the time when John was baptising until the day when He was taken up from us, and he can act with us as a witness to His Resurrection.' (Acts 1:21–22.) So for many years the message of Jesus and his teaching were passed on by word of mouth. It is impossible to know how many such *oral* accounts were passed on. Different people see and remember different things. The Mother of Jesus and some other women travelled around with Jesus and I would like to think that they had their own female *oral* tradition. Scholars also argue that there was some limited written material produced during this time. As we saw earlier writing, was a slow and difficult process.

3. The first written part of the New Testament was the first letter of St Paul to the Thessalonians during his second journey AD 50–51. The first gospel to be written was that of Mark about AD 66 or even later.

4. It was a long time before the gospels were written and so we need to look in other places to get the full picture and understanding of the teaching of Jesus. Such sources are the early liturgy, prayers and hymns, the writings of the Fathers who often comment on and refer to gospel passages, Creeds, and even church teachings and condemnations. They all help us to get the full picture of the teaching of Jesus. The gospel of John 21:25 tells us:

> There were many other things that Jesus did; if all were written down, the world itself, I suppose, would not hold all the books that would have to written.

It may be a bit exaggerated but there is also a bit of truth in it. Jesus at the Last Supper promised to send the Holy Spirit to guide his church. John 14:15:

> The Advocate, the Holy Spirit, whom the Father will send in my name, will teach you everything, and remind you of all I have said to you.
> Also cf. John 16.

Jesus founded a church that was to teach all people until the end of time. He also gave the church the Holy Spirit to guide it at all times. The church relies on and encourages biblical scholars to study the scriptures. The Church *cannot* teach anything that is opposed to scripture or tradition, but there are many problem areas that neither scripture nor tradition have anything to teach about them. They did not exist in ancient times, like embryo research, nuclear warfare, climate change etc. Catholic biblical scholarship is now recognised as very good and there is much cooperation between Catholic and Protestant scholars.

In the gospels, Jesus only mentions the word church twice, in Matthew 16:18 and 18:17. The church is often mentioned in Acts and the rest of the New Testament. However it is amazing how quickly the church and its structures came into existence after the death and resurrection of Jesus. Churches were set up, centered around the Eucharist, in various places, and the Council of Jerusalem took place in AD 49, but the first writings of the New Testament were Paul's Letters to the Thessalonians in AD 50–51. It was almost forty years after the church was up and running and teaching about Jesus before the first gospel (of Mark) was written.

The Council of Jerusalem AD 49
1. It did not require circumcision as necessary for Gentile converts.
2. It abolished dietary laws for Gentiles.
3. It recognised the so-called Gentile Christian Church which because of numbers soon became the dominant church. Many Christian Jews were not welcome in Jewish places of worship.

Scripture and tradition from the Catechism of the Catholic Church
It was the wish of Jesus before his Ascension that both he and his message would be proclaimed to the ends of the earth. Matthew 28:19–20:

> Go therefore, make disciples of all the nations; baptise them in the name of the Father, and of the Son and of the Holy Spirit; and teach them to observe all the commands I gave you.

So we need to look at how exactly this command was carried out.

1. The Apostolic tradition
Much of this material in the Catechism is quotations from the documents of Vatican II. To indicate that fact I use quotation marks but do not include the source details; they are available in the Catechism.
No. 75. 'Christ the Lord, in whom the entire Revelation of the most high God is summed up, commanded the apostles to preach the gospel, which had been promised beforehand by the prophets, and which he fulfilled in his own person and promulgated with his own lips. In preaching the gospel, they were to communicate the gifts of God to all people. The gospel was to be the source of all saving truth and moral discipline.' (Gospel equals Good News)
In the apostolic preaching:
No. 76. 'In keeping with the Lord's command, the gospel was handed on in two ways, orally by the apostles, by the spoken word of their preaching, by the

example they gave, by the institutions they established, what they themselves had received, whether from the lips of Christ, from his way of life and his works, or whether they had learned it at the prompting of the Holy Spirit in writing by those apostles and other men associated with the apostles who, under the inspiration of the same Holy Spirit, committed the message of salvation to writing.'

Continued in apostolic succession:

No. 77. 'In order that the full and living gospel might always be preserved in the church the apostles left bishops as their successors. They gave them their own position of teaching authority. Indeed, the apostolic preaching, which is expressed in a special way in the inspired books, was to be preserved in a continuous line of succession until the end of time.'

No. 78. 'This living transmission, accomplished in the Holy Spirit, is called tradition, since it is distinct from sacred scripture, though closely connected to it. Through tradition, the church, in her doctrine, life and worship, perpetuates and transmits in every generation all that she herself is; all that she believes.

The sayings of the holy Fathers are a witness to the life-giving presence of this Tradition, showing how its riches are poured out in the practice and life of the church, in her belief and her prayer.'

No. 79. 'The Father's self-communication made through his Word in the Holy Spirit, remains present and active in the church. God who spoke in the past continues to converse with the Spouse of his beloved Son. And the Holy Spirit, through whom the living voice of the gospel rings out in the church, and through her in the world, leads believers to the full truth, and makes the Word of Christ dwell in them in all its richness.'

2. The relationship between tradition and sacred scripture: One common source

No. 80. 'Sacred tradition and sacred scripture, then, are bound closely together, and communicate one with the other. For both of them, flowing out from the same divine wellspring, come together in some fashion to form one thing, and move towards the same goal. Each of them makes present and fruitful in the church the mystery of Christ, who promised to remain with his own always to the close of the age.'

Two sacred modes of transmission

No. 81. 'Sacred scripture is the speech of God as it is put down in writing under the breath of the Holy Spirit. And (holy) tradition transmits in its entirety the word of God which has been entrusted to the apostles by Christ the Lord and the Holy Spirit. It transmits it to the successors of the apostles so that, enlightened by the Spirit of truth, they may faithfully preserve, expound and spread it abroad by their preaching.'

No. 82. 'As a result the church, to whom the transmission and interpretation of revelation is entrusted, does not derive her certainty about all revealed truths from the holy scripture alone. Both scripture and tradition must be accepted and honoured with equal sentiments of devotion and reverence.'

Discussion
1. What new things did you learn about the composition of Scripture? What surprised you in its formation?
2. St Peter was also known as Simon. Did he have any other name?
3. Do you now know the connection between scripture and tradition?
4. Any other points or questions?

Final Prayer
Reflection
Read, reflect upon and pray about scripture and tradition.

   The Catechism of the Catholic Church is a book well worth having. It also has a very good index.

SESSION THREE

Galilee, Nazareth and Palestine at the Time of Jesus

Opening Prayer

Sit up in your chair and close your eyes and relax. Breathe deeply and slowly from the stomach … Today we are going to relax your lower body. Move your feet and then relax them. Feel the ground under your feet. Move up your body and move the parts gently and then relax them. Ankles … shins … knees … upper leg … hips … If you get distracted go back to breathing slowly and deeply … Now relax your tummy … It is usually the most difficult part. After about five minutes the Leader tells everybody to open their eyes, stretch and yawn if they feel like it.

Introduction

To get to know people and to understand them we need to know something about their background and the kind of social scene that they grew up in and lived in. I grew up in the country about four miles outside Mullingar and that experience of country life and a much slower-moving life have influenced me. It was a simple life and everything passed slowly. People had time to talk to one another and the whole cycle of spring, summer, autumn and winter was a clear reflection of life's normal cycle. God and religion were in the air one breathed. I do not have rose-tinted glasses as I look back at it, as it had the many problems of a poor country, but it also had its positives. In contrast with that I have lived most of my life in Japan. I have taken children from the church on summer camps out into the country and they were amazed to see the bright stars or the light of a full moon. Living in big cities you do not really see these fully because of the surrounding lights. They have never seen the first flowers of spring or much of the seasonal changes except on television. Industrial progress has also affected the social life of the people. What in Ireland are called housing estates are usually called bed towns in Japan. People head off each morning in different directions to their places of work and personal communication is greatly reduced. People have little or no interest in their locality and common purposes are few and far between, except maybe the local school. The lack of parks and social amenities in many places make the school grounds the normal focus of sporting facilities.

Nazareth, Galilee and Palestine

Nazareth was a valley open to the south. The village was on the side of a hill facing east and south-east. It was 15 miles (24 km) from the Sea of Galilee, 20 miles (32 km) from the Mediterranean, and about 85 miles (136 km) from Jerusalem. The altitude was about 1,300 feet above sea level. The climate and rainfall were favourable to vegetation, but the village seems to have had only one well which had to be supplemented by cisterns. At the time of Jesus it was a good sized village, secluded and not on any major highway or trade route. The population was probably between 1,600 to 2,000. Houses were made of stone or mud brick and very close together, sometimes two storey.

Palestine was an agricultural country. Its principal crops were wheat and barley. It also produced fruit in abundance: figs, grapes and dates. At the time of Jesus it was a well-forested country. The pasturing of sheep and goats was carried on, and also fishing. The estimated population of Palestine at the time of Jesus is two million.

Galilee

There were many Greeks in the towns, but the countryside was mainly Jewish. Both Aramaic and Greek, the language of the Roman Empire, were in use. Jesus would probably have used Aramaic most of the time. Galilee was blessed with the more fertile soil and with better communications to the outside world, and so with commerce. It was the richest part of the country as a result.

However, both religious and civil power were in Jerusalem. Galilee tended to be the nationalistic part of the country, and the source of revolts against the Romans. Jews always made efforts to maintain their unique and distinctive identity. The Jew was required by law to do business with his own, to marry his own, to enjoy social relations with his own. Any contact with a Gentile could incur ritual impurity. There were basically two classes of people, the rich and the poor. There were very few middle classes.

However any Jew who could validate his ancestry regarded himself socially as the equal of any other. St Paul who was a Pharisee was also a tent maker – Acts 18:3. The employment of the poor was in agriculture, the crafts, husbandry, fishing and unskilled labour. Joseph and Jesus as craftsmen were not on the lowest rung of the economic ladder. In a village like Nazareth they were possibly the only carpenters or woodworkers. They would have made beams for building houses, doors, door frames, lattices for windows. Also pieces of furniture such as beds, tables, stools, lamp or candle stands, boxes and closets for storage. They probably made tools for agriculture like plows and forks. Rent, taxes and tithes were paid in money or in kind. It was based on a census and then farmed out to the highest bidder among the publicans and tax collectors. The publican or tax collector was then free to collect as much as he could above his bid as his profit, and he had the Roman army, or local Jewish leader, to back him up. Collecting money for the Romans was a despised kind of work.

The poverty of the masses was appalling, but not much different from other countries at that time except that Palestine was under the domination of a foreign power which took its share of the wealth of the country. A drought, a war, an insect plague meant slavery or starvation. The sick, the crippled, the aged and the orphan who had no families to support them were at the mercy of an unfeeling society. Beggars were common. Marriages were generally arranged at an early age and took place as soon as the boy / man could support the couple. Life expectancy at the time of Jesus was about forty years. Most children got a chance to learn to read and write through a primitive school system which used the synagogue for a school house.

A poor man would scarcely have more than one set of garments, the tunic which was his normal wear, and a cloak for cold or inclement weather and also used as a blanket for sleeping. The houses of the poor were often shared by more than one family. The house of Jesus had probably two rooms and some kind of workplace or lean-to for Joseph. Work was from dawn to dusk. The food of the poor was very simple. The staples were wheat or barley bread with perhaps some dried fish. Meat was a rare treat. Some milk and cheese were available at times. Add to this some vegetables like leeks, lentils, beans etc., plus some fruit at times. Wine was produced in Palestine and in common use, if one could afford it, but the best wine was exported.

News came from passing travellers. Jewish and Roman money coins were in use. Barter was also common. The Sabbath was a day of rest. It ran from sunset on Friday evening to sunset on Saturday – hence our vigil Masses on Saturday evenings. Prayers in the synagogue in the morning were followed by a very quiet day. The synagogues were normally run by lay people with no priest present. Sacrifices, as time went on, were normally only offered in the Temple in Jerusalem, which devout Jews tried to visit at least three times a year. On the Sabbath there were all kinds of restrictions on what one could do, and it was the opposite of a day of fun and recreation. Jesus had a different interpretation of what the Sabbath should be about and it led to clashes with the authorities.

The Sabbath was made for man, not man for the Sabbath. (Mk 2:27)

(cf. *Catholic Commentary on Holy Scripture*, *Jerome Biblical Commentary*, *A Marginal Jew*, etc.)

Some social groups
In the New Testament we read of special social groups:
Pharisees: Pharisees were the 'separated ones' so named because they tried to avoid all contact with Gentiles, sinners and others less observant of the Law than themselves. They were well-educated and tried to observe all the precepts of the Law. They usually fasted twice a week. They were in some ways the liberals of their time as they were open to accepting oral interpretations, and hence able to adjust to new situations. They were opposed to the Romans but not openly in most cases. They were admirable people in many ways but were

inclined to parade their piety openly at times. Their fundamental religious outlook, rooted in the Old Testament, helped the Jews survive the destruction of Jerusalem. Pope Benedict XVI, in his book *Jesus of Nazareth* on page 13 says:

> The pattern of life practised by the Pharisees found an enduring form in the sort of Judaism shaped by the Mishnah and the Talmud.

(The Talmud is the body of Jewish Law and legend comprising the Mishnah [precepts of the elders] codified about AD 200. Mishnah is the basic text of rabbinical teaching composed around AD 200.)

Sadducees: They represented a priestly and aristocratic movement among the Jews, although there were some priests among the Pharisees. They were materialistic and had no problem dealing with the Romans. They regarded the Pharisees as laity, and resented their interference into religious matters. They were more influenced by Hellenistic (or Greek) thought and culture than the Pharisees. They accepted only the first five books of the Old Testament, namely: Genesis, Exodus, Leviticus, Numbers and Deuteronomy. More secular than the Pharisees and, as the New Testament shows, they did not believe in angels or in a resurrection into another life after death. In Acts 23:6–10 Paul gets his accusers, who were both Pharisees and Sadducees, fighting with each other about these points. The Sadducees disappeared after the destruction of Jerusalem and the Temple in AD 70.

Scribes: Their first duty was to study the scriptures and to try to interpret them. True wisdom consists basically in the Law, and it was their duty to try and elucidate it. They were also interested in oral traditions and approached their work in a prayerful manner.

Essenes: Their documents were discovered by two shepherds in Spring 1947 at Qumran near the Dead Sea. Some translate their name as 'the pure ones'. They may have withdrawn from the regular Jewish community in 152 BC when there was a dispute about the legitimacy of the High Priest. They were a pious group who kept themselves away from worldly things. Some were celibate and there also seem to have been family groups. They amounted to about 400–500 members. Pope Benedict XVI, in his book *Jesus of Nazareth* says on page 14:

> The earnest religiosity of the Qumran writings is moving; it appears that not only John the Baptist but possibly Jesus and his family as well were close to the Qumran community. At any rate, there are numerous points of contact with the Christian message in the Qumran writings. It is a reasonable hypothesis that John the Baptist lived some time in this community and received part of his religious formation from it. They were nationalistic in their outlook and were wiped out by the Romans in AD 68.

Discussion
1. What struck you about the world that Jesus was born into? Any new knowledge or understanding about the life of Jesus?
2. Imagine you were living in Nazareth at the time when Jesus was a child. What would life have been like for you? Make your answers as concrete as possible.
3. Have you ever been in a developing country and seen great poverty? Share your experience.

Final Prayer
Prayer of St Francis

> Lord, make me an instrument of your peace,
> Where there is hatred, let me sow love.
> Where there is injury, pardon.
> Where there is doubt, faith.
> Where there is darkness, light.
> Where there is sadness, joy.
> O Divine Master,
> Grant that I may not seek,
> To be consoled as to console;
> To be understood, as to understand;
> To be loved as to love.
> For it is in giving that we receive;
> It is in pardoning that we are pardoned;
> It is in dying that we are born to eternal life.

Reflection

> *Slow me down, Lord*
> Slow me down, Lord
> Ease the pounding of my heart;
> By the quieting of my mind;
> Steady me with the vision
> Of the eternal reach of time.
> Give me, amid the confusion of my days
> The calmness of the eternal hills.
> Break the tension of my nerves
> With the soothing of the streams.
>
> Help me to know the restoring power
> Of sleep, and teach me
> The art of taking one minute holidays.
> Slow me down to look at a flower;
> To chat with a friend;
> To read a few lines in a book.

Remind me each day,
That there is more to life
Than increasing its speed.

Let me look into the branches
Of the towering trees;
And to know that they grew slowly and well.
Slow me down, Lord
And inspire me to send my roots down into the soil
For life's enduring values;
That I may grow towards the stars of my greater destiny.
Slow me down, Lord.
Slow me down, Lord.
Slow me down …

Homework

From now on, we will be using the Bible a good deal and I would like you to read a short passage each day. If you miss a day or two then read two or three sections the next day. (Also please read the next Session.)

Readings from Luke

Day	1	2	3	4	5	6	7
Chapter	1	1	1	1	1	1	1
Verses	1–4	5–25	26–38	39–45	46–56	57–66	67–80

The gospel of Luke is part of a two-volume work, namely, Luke and Acts of the Apostles. The works of Luke are more in a narrative form than the other synoptics. He wrote a narrative account that is thorough, accurate and in good Greek.

Luke and Acts are attributed to Luke, the companion of Paul. From a study of his work we get the impression that Luke was a gentile convert, well-educated in Hellenistic (Greek) literary techniques. He is a great storyteller and this enables him to make the account of Jesus and the beginning of the church into a coherent, interconnected narrative. His substitution of Greek names for Hebrew ones, his less than adequate knowledge of Palestine geography, customs and practices suggest that he was a non-Palestinian, writing for a largely Gentile–Christian audience, probably in Greece, but one that was sufficiently steeped in the Old Testament to grasp his allusions to it. It was written about AD 80–85.

A general breakdown of the gospel of Luke is as follows:

1. Prologue – dedication to Theophilus.
2. Infancy and boyhood of Jesus.

3. Preparation for public ministry.
4. Ministry in Galilee.
5. Journey to Jerusalem.
6. Ministry in Jerusalem.
7. Last Supper, Passion, Death, Burial.
8. Resurrection Appearances.

It is always helpful to have an oversight of the plan of the gospel that the writer was working with.

Discipleship for Luke is:

1. Jesus is the One who chooses.
2. A true disciple will follow the Master wherever he goes.
3. The disciples will inherit the Master's spirit, who will remain with them, and will be a sign that they are his disciples. (Fr Fuellenbach, SVD) It is too simple to explain the gospels as follows but it can be helpful. Mark tells us who Jesus is, Matthew tells us what he taught, Luke deals with both of these points and shows Jesus' compassion, and John emphasises the divinity of Jesus.

SESSION FOUR

Birth and Early Years of Jesus

Opening Prayer

Do the usual relaxing process. Start with your feet feeling the ground and go up to your tummy ... Then do it from the top of your head to your tummy ... Finally relax your tummy ... If distracted go back to breathing deeply from the tummy ... Now I want you to do something new. As you breathe in, breath in the name Jesus and as you breathe out, breath out the word Love. You do it noiselessly. After five minutes the Leader tells everybody to finish in the usual way.

In the Orthodox prayer the monks wanted to die with the name of Jesus on their lips. Use whatever words you like, for instance, Jesus and Love, Jesus and Mercy, Jesus and God, Father and God, Jesus and Mary and so on.

Introduction

I use the *Jerusalem Bible*. I have been using it for forty years and I have many notes written in it but feel free to use your own Bible of choice.

The Annunciation

In the sixth month the angel Gabriel was sent by God to a town in Galilee called Nazareth, to a virgin betrothed to a man named Joseph, of the house of David; and the virgin's name was Mary. He went in and said to her: 'Rejoice, so highly favoured! The Lord is with you.' She was deeply disturbed by these words, and asked herself what the greeting could mean, but the angel said to her, 'Mary, do not be afraid, you have won God's favour. Listen! You are to conceive and bear a son, and you must name him Jesus. He will be great and will be called the Son of the Most High. The Lord God will give him the throne of his ancestor David; he will rule over the House of Jacob for ever and his reign will have no end.'

Mary said to the angel, 'But how can this come about, since I am a virgin?' 'The Holy Spirit will come upon you,' the angel answered, 'and the power of the Most High will cover you with its shadow. And so the child will be holy and will be called Son of God. Know this too, your kinswoman Elizabeth has, in her old age, herself conceived a son, and she whom people called barren is now in her sixth month, for nothing is impossible to God.' 'I am the handmaid of the Lord,' said Mary, 'let what you have said to me be done to me.' And the angel left her.

It might seem strange to us but arranged marriages were the norm at that time in Palestine. They were normally arranged quite a while before the actual marriage took place. After the betrothal, the bridal pair were considered to be married. After some time, the woman went in a bridal procession to the bridegroom's house. According to the custom of the time, the girl was a wife before she became a bride! Allowing for all this Mary was probably about seventeen years of age when she gave birth to Jesus which would be normal for that time and place. An ancient tradition going back to the first half of the second century tells us that the parents of Mary were called Joachim and Ann. Their feast day is on the 26th of July.

We would like to know more details of who told Joseph of the situation of Mary's pregnancy. We know a little from Matthew 1:18–25. Joseph decided to divorce her informally as he was a man of honour and wanted to spare her publicity. He could have invoked Mosaic law and had her stoned to death. However an angel appeared to him in an dream and said: 'Joseph son of David, do not be afraid to take Mary home as your wife, because she has conceived what is in her by the Holy Spirit. She will give birth to a son and you must name him Jesus, because he is the one who is to save his people from their sins.' (Matthew 1:20–21) Despite this it must have been a very worrying time for Mary as she waited for Joseph's decision.

The Visitation

> Mary set out at this time and went as quickly as she could to a town in the hill country of Judah. She went into Zechariah's house and greeted Elizabeth. Now as soon as Elizabeth heard Mary's greeting, the child leapt in her womb and Elizabeth was filled with the Holy Spirit. She gave a loud cry and said, 'Of all women you are the most blessed, and blessed is the fruit of your womb. Why should I be honoured with a visit of my Lord? For the moment your greeting reached my ears, the child in my womb leapt for joy. Yes, blessed is she who believed that the promise made her by the Lord would be fulfilled.' (Luke 1:39–45)

This was a remarkable journey because Elizabeth lived near Jerusalem. Mary would have needed to find a group going that way and go with them for safety as the journey would have taken about a week. Luke tells us that Mary stayed with Elizabeth for about three months or probably until the birth of John the Baptist. (At the Annunciation the angel had mentioned to Mary that Elizabeth was six months pregnant.) I have been told that this picture of Mary at the Visitation is one of the most common pictures of Mary drawn or painted over the centuries. Of course it is a happy one as the two women share the wonderful news of what God has done for them, and wonder about his plans for the future of humankind. It is also a challenge for us to share the good news of God's love with others.

The Nativity

> Now at this time Caesar Augustus issued a decree for a census of the whole world to be taken. This census, the first, took place while Quirinius was governor of Syria, and everyone went to his own town to be registered. So Joseph set out from the town of Nazareth in Galilee and travelled up to Judaea, to the town of David called Bethlehem, since he was of David's House and line, in order to be registered together with Mary, his betrothed, who was with child. While they were there the time came for her to have her child, and she gave birth to a son, her first-born. She wrapped him in swaddling clothes, and laid him in a manger because there was no room for them in the inn. (Luke 2:1–8)

There were several caves around Bethlehem which were used for stock, and also travellers or shepherds could sleep in them. It would have been fairly primitive conditions for the birth of a child as the most they would have had were a few candles and a fire to boil water. Probably some other women staying around the place helped.

We do not know exactly when Jesus was born but it was probably around the time that we celebrate it. It would have been a quiet time of the year when Joseph and others could take time off from work and travel together to Bethlehem. The feast of Christmas was not celebrated in the church to any great extent until the beginning of the fifth century. Before that the emphasis was on Easter. The Romans celebrated a feast around the 25th to celebrate the return of the sun as the days got a little longer. The Orthodox celebrate Christmas on the 6th of January.

Luke goes on to tell us about an angel of the Lord appearing to some shepherds. (Luke 2:8–20) He tells them to go to Bethlehem: 'Today in the town of David a saviour has been born to you; he is Christ the Lord.' (Luke 2:11) They go and find Mary and Joseph and Jesus and are delighted and start telling people about what has happened and glorifying and praising God. The shepherds as the first people to visit Jesus are very interesting. They were considered to be sinners. Because of their work they could not keep the Sabbath and other Jewish laws.

Next we read in Luke about the circumcision of the child and how he is given the name Jesus. Some days later he is presented in the Temple because every first-born was considered to belong to God. Joseph and Mary made a sacrificial offering of turtledoves or two young pigeons which would be the offering of poor people.

Finally in the Temple we have the prophecy of Simeon: 'You see this child; he is destined for the fall and for the rising of many in Israel; destined to be a sign that is rejected, and a sword will pierce your own soul too, so that the secret thoughts of many may be laid bare.'(Luke 2:33–35)

Then after that, in the Temple a prophetess called Anna came by and as Luke tells us: 'She came by just at that moment and began to praise God; and she spoke of the child to all who looked forward to the deliverance of Jerusalem.' (Luke 2:38)

The visit of the Magi

After Jesus had been born at Bethlehem in Judaea during the reign of King Herod, some wise men came to Jerusalem from the east. 'Where is the infant king of the Jews?' they asked. 'We saw his star as it rose and have come to do him homage.' '… And there in front of them was the star they had seen rising; it went forward and halted over the place where the child was. The sight of the star filled them with delight; and going into the house they saw the child with his mother Mary, and falling to their knees they did him homage. Then, opening their treasures, they offered him gifts of gold, frankincense and myrrh. But they were warned in a dream not to go back to Herod, and returned to their country by a different way.' (Matthew 2:1–12)

a) They are referred to as both Magi and wise men and were probably astrologers. They are the first foreigners to recognise the Lord and, in a religious sense, our ancestors.
b) The text tells us that Mary and Jesus were living in a house and not in a cave, so some time must have passed. Maybe Joseph had decided to settle there as Bethlehem was his ancestral home. When Joseph and the holy family came back from Egypt he seemed to have planned to settle in Judaea but as Matthew tells us: 'When he learned that Archelaus had succeeded his father Herod as ruler of Judaea he was afraid to go there, and being warned in a dream he left for the region of Galilee. There he settled in a town called Nazareth. In this way the words spoken by the prophets were to be fulfilled: 'He will be called a Nazarene.' (Matthew 2:22–23)

The flight into Egypt

To go back a little after the Wise Men left, Joseph was warned in a dream to flee into Egypt as Herod was seeking the child's life. He immediately left for Egypt. Herod by this time had realised that the Wise Men had deceived him, and had not come back to tell him where the child was. He was a tyrant and he had all the male children who were two years old or under in Bethlehem and its surrounding districts killed. Herod was so jealous of his power that he even had members of his own family murdered. Eventually, after the death of Herod, Joseph was told in a dream that it was safe to come back, but as we saw earlier he decided that it was safer to go north from Jerusalem and Bethlehem to Nazareth where he settled down. (cf. Matthew 2:12–23)

Jesus among the doctors of the Law in Jerusalem

When Jesus was twelve years old he went with Mary and Joseph to celebrate the feast of the Passover (Exodus) in Jerusalem. When they left to return home they thought Jesus was with some of his companions in the group, and it was only after a day's journey that they realised that he was not in the party. They hurried back to Jerusalem and after a three-day search they found him in the Temple. He was sitting among the doctors, listening to them, and asking them questions, and all those who heard them were astounded at his intelligence and his replies. We sometimes hear of a child who is a kind of genius, and we would expect the same or more from a child who was the most perfect human being who was ever born. Mary said to him: '"My child, why have you done this to us? See how worried your father and I have been, looking for you." "Why were you looking for me?" he replied, "Did you not know that I must be busy with my Father's affairs?" But they did not understand what he meant.

'He then went down with them to Nazareth and lived under their authority. His mother stored all these things in her heart. And Jesus increased in wisdom, in stature, and in favour with God and men.' (Luke 2:48–52)

Just as a concluding word, Joseph is never mentioned again and so it is generally concluded that he died some time during the hidden years in Nazareth. He is considered the patron of a happy death as he had Mary and Jesus with him at his death.

Discussion

1. What part of the Infancy Narrative appeals to you most?
2. Can you understand why the Visitation has been so popular over the years?
3. Why did Jesus spend so much of his life in Nazareth? There is no answer in scripture and so you must try to come up with some reasons of your own.
4. Is the flight into Egypt a challenge to us as to how we deal with migrants today? There were never so many migrants, both external and internal, in the history of the world as today.

Final Prayer

This prayer of Mary is made up of a series of quotations from the Old Testament.

The Magnificat

My soul proclaims the greatness of the Lord and my spirit exults in God my saviour; because he has looked upon his lowly handmaid. Yes, from this day forward all generations will call me blessed, for the almighty has done great things for me. Holy is his name, and his mercy reaches from age to age for those who fear him. He has shown the power of his arm, he has routed the proud of heart. He has pulled down princes from their thrones and exalted the lowly. The hungry he has filled with good things, the rich sent empty away. He has come to the help of Israel his servant, mindful of his mercy, according to the promise he made to our ancestors, of his mercy to Abraham and to his descendants for ever.

Reflection

The following of the star

As into the skies of Melchior,
Gaspar and Balthasar,
Into the skies of everybody,
There flashes forth a star.

It shone in the eyes of a people,
It stood in a nation's ken,
But the only fools that followed it
Were three Wise Men.

And they rode with the hearts of children,
Till to the walls they came,
First of the Christ's Crusaders,
To the walls of Jerusalem.

And half-roused sleepers wondered,
And village dogs would bark,
To hear the Wise Men's caravan,
Go blundering through the dark.

But never a doubt in Melcior,
In Gaspar or Balthasar,
The ways were wild, but they heeded not,
For their eyes were on the Star.

And they went with the treasures of frankincense;
They went with their myrrh and gold,
While over the feast of their jesting kin,
The mad thing was told.

Yet deeper they plunged in folly,
And heaven and earth seemed lost,
But there marched, unseen, beside them,
God's flame-winged battle host.

And they found their peace and their healing
As they knelt in the stable bare;
And the day would come when their kin in the East
Would curse that they were not there.

As into the skies of Melchior,
Gaspar and Balthasar
Into the lives of you and me
There flashes forth a star.
Fr Patrick O'Connor, SSC

Homework
Readings from Luke

Day	1	2	3	4	5	6	7
Chapter	2	2	2	2	2	3	3
Verses	1–20	21–32	33–40	41–50	51–52	1–6	7–14

Jesus Starts His Public Life

Opening prayer

Do the usual relaxing process.

Some people find it easier to start with their feet and then move to their head and end up with the tummy which is the most difficult and usually has the most tension. Start either with your head or feet as you feel like it. Experiment!

Today I want you to do something new. When you find yourself relaxed, I want you to think of the following words of scripture: 'Jesus left the house and sat by the lakeside.' (Matthew 13:1)

Go and sit beside him. See what he is seeing and hear what he is hearing and so on. In many cases, there is no need for words among friends but maybe at some stage you will feel like saying something or something from him may come into your mind. It can be very interesting what comes up in silence and sitting.

Again two of John the Baptist's disciples had Jesus pointed out to them by John and they followed Jesus. He turned and asked them what they wanted and they asked him where he was staying. He told them to come and see and the scripture tells us that they spent the rest of the day with him. Picture the scene on the banks of the Jordan river; maybe they caught some fish and made a meal. Join them and listen. I do not want to give you any more examples. Pick your own and join in. Talk/listen to Mary at some stage of her life if you like.

There is a story told about St John Vianney, the Curé of Ars – feast day 4 August. There was a man who each evening spent a couple of hours before the Blessed Sacrament praying. St John Vianney asked him what kind of prayers he used and he told him that he did not use any prayers. Instead he said the he just looked at Jesus and Jesus looked at him.

If you use this kind of prayer in private I would suggest that you limit yourself to about 15–20 minutes for some time until you get used to it.

Introduction

There is so much that we would like to know about the life of Jesus in Nazareth but there are no details. However we can say the following with some degree of accuracy:

1. St Joseph died sometime during the hidden life as he is never mentioned after the incident of Jesus getting himself lost in the Temple at the age of twelve.

2. It is possible that sometime during this period Jesus and his family moved from Nazareth. We read in Luke 4:16: 'He came to Nazara where he had been brought up ...' There is an implication here that he could have moved but it is not definite. Nazara is a rare form of Nazareth. Again in John 2:12 after his first miracle at Cana of changing water into wine we read: 'After this he went down to Capernaum with his mother and the brothers, but they stayed there only a few days.' Not definite proof but he must have had somewhere to stay there.

3. Before Jesus started out on his own public life he may have been a disciple of John the Baptist for a short time, or did he just stay with him? John's disciples were not happy when Jesus set up with his disciples. John 3:26–27 tells us about John's disciples complaining to John: 'Rabbi, the man who was with you on the far side of the Jordan, the man to whom you bore witness, is baptising now; and everybody is going to him.'

An interesting footnote to this is found in John 4:1–3 where it says: 'When Jesus heard that the Pharisees had found out that he was making and baptising more disciples than John, though in fact it was his disciples who baptised not Jesus himself, he left Judaea and went back to Galilee.' This shows the difference between the baptism of repentance and purification of that early period, and the sacramental baptism Jesus would establish later.

John the Baptist
We know that he was a relation of Jesus. At the Annunciation the angel told Mary that her kinswoman Elizabeth was six months pregnant, and hence Jesus and John were related in some way. There was a belief among Jews that before the coming of the Messiah, Elijah who had been taken up to heaven in a fiery chariot would come back to earth. (2 Kings 2:1–12) Jesus in Matthew 11:2–15 is full of praise for John and says that he is the one who has taken the place of Elijah. It must have taken some time for John to build up his reputation so that people travelled from all over to hear him. He was a striking man as Matthew describes in 3:4: 'This man John wore a garment made of camel-hair with a leather belt around his waist, and his food was locusts and wild honey.' He was fearless in condemning evil. His advice to people was very down to earth and practical for their state of life. (Luke 3:10–14) Baptism was *not* something unique to John the Baptist. It meant asking God's pardon for past sins, a kind of purification ceremony, and a pledge to do better in the future.

John is the last prophet of the Old Testament era, and we need to keep in mind that the main function of a prophet was to teach the truth, to warn about evil practices, and prepare for the coming of the saviour. He might on occasion foretell something about the future. Isaiah had foretold the function of John the Baptist:

A voice cries in the wilderness;
Prepare the way of the Lord,
make his paths straight.
Every valley will be filled in,
every mountain will be laid low,
winding ways will be straightened
and rough roads made smooth.
And all humankind shall see the salvation of God.
(Isaiah 40:3–5 & Luke 3:5–6)

John was a great person in God's plan of salvation but he missed knowing the depth of God's love as manifested in the life and words of Jesus.

The Baptism of Jesus by John
It was only when Jesus came to be baptised by John that John by some sign from God recognised him as the one he had come to prepare the way for. He was reluctant to baptise him but Jesus persuaded him to do so. There followed the manifestation of the Father and the Holy Spirit. As far as Jesus was concerned there was no need for forgiveness of sin, and I suppose the best way to look at the ceremony was that it was an induction into his public life, a public start to a new way of life for Jesus, and also a gesture of solidarity with sinners on their way back to God.

John does tell us of the difference between his baptism and the one that Jesus would bring in Matthew 3:11: 'I baptise you in water for repentance, but the one who follows me is more powerful than I am, and I am not fit to carry his sandals; he will baptise you with the Holy Spirit and with fire.'

Temptation in the Wilderness
This is an interesting story as it shows us the humanity of Jesus and that he could be tempted as an ordinary human being. Many people are overly-worried about temptations and often consider the temptations to be sins. We will deal with the whole matter of temptation and sin later.

Here there is a story behind the story. We always need to look out for symbols in scripture stories, try and look at it as a Jew of many centuries ago would look at it. The mention of forty days in the desert would immediately remind a Jew of the forty years wandering in the desert with Moses after the Exodus from Egypt. He would be thinking that in Jesus we have a new 'Moses' leading us to the Promised Land. He would be thinking of a new Covenant and new laws. As we will see later this would all happen in the case of Jesus. (cf. Luke 4:1–12)

The Ancestry of Jesus: Luke 3:23–38
As I mentioned earlier in regard to genealogies, that of Luke is interesting in that it starts with Joseph and goes back to Adam who is stated to be a son of

God. Luke makes use of the number seven in his genealogy. There are eleven series of seven names. There are differences between the two genealogies but no definite explanation from scholars. (Matthew also uses a series of sevens.) One of the best explanations that I have come across is that genealogies can be an ancient literary device to span centuries. People then did not expect the precision that we want and expect today. In some ways I prefer the genealogy of Matthew as it mentions three women. Two of them were not very good people while Ruth was an excellent foreign woman. All kinds of people are mentioned in the genealogies and it should help us to accept our own ancestors whether they were good, bad or indifferent.

The Disciples of Jesus

The scripture highlights in a few places John the Baptist, pointing his disciples in the direction of Jesus. It is also clear that others went to Jesus of their own volition, because they probably heard of him and his teaching and miracles or to use the more scriptural word 'signs' for miracles. We also read of Jesus calling certain people to follow him. Men, women and children are mentioned in close proximity to him.

Discussion

1. Compare John and Jesus from the announcements of their conceptions to the death of John the Baptist. Scholars often like to compare the similarities of the announcements of their conceptions, births etc.
2. Did you learn anything new? It is by sharing such ideas that we learn.
3. Any other questions? There is no way that I can possibly cover everything. It is sometimes difficult to accept that neither we nor scholars have all the answers. The church is very dependent on the research of biblical scholars.

Final Prayer

The Benedictus of Zachary the father of John in Luke 1:68–79

Blessed be the Lord, the God of Israel,
for he has visited his people and come to their rescue
and he has raised up for us a power of salvation
in the house of his servant David,
even as he proclaimed,
by the mouth of his holy people from ancient times,
that he would save us from our enemies
and from the hands of all who hate us.
Thus he shows mercy to our ancestors,
thus he remembers his holy covenant,
the oath that he swore to our father Abraham
that he would grant us, free from fear,

to be delivered from the hands of our enemies,
to serve him in holiness and virtue
in his presence, all our days.
And you, little child,
you shall be called Prophet of the Most High,
for you will go before the Lord
to prepare the way for him.
To give his people knowledge of salvation
through the forgiveness of their sins;
thus by the tender mercy of our God
who from on high will bring the rising Sun to visit us,
to give light to those who live in darkness
and the shadow of death,
and to guide our feet into the way of peace.
(*My Memo: This is not ancient history but has meaning today for us*)

Reflection
   The life of this one man
   He was born of a simple virgin in a village of no importance.
   He worked there for some thirty years as a carpenter.
   Then for three years he travelled around and preached.
   He never published a book.
   He never held public office.
   He had no wife, no children, no home.
   He did not go to school.
   He never left his native land.
   He never went far from the place of his birth.
   There was nothing remarkable about him,
   as these things are measured.
   He built no empires, conquered no enemies, led no armies.
   He did not win the independence of his country,
   nor leave behind memorial plaques.
   He had no title beyond his name.
   He became the centre of fierce controversy
   around the age of thirty-three,
   and clashed with the religious authorities.
   He was handed over to his enemies,
   and deserted by every one of his friends.
   He was taken to court and condemned to death.
   He was nailed to a cross between two thieves.
   As he was about to die the soldiers
   who nailed him to the cross cast lots
   for his one remaining possession, his cloak.

After his death his body was placed in the burial crypt
of a sympathetic friend.
Two thousand years have come and gone
since all this happened.
Yet even today he remains the pivotal,
central figure for humankind.
No invasion, no incursions by land or sea,
no navy or parliament, dictator or king
will ever have the influence on human affairs,
of the life of this one man.
(Author unknown)

Homework
Readings from Luke

Day	1	2	3	4	5	6	7
Chapter	3	3	3	3	4	4	4
Verses	15–18	19–20	21–22	23–38	1–13	14–15	16–22

Afterword
It may take some time for you to be able to do so, but I would like you to read
the gospel of Mark. It is the shortest and it should be possible to do it in about
two hours or a little more. It is to give you an overall picture of the life of Jesus.

SESSION SIX

Jesus and the Good News

Opening Prayer
In the name of the Father and of the Son and of the Holy Spirit. Amen.
Come, O Holy Spirit, fill the hearts of your faithful,
and enkindle in them the fire of your love.
V. Send forth your Spirit, and they shall be created.
R. And you shall renew the face of the earth.
Let us Pray. O God, who by the light of the Holy Spirit, did instruct the
hearts of the faithful, grant that in the same Spirit we may be truly wise,
and ever rejoice in his consolation. Through Christ Our Lord. Amen.
(You could use this prayer to start other sessions.)

Introduction
a) The meaning of gospel is Good News. I will deal with various points in regard to the Good News of Jesus, but they are not necessarily in order of importance. One could easily say that Jesus himself is the Good News. Jesus
becoming a human being and taking on our human nature is Good News in itself. It adds a new dignity and value to the lives of each and every one of us.
Teaching catechism over many years in Japan I missed this obvious point for a
long time. In modern terminology when I later studied mass media it would
mean saying the medium is the message.

Much of the hidden life in Nazareth was very ordinary and humdrum but
in the sight of God it was important. It means that any kind of work has meaning in the sight of God. Ordinary, everyday things like meeting and talking to
people have meaning and value.

The God of the Jews in the Old Testament was rather a distant God in Jewish
thinking, even if he had a special regard for, and connection with the Jewish
people. However, God can hardly come closer to us than in a simple child like
the child Jesus or in his simple ordinary adult life. We need to ask ourselves
from time to time if our image of God is that which Jesus showed us from Bethlehem to Nazareth to Jerusalem – by action and by words.

How do I let such an image of God impact on my life? The martyred Archbishop Oscar Romero said: 'Christianity is not a collection of laws to be obeyed,
or prohibitions. That makes it distasteful. Christianity is a person, one who
loved us so much, one who calls for our love. Christianity is Christ.

It is through reading – especially scripture/New Testament/gospels, and
prayer and discussion that we get to know Christ.

b) The things of this world are good and it is right to enjoy them. There is a refrain running through the account of the creation of the world in the first chapter of Genesis. The work of each day is concluded by the words, 'God saw that it was good.'

We read of Jesus being at parties of various kinds. Luke 7:33–34 quotes Jesus: 'For John the Baptist comes, not eating bread, not drinking wine, and you say, "He is possessed." The Son of Man comes, eating and drinking, and you say, "Look, a glutton and a drunkard, a friend of tax collectors and sinners."' Jesus worked to make this world a better place for those who lived around Him. We have a duty and obligation to look after the world around us, namely the environment, society etc., and make sure that we pass something worthwhile on to those who will come after us. Never before in the history of humankind have we had the possibility of destroying the environment and the world in which we live.

Jesus starts his Mission
c) Mark 1:14–15: After John had been arrested, Jesus went into Galilee. There he proclaimed the Good News from God. 'The time has come,' he said, 'and the Kingdom of God is close at hand. Repent, and believe the Good News.'

As I deal with the Good News I bring up different points, but, I repeat, not in order of importance. First of all, very often when we hear the word repent we think of going and doing some penance or fasting or something like that. We can end up looking backwards instead of looking forwards. We may have done something bad in the past, but if we are sorry for it God has already forgiven us. We are all weak human beings and sinners but Jesus did not condemn sinners, he welcomed them into his company. His welcoming of sinners and eating and drinking with them was a continual source of conflict with the authorities. It was one of the factors that would eventually lead to his death. Eating with them showed that they were forgiven. The decision to follow Jesus and his teaching of love is the important factor in repenting. When we think of the meaning of the Good News of Jesus we realise that first of all Jesus spoke of many things, and secondly besides words we need to think of what Jesus did. We need to remember that the Good News is linked to the Paschal Mystery of the death-resurrection of Jesus. There we see the love of God for us manifested. *The Catechism of the Catholic Church* tells us in No. 571: 'The Paschal Mystery of Christ's cross and resurrection stand at the centre of the Good News that the apostles, and the church following them, are to proclaim to the world.'

d) When we think of the Good News that Jesus brought we need to think of the needs of people of his time. What were the hopes and desires of the Jewish and Gentile peoples at that time? We need to ask ourselves about the needs of the people of the world at the present time and how the message and the deeds of Jesus help them to cope in the world of today?

e) In Acts 10:37–43 we read of Peter's address in the house of Cornelius which tells us about the Good News in the early church: 'You must have heard about the recent happenings in Judaea; about Jesus of Nazareth and how he began in Galilee, after John had been preaching baptism.

1. God had anointed him with the Holy Spirit and with power, and because God was with him, Jesus went about doing good and curing all who had fallen into the power of the devil.
2. Now I, and those with me, can witness to everything he did throughout the countryside of Judaea and in Jerusalem itself; and also to the fact that they killed him by hanging him on a tree.
3. Yet three days afterwards, God raised Him to life and allowed Him to be seen, not by the whole people but only by certain witnesses God had chosen beforehand.
4. Now we are those witnesses, we have eaten and drunk with him after his resurrection from the dead, and he has ordered us to proclaim this to his people, and to tell them that God has appointed him to judge everybody, alive or dead.
5. It is to him that all the prophets bear witness; that all who believe in Jesus will have their sins forgiven through his name.'
   (Numbering by me.)

In this passage Peter talks about what he and the other disciples had seen and experienced. He gives a more detailed description in his address to the Jews after the descent of the Holy Spirit at Pentecost in Acts 2:14–41.

f) One of the most basic desires in the human soul is for life and eternal life. Jesus tells Nicodemus in John 3:16: 'Yes, God so loved the world that he gave his only Son, so that everybody who believes in him may not be lost but may have eternal life.' Peter and the other disciples saw their mission as going to people and telling them about Jesus and His teaching, and then baptising them so that they could share in the life of God as adopted children of God. Each one of us, Jew or Gentile, is invited to share in the salvation of Jesus. It took some time and a vision from God to Peter for the early church to realise that the message of Jesus was for all of humankind and not just for the Jews.

Speaking of life, Jesus says in John 10:10: 'I have come that they may have life and have it to the full.' Speaking of the eternal life of heaven Jesus liked to compare it to a great banquet or a great wedding feast. He wanted to give a concrete example that the people of that time could understand. From about two hundred years previously Greek philosophy had brought some hope about life after death into Jewish thinking, but its influence was rather limited. At that time the best that they had from the Old Testament era was some vague hope for a life after death. At the Last Supper when the disciples were sad as Jesus spoke of his imminent departure he told them in John 14:1–4: 'Do not let your hearts be troubled. Trust in God still, and trust in me. There are many rooms in my Father's house; if there were not, I should have told you. I am going now to prepare a place for you, and after I have gone and prepared you a place, I shall return to take you with me; so that where I am you may be too.'

g) Another basic human desire is to be loved and to love. It adds dignity to a person's life, gives it new meaning and as the Japanese would say, it adds colour to an individual's life. To be loved and to love are core values of human life. Jesus came to tell us how much God loved each and every one of us. It was not a general love of human beings but a particular, personal love for each one of us. He told us to call God Abba which is a child's word and which shocked and angered the Jewish elders. We saw how they were not prepared to use Yahweh, the personal name of God given to Moses. To call God Abba or Daddy was not acceptable to them and another reason for their dislike and hatred of Jesus. Isaiah tells us in 49:15–16: 'Does a woman forget her baby at the bosom, or fail to cherish the child of her womb? Yet even if these forget, I will never forget you. See I have branded you on the palm of my hands.' We can enter into a new relationship with God as Jesus told us at the Last Supper in John 15:15:

> I shall not call you servants anymore,
> because a servant does not know
> his master's business.
> I call you friends
> because I have made known to you
> everything that I have heard from the Father.

h) Jesus also spoke of his Good News which would take time to be actualised.
1. A church that would lead and guide people and be a place of fellowship and community.
2. Baptism as entrance into God's new eternal world for us.
3. Forgiveness of sin.
4. Meaning in life and peace of mind.
5. The Mass as the one true way to worship God and Eucharist as spiritual nourishment.
6. A basis for true peace and justice based on love.
7. A true basis for democracy which recognises the importance of each individual as a child of God.

There are more points from the teaching of Jesus that some individual might like to quote. For the Jews it was the coming of the Messiah but sadly most did not recognize him.

Jesus by word and deed taught us that we are accepted, loved and forgiven. We find it hard to accept this unconditional love. We compare divine love with human love where there is often a quid pro quo. We are often hoping in human love, often unconsciously, for something in return. In order to help us understand

God's unconditional love Jesus became man. He lived like us and died like us. He transformed everything when he rose from the dead. We are freed and saved for an eternal destiny of joy and happiness and love. The Good News of Jesus sets us free to accept, to love and to forgive others as God accepts, loves and forgives us. God's power is greater than any weakness that we may have.

Fr John Fuellenbach, SVD, in his book *Throw Fire* writes what he calls a 'credo' or creed for a disciple of Jesus, on page 64:

> I believe in the God of Life who loves me at each moment without any conditions whatsoever, and who wants to see me alive and well. I believe in the God who always forgives me and opens to me a future full of life and hope. I believe in the God who is with me every second of my life to help me, heal me, console me, strengthen me, suffer with me and be my best friend. I believe in the God who only knows love and compassion; who is a lover of life and who begs me to choose life. In this faith I find joy and peace in the present life and hope for the life to come.

Summary
1. We are loved, accepted and forgiven by God.
2. Through faith, we can enter into the life and love of God.

In regard to the Good News, Jesus is both medium and message: The medium, namely Jesus and his life, actions, words, passion, death, resurrection are of vital importance to all of us. Many people spend too much time looking at his teachings rather than looking at the teacher/medium.

At different points in our life various aspects of the life of Jesus, and also different aspects of his teaching, will have a special meaning for us. Hence getting to know Jesus and his teachings are vital for us to have peace of mind, and meaning in our lives.

Medium or message, which do you usually think about? Hopefully both.

Afterword
If someone asks you what is the Good News of Jesus you can simple answer 'God loves me.' It may well take you a whole lifetime to begin to realise the full meaning of those three simple words.

From a human point of view it was a good time for Jesus to start his work. There was relative peace in the known world at that time. Moreover, Greek was widely spoken throughout the Roman Empire and this would facilitate the spread of the gospel/church to other countries.

Discussion
1. What parts of the Good News of Jesus appeal most to you?
2. Any other Good News, besides the above, from the words and actions of Jesus that appeals to you?

3. Why did Jesus spend so much time in Nazareth working as a carpenter while the whole world was waiting for his coming?

Reflection and Final Prayer
Traditional Native American Prayer

O Great spirit
whose voice I hear in the winds,
and whose breath gives life to all the world,
hear me! I am small and weak,
I need your strength and wisdom.
Let me walk in beauty, and make my eyes
ever behold the red and purple sunset.
Make my hands respect
the things you have made,
and my ears sharp to hear your voice.
Make me wise
so that I may understand the things
you have taught my people.
Let me see the lessons
you have hidden in every leaf and rock.
I seek strength, not to be greater than my brother,
but to fight my greatest enemy – myself.
Make me always ready to come to you
with clean hands and straight eyes.
So when life fades, as the fading sunset,
my spirit may come to you without shame.

Homework
Readings from Luke

Day	1	2	3	4	5	6	7
Chapter	4	4	4	4	5	5	5
Verses	25–30	31–37	38–41	42–44	1–11	12–16	17–26

Scripture Memos
1. Many lepers are mentioned. In many cases it was just some skin disease and when it cured the victim showed the clear skin to a priest and was let back into the community. (cf. Luke 10:11-19)
2. Many devil-possessed people are mentioned in scripture. That was how mental disease was seen and described at that time. We even say there is a devil in him/her when a person is in bad humour. The gospels at times clearly distinguish mental illness from devil possession.

3. Furthermore, numbers need to be treated with caution as numbers can have
    special meanings. Also exaggeration can be used to indirectly state some-
    thing was great or big in the sight of the people. For instance Exodus 12:27
    says: 'The sons of Israel left Rameses for Succoth, about six hundred thou-
    sand on the march, all men, not counting their families.' If there had been
    that many Israelites in Egypt they would not have left but would have taken
    over the country. Biblical experts estimate that about five thousand crossed
    the Sea of Reeds in the Exodus.
4. Do not expect our emphasis on exact time, place, numbers etc. to be present.
    It was not part of the culture or writing at that time. Simple fact, nobody
    had watches.

SESSION SEVEN

The Prodigal Son

Opening Prayer
Use one of the previous prayers, use you own prayer or use any prayer that appeals to you.

Introduction
This is one of the most famous parables that Jesus gave us. It is also the worst named parable. Another name like the 'All-Merciful Father' or the 'All-Forgiving Father' would be a much better name for it. However it does tell us a good deal indirectly about our heavenly Father whom Jesus told us to call Abba, Daddy.

This parable, which for convenience I will call the Prodigal Son parable, is found only in Luke 15:11–32. When I did some short studies on mass media the first thing that was emphasised to us was the difference between written and spoken English. If I am writing something I must be careful about writing full and proper sentences. I must make sure the grammar is correct. If I am speaking, I can use half sentences at times or repeat words for emphasis, use gestures etc. When Jesus gave us this parable it was spoken in Aramaic and what we are dealing with is a written form in English. It might seem a small point but it helps us to understand the parable if we keep this background in mind. (Materials found only in Luke are the parables of The Good Samaritan, The Prodigal Son, The Rich Man and Lazarus, The Raising of the Widow's Son, The Healing of the Ten Lepers and The Story of Zacchaeus.) I intend to try and tell this parable as Jesus would have done and explain the background as we go along.

The first thing we need to keep in mind is that his audience would not have been silent. There would have been all kinds of interruptions, of approval or disapproval, questions, suggestions etc. The audience would have participated in the story, like children at a movie shouting to the hero to watch out behind him, or cheering him on.

Luke 15:11ff.: 'He also said, "A man had two sons. The younger said to his father, 'Father, let me have the share of the estate that would come to me.' So the father divided the estate between them."'

At this stage the audience would shout 'Beat him up.' There is no way such a demand would be accepted by a father at that time. It was incomprehensible. A father at that time would have had almost the power of life and death. In Japan the father up to modern times was known as the 'o-yagi' and put in the

same category as fire, typhoons and earthquakes. This lasted up to the second
World War and is a good way of knowing what the situation would have been
like in Israel at the time of Jesus.

Obviously the father was a very gentle and good person and half of the
tenants and workers would not have been happy to come under the domination of the younger son or anybody else, and the audience would have pointed
this out to Jesus. Despite the interruptions Jesus continues the parable.

'A few days later, the younger son got together everything he had and left
for a distant country where he squandered his money on a life of debauchery.
When he had spent it all, the country experienced a severe famine, and now he
began to feel the pinch, so he hired himself out to one of the local inhabitants
who put him on his farm to feed the pigs. And he would willingly have filled
his belly with the husks the pigs were eating but no one offered him anything.'
His so-called friends disappeared when his money ran out.

By this stage the audience would be cheering about the younger son not
having any friends, and also having to look after pigs as such work was considered to defile a person. The fact that he wanted to even eat the food the pigs
were getting was absolutely defiling for a Jew, but as far as Jesus' audience
were concerned it was great news, and their reaction would be to hope that it
would get even worse for him, and they would be expressing such a hope to
Jesus. We need to keep in mind how engrossed they would have been in the
parable story.

'Then he came to his senses and said, "How many of my father's paid servants have more food than they want, and here I am dying of hunger? I will
leave this place and go to my father and say: 'Father, I have sinned against
heaven and against you; I no longer deserve to be called your son; treat me as
one of your paid servants.'" So he left the place and went back to his father.'

The younger son is still very selfish and only thinking of himself. There is
no mention of paying back his father. His audience would soon let Jesus know
that the proposal was not acceptable. If he did go home he should plan to work
as a slave as slavery was normal at that time, and not as a paid servant. No
father would accept the proposal of him being a hired servant and getting paid.
The audience would have been very definite that he should be a slave or get a
job and pay back his father.

'When he was still a long way off, his father saw him and was moved with
pity. He ran to the boy, clasped him in his arms and kissed him tenderly. Then
his son said, "Father, I have sinned against heaven and against you. I no longer
deserve to be called your son." But his father said to his servants, "Quick! Bring
out the best robe and put it on him; put a ring on his finger and sandals on his
feet. Bring the calf we have been fattening, and kill it; we are going to have a
feast, a celebration, because this son of mine was dead, and has come back to
life; he was lost and is found." And they began to celebrate.'

Shouts from the audience of 'No, No, No, No way, Send him away etc.' His father's conduct was unbelievable to them. The father was obviously waiting and hoping for his return and keeping a watch for him. The son was probably walking very slowly as he lost courage, and became fearful about the kind of reception he would get. The father did not even give him time for an apology but called for a new robe and sandals for him. The father then did two very significant things.

First, he put a ring on his finger. This gave him back his previous status and power in his father's house. In all my years in Japan, my registered seal was all-important for signing documents. In a marriage ceremony the bridal pair would sign their names, but they would also put their seals on the marriage document. The second significant thing that the father did was to put on a special feast to celebrate the return of the younger son. It meant that all was forgiven and he was welcome back. A meal does not have the same deep significance for us that it had for people of that time and place. All the time the audience would have been saying to Jesus that they did not believe what they were hearing. Jesus was probably well used to hearing such things as he had to put up with complaints of eating with sinners and tax collectors.

'Now the elder son was out in the fields, and on his way back, as he drew near the house, he could hear music and dancing. Calling one of the servants he asked him what it was all about. "Your brother has come," replied the servant, "and your father has killed the calf we had fattened because he has got him back safe and sound." He was angry then and refused to go in, and his father came out to plead with him, but he answered his father: "Look, all these years I have slaved for you and never once disobeyed your orders, yet you never offered me so much as a kid to celebrate with my friends. But, for this son of yours, when he comes back after swallowing up your property, he and his women, you kill the calf you had been fattening."'

I think that we are inclined to feel some sympathy with the elder son and agree with his viewpoint. This shows that God's way of thinking is different from ours. When he refused to go in, his conduct would have lost him sympathy with the onlookers. However, when the father came out to plead with him to go in he would completely lose the sympathy of the crowd. There would have been shouts of 'Disown him' and 'I don't believe it.' The father, by coming out to plead with him, meant that he was losing face and authority in a way that was not believable or acceptable at that time and place.

The father said, 'My son, you are with me always and all I have is yours. But it is only right that we should celebrate and rejoice, because your brother here was dead and has come to life; he was lost and is found.'

This shows us God's way of thinking and not our human one. It is interesting to note that the elder son refers to this son of yours, whereas the father refers to your brother here.

Fr John Fuellenbach, SVD tells the following interesting story:

On the island of Bali, a local well-known dancing group presented the parable of the Prodigal Son to a native audience composed of Christians, Buddhists and Muslims. Instead of presenting the biblical story as recorded in the Bible, they altered the parable in an unusual way. When the Prodigal Son approached his father's house the servants see him coming, and they run to meet him. However, it is not to greet him or welcome him. They start mocking him, making fun of his wretchedness and then beat him up badly. The father watches all this from afar without interfering. Only when the servants have done their part does he step in and declare it to be enough.

This is rather different from the story in the Bible, and I pointed this out to my confrere, who was the producer of the play, and also that this did not convey the message of the Parable. He replied, 'The native people would not have understood the story without such an addition. There was no way to make it clear to them that the younger son could go free from punishment after his episode into disgrace and sin. If we play the story as recorded in the Bible the people would feel offended that this might become a pattern for dealing with a wayward son. If God was not prepared to deal properly with the son and punish him, they would do it for God.'

Discussion
1. Did you find it useful to look at the spoken word and consider the reaction of the listeners?
2. Compare God's reaction as Abba and an ordinary father's reaction.
3. Any other questions?

Final Prayer
From now onwards use any prayer that you like but I would suggest Intercessory Prayers like in the Mass before the Offertory. Anybody can make them up. Start with 'Father in heaven,' or 'Lord Jesus …' or whatever you like. End with 'Lord hear us' and the response could be 'Lord graciously hear us.'

Reflection
Courage to accept acceptance
All human beings crave to be accepted as they are.
A human life without acceptance is a life
in which a most basic need goes unfilled.
Acceptance means that I am welcome to be myself.
I am not locked into my past or present.
Acceptance liberates everything that is in me.

Only when I am loved in that deep sense of complete acceptance can I
become myself.
When a person is loved for what he/she *does*,
he/she is not unique.
When a person is accepted and loved for what he/she *is*,
then he/she becomes unique and an irreplaceable personality.
I am accepted by God as I am,
as I am, and not as I should be.
God is a friend who knows everything about me and still accepts me.

1 John 4:10: 'This is the love that I mean: not our love for God but God's love
for us.' We have love but God *is* love. His love is not an activity but his whole
self. Paul Tillich (Lutheran theologian 1866–1965) defines faith as the courage
to accept acceptance. Self-acceptance is like an act of faith. When God loves and
accepts me, I must do the same. I cannot be more demanding on myself than
God. What do you want? An illusion of yourself that you can only admire or
hate or the reality of yourself that you can only love? Life is not a problem to
be solved, a question to be answered. Life is a mystery to be contemplated,
wondered at and savoured.

Homework

Readings from Luke

Day	1	2	3	4	5	6	7
Chapter	5	5	6	6	6	6	6
Verses	27–32	33–39	1–11	12–19	20–26	27–35	36–38

Scripture Memos
1. When you read a parable try to imagine the reaction of the crowd. It could
   be very simple like 'Good' or 'Well said.'
2. In the story of the Good Samaritan, which is only in Luke (10:29–37), a priest
   and a Levite passed by on the other side of the road and ignored the man
   who had fallen into the hands of brigands. The probable reason is that he
   was covered in blood or they thought him to be dead. According to the Law,
   to touch him would defile them and they would need a purification ceremony. They put the Law ahead of pity and love and ignored him.
3. Matthew, Mark and Luke are known as the synoptic gospels. This means
   that because of the extensive agreement of their material they can be put in
   parallel columns for the sake of comparison. This kind of arrangement is
   called a synopsis.
4. The gospel of Luke that we are reading at present starts and finishes in
   Jerusalem. It starts in the Temple and ends at Bethany just outside Jerusalem.

SESSION EIGHT

The Kingdom of God

Opening Prayer
Use one of the previous prayers, use your own prayer or use any prayer that appeals to you.

Introduction
After John had been arrested, Jesus went into Galilee. There he proclaimed the Good News. 'The time has come,' he said, 'the Kingdom of God is close at hand. Repent and believe the Good News.' (Mark 1:14–15) With these words the kingdom broke into history.

Previously we dealt with the Good News and now we will deal with the kingdom of God. We often do not think much about it even if we pray regularly for it in the Lord's Prayer: 'Thy Kingdom come …' As you will find out, it is not that easy to define it or get a good understanding of it but Jesus spoke a great deal about it.

Jesus uses the phrase 92 times and it appears in other places in the scriptures. The problem is that Jesus never defined it. Sometimes it is translated as the kingdom of God, other times as the kingdom of heaven or the reign of God or simply as the kingdom. You can also get the impression that Jesus himself is the kingdom. It is all of these and more. (See especially Matthew 13 and Mark 4.) We also have concepts like life, glory, joy and light to describe it. We have the parable of the sower of seed that falls on different kinds of ground with different results. Again there is the parable of the enemy sowing darnel among the good seed. Also the mustard seed, the yeast, the treasure hidden in the field, the merchant selling all that he has to buy a pearl of great price, the dragnet thrown into the sea that brings in all kinds of fish, the parable of the lamp, the parable of how a man uses a measure, as he measures his reward will be measured to him (Luke 6:38), how a seed in the ground grows in a secret way both day and night, that the kingdom of God is open to sinners and all people, and so on. Jesus also tells Nicodemus that he cannot enter the kingdom of God unless he is born again of water and the Holy Spirit. The kingdom of God can be close at hand (see opening quotation), here present or in the future.

Of the many parables that Jesus used to explain the kingdom of God, my personal favourite is probably the parable of the mustard seeds as related in Luke 13:18–19: 'He went on to say, "What is the kingdom of God like? What shall I compare it with? It is like a mustard seed that a man took and threw into his garden: it grew and became a tree, and the birds of the air sheltered in its branches."'

As Jesus wonders what to compare the kingdom of God with he almost seems to be frustrated. I like the parable of the Mustard Seed because it has a beginning, death of the seed leading to life, life and growth and it can change and adapt to its environment. It has a past, a present and a future. The kingdom of God is still growing like the mustard seed even when it is not obvious. There is, as Fr Fuellenbach says, an already and not yet part in it. What we have now guarantees the future full growth.

The Catechism of the Catholic Church tells us about the start of the kingdom in Nos 541–542. Mark 1:14–15 tells us how Jesus started off his mission on earth. 'The time is fulfilled, and the kingdom of God is at hand, repent and believe the Good News.' To carry out the will of the Father, Christ inaugurated the kingdom of God on earth (*Lumen Gentium* or *Dogmatic Constitution on the Church*, No. 3.). Now the Father is to raise up a people to share in his own Life (*Lumen Gentium* 2). He does this by gathering people around his Son Jesus Christ. This gathering is the church on earth, the seed and beginning of the kingdom (*Lumen Gentium* 3).

Christ stands at the heart of this gathering of people into the family of God. By His word, through signs (miracles) that manifest the reign of God, and by sending out his disciples, Jesus calls all people to come around him. But above all in the great Paschal Mystery, his death on the cross and his resurrection, he would accomplish the coming of the kingdom. 'And I, when I am lifted up from the earth, will draw all people to myself' (John 12:32). Into this union with Christ all people are called. (*Lumen Gentium* 5)

The Catechism of the Catholic Church in Nos 554 and 556 states that the transfiguration was a foretaste of the kingdom. The transfiguration gives us a foretaste of Christ's glorious coming, when he will change our lowly bodies to be like his glorious body. (Philippians 3:21)

Fr Fuellenbach gives us a good idea of what the values of the kingdom should be in his book *Throw Fire*, pp. 193–218. He quotes St Paul's definition of the kingdom in Romans 14:17: 'After all, the kingdom of God is not a matter of whether you get what you like to eat or drink, but the kingdom of God is a matter of justice, peace and joy in the Holy Spirit.'

(*Justice* = right relations or life-giving relationships with God, Oneself, Others and Creation. *Peace* = a reality wherever justice reigns. The opposite of Shalom in Hebrew is not war but injustice. *Joy* = means life. It means an expression of fullness of life and love.)

Fuellenbach explains these three terms in their full biblical meaning, and stretches the meaning of the words as far as possible to include integrity of creation etc. I do not think that in his time St Paul knew much about or worried about the integrity of creation. I think that St Paul did not intend the kingdom of God to be limited to these three things, but meant them more as primary examples. Jesus spoke a great deal of love, hope, peace in its various forms, e.g.

peace of mind, compassion, gentleness, empathy, fellowship, sharing, trust in God, forgiveness, living a God-entered life etc. Anything that would make our world more human and imbued with a sense of the presence and purpose of God for it and for us would advance the kingdom of God.

Here on earth we live in the kingdom of God but it has not arrived in its fullness and we are called to help its advance. It is in the small things that we do in our immediate locality of family, friends, church, work and so on that we help to make the kingdom of God a reality that will only reach its fullness at the end of time. At present we can find comfort in it, but it is also a challenge to us to work for it. We are also linked through the kingdom with those outside the church who share kingdom values with us, and who through those values are linked to God and to us.

We should also remember that the church is temporal and will cease at the end of time, but the kingdom of God is eternal. It is because of this eternal, heavenly quality that I am satisfied with glimpses and experiences of the king-dom here on earth. Jesus often compared heaven to a banquet or a wedding feast, and he also practised table fellowship with all kinds of people. These things are inadequate to describe heaven but give us a glimpse. St Paul tells us: 'No eye has seen and no ear has heard, things beyond the mind of man, all that God has prepared for those who love him.' (1 Corinthians 2:9) Jesus told us that God was our all-loving, all-forgiving, all-understanding Abba Father who is always on our side, leading us to his kingdom. As children of such a Father we are encouraged and comforted at all times, but it does not mean that we can understand the greatness of our destiny in the kingdom of God, but can only glimpse it in a limited way, maybe sometimes more clearly than others.

Different people will find comfort in varying aspects of the kingdom, and also find themselves challenged by different aspects according to their situation in life. The most important thing in regard to the kingdom of God is the central message of the gospel or the Good News of Jesus that God is Abba Daddy God and that he is always on our side forgiving, helping, encouraging us as we travel on our way to the eternal kingdom that he has prepared for us. It is both a challenge and a consolation.

Every time we pray the Our Father we are praying 'Thy Kingdom come' and that prayer means that we are praying for the coming of the kingdom both now and at the end of time. To know more about what is involved it is helpful to read Jesus' Sermon on the Mount in Matthew 5:1–7, 29. We will be studying that shortly.

Pope John Paul II in *Redemptoris Missio* No. 18 says: 'The Kingdom of God is not a concept, a doctrine or a programme subject to free interpretation, but before else a Person with the face and name of Jesus of Nazareth, the image of the invisible God. If the kingdom is separated from God, it is no longer the kingdom of God which he revealed.'

This could also mean that a person might know little or nothing about Jesus but still be imbued with kingdom values. Through those kingdom values in some way he/she knows Jesus. We cannot set limits to the workings of God among non-Christians.

Some Closing Remarks

1. The Kingdom of God is a free gift from God. In Mark 10:15 Jesus says: 'I tell you solemnly, anyone who does not welcome the kingdom of God like a little child will never enter it.'
2. The building of the kingdom of God is always a task or challenge for all of us as well as a gift. God has put himself in the weak position of needing people to carry out his tasks. The kingdom can only become a reality with human assistance. (Parable of the Talents, Matthew 25:14–30.)
3. We should enjoy the kingdom in our Eucharistic celebration or sharing in God's word. Jesus often enjoyed the kingdom in table sharing. The Eucharist is an opportunity for us to share the kingdom in joy, companionship, praise, thanksgiving, mutual support etc.
4. We should not get depressed as the kingdom is growing all the time. At one place it may be like the seed in the ground and in another place it may be the slowly growing mustard tree.
5. The kingdom is wider than the church and is aimed at all of humankind.
6. The first part of God's plan is to make us all his children. The second part of His plan is that we all share in fellowship with others as brothers and sisters.

I am consoled that the coming of the kingdom does not depend on my/our achievements, but it still remains basically the work of our loving Father.

Fr Fuellenbach quotes a definition of the Kingdom from Fr E. Schillebeeckx, another prominent theologian, in the latter's book, *Church the Human Story of God*:

> *The kingdon of God* is the saving presence of God, active and encouraging, as it is affirmed or welcomed among men and women. It is a saving presence offered by God and freely accepted by men and women which takes concrete form above all in justice and peaceful relationships among individuals and peoples, in the disappearance of sickness, injustice and oppression, and in the restoration of life of all that was dead or dying.
>
> *The kingdom of God* is a new world in which suffering is abolished, a world of completely whole or healed men and women in society where peace reigns and there are no master–slave relationships, quite a different situation from that of the society of this time. In Luke 22:25–27 Jesus tells us: 'Among pagans it is the kings who lord it over them, and those who have authority over them are given the title Benefactor. This must not happen with you. No; the greatest among you must behave as if he were the youngest, the leader as the one who serves.'

The *kingdom of God* is a changed new relationship (*metanoia*) of men and women with God, the tangible and visible side of which is a new type of liberating relationship among men and women with a reconciling society, in a peaceful natural environment.

Discussion
1. Since Jesus spoke so often about the kingdom of God we need to get some ideas about it that we could work on individually or with others. Discuss.
2. List some priorities and possible solutions for the progress of the kingdom of God in your locality.
3. What appeals to you in the kingdom of God present and future?

Final Prayer
Whatever you wish. You might use the prayer in the Reflection.

Reflection
A Prayer of Archbishop Oscar Romero
It helps now and then to step back and take the long view.
The kingdom is not only beyond our efforts,
It is even beyond our vision.
We accomplish in our lifetime only a tiny fraction
of the magnificent enterprise of God's work.
Nothing we do is complete, which is another way of saying
that the kingdom always lies beyond us.
No statement says all that could be said.
No prayer fully expresses our faith.
No confession brings perfection.
No pastoral visit brings wholeness.
No programme accomplishes the church's mission.
No set of goals and objectives includes everything.

This is what we are about:
We plant the seeds that one day will grow.
We water the seeds already planted,
knowing that they hold future promise.
We lay foundations that will need further development.
We provide yeast that produces effects,
far beyond our capabilities.
We cannot do everything,
and there is a sense of liberation in realising that.
This enables us to do something and do it very well.
It may be incomplete, but it is a beginning,
a step along the way,
an opportunity for the Lord's grace to enter and do the rest.

We may never see the end results, but there is a difference
between the master builder and the worker.
We are workers, not master builders,
ministers, not messiahs.
We are prophets of a future not our own. Amen.

A succinct definition of the kingdom is: The kingdom is a vision of reality, creation, God and humankind, of God bringing about his purpose in history that Jesus came to communicate.

Homework
Readings from Luke

Day	1	2	3	4	5	6	7
Chapter	6	6	7	7	7	7	7
Verses	39–45	46–49	1–10	11–17	18–30	31–35	36–50

The Sermon on the Mount: Part I

Use one of the previous prayers, use your own prayer or use any prayer that appeals to you.

Introduction

I am going to use the account of the Sermon on the Mount in Matthew 5:1–7, 27 rather than Luke's, because I prefer it. There are many parallels between the two accounts. I will also give the text according to my *Jerusalem Bible*. In a group there can be different Bibles and slightly different translations, and there is no point in arguing/discussing trivialities.

I would suggest that in a group somebody read the scripture section and then pause for any comments. Of course the members of the group should have read it before the Session. I have inserted 'any comments?' in several places which would be a good place to pause.

Matthew 5:1–2: 'Seeing the crowds, he went up the hill. There he sat down and was joined by his disciples. Then he began to speak. This is what he taught them:'

This is a description of a solemn setting for important teachings which may not all have been delivered on this one occasion. It is possible that much of it was repeated on many occasions with new people in attendance. Jesus would have had to repeat and explain many times what he had previously said. The mention of Jesus going up the hill is very significant. For the Jews they would immediately think of Moses getting the Ten Commandments on Mount Sinai and also the Old Covenant. (Luke for some unknown reason has the talk on level ground. He also eliminates passages referring to Jewish laws and practices which would not be of interest to his non-Jewish readers.)

According to the notes in my *Jerusalem Bible* there are five main subjects dealt with in this discourse and which deals with the spirit of the new kingdom:

1. The spirit that should animate the children of the kingdom. (Mt 5:3–48)
2. The spirit in which they are to fulfill the laws and practices of Judaism. (Mt 6:1–18)
3. Detachment from riches. (Mt 6:19–34)
4. Relations with one's neighbour. (Mt 7:1–12)
5. The decisive act of choice that must be made, and the practical consequences that must be accepted, in order to enter the kingdom. (Mt 7:13–27)

I am going to follow these five sections as it makes the message of Jesus clearer in regard to the kingdom of God, and also his other teachings.

The spirit that should animate the children of the Kingdom (Mt 5:3–12)
a) The Beatitudes

How happy are the poor in spirit:
theirs is the kingdom of heaven.
Happy the gentle:
they shall have the earth for their heritage.
Happy those who mourn:
they shall be comforted.
Happy those who hunger and thirst for what is right:
they shall be satisfied.
Happy the pure in heart:
they shall see God.
Happy the peacemakers:
they shall be called children of God.
Happy those who are persecuted in the cause of right:
theirs is the kingdom of heaven.
Happy are you when people abuse you and persecute you and speak all
kinds of calumny against you falsely on my account. Rejoice and be glad,
for your reward will be great in heaven; this is how they persecuted the
prophets before you.

Sometimes 'happy' is translated in the Old Testament as 'blessed'. In regard to
the poor in spirit, many scholars say that it needs to be taken literally. In the
society that Jesus lived in most people were poor. There were the rich and a
very small middle class. Moreover, Jewish thinking was also a problem as the
rich were considered to be blessed by God. That is why the disciples were
shocked when Jesus said: 'It is easier for a camel to pass through the eye of a
needle than for a rich man to enter the kingdom of God.' (Mt 19:24) Riches and
power are what are usually admired in this world of ours. We have just done
the kingdom of God and we need to remember it is both here on earth and also
in heaven.

These Beatitudes are a challenge for all of us. As I mentioned earlier, try to
imagine the reaction of the crowd when they heard them from Jesus. Another
point to remember is that 'Happy are you when people abuse …' is not a ninth
Beatitude. It identifies Jesus with the Law and his followers with the prophets
of old. Maintaining good relations with Jesus is a good moral thing and the
only thing that really matters.

Any comments about the Beatitudes?

b) Salt of the earth and light of the world (Mt 5:13–16)
'You are the salt of the earth. But if salt becomes tasteless, what can make it
salty again? It is good for nothing, and can only be thrown out to be trampled
underfoot by men.'

'You are the light of the world. A city built on a hill-top cannot be hidden. No one lights a lamp to put it under a tub; they put it on the lamp-stand where it shines for everyone in the house. In the same way your light must shine in the sight of people, so that, seeing your good works, they may give the praise to your Father in heaven.'

These are two simple examples of what a disciple of Jesus should be like. They may have lost some of their original power because of the kind of world that we live in. For the people of that time salt was a necessary part of their diet and not readily available. Our problem is avoiding taking too much salt. A common way of getting salt then was to flood some low-lying land with seawater and then after the water had evaporated to collect the salt. If there was a salt mine available that made it much easier. Salt preserved food and kept people alive. Again we take light for granted, but it was different for people who were dependent on home-made candles or perhaps an oil lamp. It is worth thinking of the difference a light makes in a room. Not only does it give light but it removes fear and also gives a feeling of warmth to the room. Children of the kingdom are called to bring light and warmth to others. I mentioned before to think of the reaction of the listeners. Probably someone said: 'Teacher, well said.' Another may have asked: 'Teacher, how do I become the salt of the earth or the light of the world?'

Any comments?

c) The fulfillment of the law (Mt 5:17–19)

'Do not imagine that I have come to abolish the Law or the Prophets. I have come not to abolish but to complete them. I tell you solemnly, till heaven and earth disappear, not one dot, not one little stroke, shall disappear from the Law until its purpose is achieved. Therefore, the person who infringes even one of the least commandments and teaches others to do the same will be considered the least in the kingdom of heaven; but the person who keeps them and teaches them will be considered great in the kingdom of heaven.'

The difficult words here are at the beginning when Jesus says that he has not come to abolish the Law or the Prophets, these two are usually linked together. The Law had a great value for the Jewish people, and when we remember that Matthew's gospel was written up to fifty years after the death–resurrection of Jesus for Jewish people we realise the amount of discussion that took place before the actual writing of the gospel. We also must remember that the Law for the Jews was the summary of all wisdom and directly connected to God. From the Ten Commandments of Moses they had developed 613 precepts. They made a distinction between serious and light precepts. Jesus did not put the same weight on the Law as the Jewish elders did. He did not seem concerned when his disciples did not keep the Levitical laws on cleanliness – washing their hands. Moreover we have the incident when His disciples were reprimanded for rubbing corn in their hands on the Sabbath and eating the corn.

Jesus said: 'The Sabbath was made for man and not man for the Sabbath.' (Mark 2:23–28) How do we reconcile Jesus' actions and words with his words here: 'I have come not to abolish but to complete them.' *The Jerome Biblical Commentary* suggests that a better translation for 'complete' would be 'perfect them'. The Law will not pass until it has been finished and perfected by the Messianic work of Jesus. It is probably better to look at it as a continuum rather than an ending and a new start. We also need to remember that Matthew was writing for Jewish Christians, and another point worth remembering is that we should keep both the letter and the spirit of the Law in mind.

The righteousness of the disciples of Jesus must exceed the righteousness of the scribes and Pharisees; it is a submission to the will of God that goes beyond the observance of the Law.

What this departure from the Law means is illustrated in the following six examples (5:20–48). Paul also speaks of a righteousness of the Law that is not true righteousness and does not save; but true righteousness is achieved through faith in Jesus Christ (Romans 3:20; 10:3; Galatians 2:26; 3:21).

Any comments?

d) The new standard higher than the old (Mt 5:20–48)
We are still reading about the spirit that should animate the children of the kingdom. 'For I tell you that if your virtue goes no deeper than that of the scribes and Pharisees, you will never get into the kingdom of heaven.'

1. You have learnt how it was said to your ancestors: 'You must not kill: and if anyone does kill he must answer for it before the court. But I say to you anyone who is angry with his brother will answer for it before the court; and if a man calls his brother "Fool" he will answer for it before the Sanhedrin; and if a man calls him "Renegade" he will answer for it in hell fire. So then if you are bringing your offering to the altar and there remember that your brother has something against you, leave your offering there before the altar, go and be reconciled with your brother first, and then come back and present your offering. Come to terms with your opponent in good time while you are on the way to the court with him, or he may hand you over to the judge and the judge to the officer, and you will be thrown in prison. I tell you solemnly, you will not get out till you have paid the last penny.'
2. 'You have learnt how it was said: You must not commit adultery. But I say this to you; if a man looks at a woman lustfully, he has already committed adultery with her in his heart. If your right eye should cause you to sin, tear it out and throw it away; for it will do you less harm to lose one part of you than to have your whole body thrown into hell. And if your right hand should cause you to sin, cut it off and throw it away; for it will do you less harm to lose one part of your body than have your whole body go to hell.'

This shows us that we have to make choices for God that will involve effort and sacrifice.

3. 'It has also been said: Anyone who divorces his wife must give her a writ of dismissal. But I say this to you: everyone who divorces his wife, except for the case of fornication, makes her an adulteress; and anyone who marries a divorced woman commits adultery.'

    The mention of divorce as alright in the case of fornication is very unclear and generally questioned. In Mark 10:11–12 and Luke 16:18, Jesus clearly condemns and forbids divorce. The best explanation that I have found is that even in Deuteronomy the reasons for divorce in the Old Testament era were unclear, and that in this particular case there is a problem with the Greek, and that instead of 'fornication' the word should be 'concubinage' which would make it clear. This makes more sense as the children of the kingdom are called to higher standards. (*Jerome Biblical Commentary*) Moreover, a married person would commit adultery and not fornication.

4. 'Again, you have learnt how it was said to your ancestors: You must not break your oath, but must fulfill your oath to the Lord. But I say this to you: do not swear at all, either by heaven, since that is God's throne; or by the earth, since that is his footstool; or by Jerusalem, since that is the city of the great king. Do not swear by your own head either since you cannot turn a single hair white or black. All you need say is 'yes' if you mean yes, 'no' if you mean no; anything more than this comes from the evil one.'

5. You have learnt how it was said: 'Eye for eye and tooth for tooth. But I say this to you: offer the wicked man no resistance. On the contrary, if anyone hits you on the right cheek, offer him the other as well; if a man takes you to law and would have your tunic, let him have your cloak as well. And if anyone orders you to go a mile, go two miles with him. Give to anyone who asks, and if anybody wants to borrow, do not turn away.'

    We are forbidden to return evil for evil as in the first verse which quotes the Jewish law of *talio*. Christ does not forbid us to resist unjust attack or to fight for the elimination of injustice.

6. 'You have learnt how it was said: You must love your neighbour and hate your enemy. But I say to you: love your enemies and pray for those who persecute you; in this way you will be children of your Father in heaven, for he causes his sun to rise on bad people as well as good, and his rain to fall on honest and dishonest people alike. For if you love those who love you, what right have you to claim any credit? Even the tax collectors do as much, do they not? And if you save your greetings for your brothers, are you doing anything exceptional? Even the pagans do as much, do they not? You must therefore be perfect just as your heavenly Father is perfect.'

    The 'hate your enemy' words are too strong in comparison to the original version in the Law. Any comments on these six points? There was a chance to comment in places along the way but someone may like to make a general comment.

Discussion
It can be in regard to any point of the material here or elsewhere.

Final Prayer
I would suggest the Our Father, but use whatever you like.

Reflection
Hero Worship
I know of a princely Hero
who has set my heart aflame:
I cherish the thought of his glory,
And love the sound of his name.

Pure and splendidly winning,
He casts a wondrous spell,
And the lure of his perfect goodness
Is a thing no tongue can tell.

He comes of a royal lineage,
There is none so royal as he,
And thronged with his battle-legions
Are the fields of eternity.

He is mightier than the mighty,
He had lit the blazing stars,
He cages the wrath of the tempest
Within his will's strong bars.

Yet tender is he, and child-like,
No gentle grace he lacks;
He would not break the bruised reed,
Nor quench the smoking flax. (Mt 12:30)

He had seen the grief of my sickness,
And my burden of poverty,
And had leapt from the throne of his kingdom
To offer himself for me.

He has borne the weight of my sorrow,
He hath made him lowly and poor;
He had prayed and toiled and suffered,
And made my peace secure.

And he went from the hearth of his mother,
To die upon a tree,
For me and for mine, who are dust and clay,
And yet a King was he.

And when his deeds are counted
Thus did the people tell:
'He spoke as no man ever spoke,'
And 'He did all things well.'

Oh, I thought that I could serve him blindly,
Could watch like a dog at his door,
Aye, from the blaze of a thousand swords,
So he be honoured more.

But the days came when I struck him,
And wounded him bloodily,
Ah Christ! You are goodness infinite,
For still you bore with me.

Oh, He is my hero of heros,
Whom I worship and confess,
From the earthly depths of my weakness,
From the slough of my sinfulness.

Pure-souled, generous, kingly,
Splendidly winning is he,
With the lure of his perfect goodness,
With his grand divinity.
Fr Patrick O'Connor SSC

Homework
Readings from Luke

Day	1	2	3	4	5	6	7
Chapter	8	8	8	8	8	8	9
Verses	1–8	9–15	16–21	22–23	26–39	40–56	1–9

SESSION TEN

The Sermon on the Mount: Part II

The spirit in which they are to fulfill the laws and practices of Judaism (Mt 6:1–18)

a) Almsgiving in Secret (Mt 6:1–4)
'Be careful not to parade your good deeds before people to attract their notice; by doing this you will lose all reward from your Father in heaven. So when you give alms, do not have it trumpeted before you; this is what the hypocrites do in the synagogues and in the streets to win peoples admiration. I tell you solemnly, they have had their reward. But when you give alms, your left hand must not know what your right hand is doing; your almsgiving must be secret, and your Father who sees all that is done in secret will reward you.'

Blowing a trumpet before giving out alms was literally true at times. Almsgiving was regarded as a very laudable practice, of course there was no social welfare at that time.

b) Prayer in secret (Mt 6:5–6)
'And when you pray, do not imitate the hypocrites: they love to say their prayers standing up in the synagogue and at street corners for people to see them. I tell you solemnly, they have had their reward. But when you pray, go to your private room and, when you have shut your door, pray to your Father who is in that secret place, and your Father who sees all that is done in secret will reward you.'

It might be worth reading the parable of the Pharisee and the Tax Collector in Luke 18:9–14. The Tax Collector was the one who went away justified.

c) How to pray. The Lord's Prayer (Mt 6:7–15)
'In your prayers do not babble as the pagans do, for they think that by using many words they will make themselves heard. Do not be like them; your Father knows what you need before you ask him. So you should pray like this:

Our Father in heaven,
may your name be held holy,
your kingdom come,
your will be done,
on earth as in heaven.
Give us today our daily bread.
And forgive us our debts,
as we have forgiven those who are in debt to us.
And do not put us to the test,
but save us from the evil one.

Yes, if you forgive others their failings, your heavenly Father will forgive you yours; but if you do not forgive others, your Father will not forgive your failings either.'

I am not going to do a write-up on the Our Father but it is worth a little discussion. Note how the first part is directed towards God, and the second part towards other people. Note also God's condition for forgiving us in the last part.

Any comments?

d) Fasting in secret (Mt 6:16–18)
'When you fast do not put on a gloomy look like the hypocrites do: they pull long faces to let people know they are fasting. I tell you solemnly, they have had their reward. But when you fast, put oil on your head and wash your face, so that no one will know you are fasting except your Father who sees all that is done in secret; and your Father who sees all that is done in secret will reward you.'

Continues the theme of doing things for God and not for public admiration. Any comments/discussion?

Detachment from riches (Mt 6:19–34)

a) True treasures (Mt 6:19–21)
'Do not store up treasures for yourselves on earth, where moths and wood-worm destroy them, and thieves can break in and steal. But store up treasures for yourselves in heaven, where neither moth nor woodworm destroy them and thieves cannot break in and steal. For where your treasure is, there will your heart be also.'

The last sentence really sums it all up as it asks us where our priorities really lie? How would you place your priorities? After a major back operation and two serious eye operations, I would place health at the top of my priorities.

b) The eye, the lamp of the body (Mt 6:22–23)
'The lamp of the body is the eye. It follows that if your eye is sound your whole body will be filled with light. But if your eye is diseased, your whole body will be all darkness. If then, the light inside you is darkness, what darkness that will be.'

The knowledge that influences us often comes through our eyes as well as our ears. We also see reality through our eyes.

c) God and money (Mt 6:24)
'No one can be the slave of two masters; he will either hate the first and love the second or treat the first with respect and the second with scorn. You cannot be the slave both of God and money.'

There is a common theme here that the true disciple cannot have a divided loyalty.

d) Trust in Providence (Mt 6:25–34)

'That is why I am telling you not to worry about your life and what you are to eat, nor about your body, and how you are to clothe it. Surely life means more than food, and the body more than clothing. Look at the birds in the sky. They do not sow or reap or gather into barns; yet your heavenly Father feeds them. Are you not worth more than they are? Can any of you, for all your worrying, add one single cubit to your span of life? And why worry about clothing? Think of the flowers growing in the field; they neither have to work or spin; yet I assure you that not even Solomon in all his regalia was robed like one of these. Now if that is how God clothes the grass in the field which is there today and thrown into the furnace tomorrow, will he not much more look after you, you people of little faith? So do not worry; do not say, 'What are we to eat? What are we to drink? How are we to be clothed?' It is the pagans who set their hearts on all these things. Your heavenly Father knows that you need them all. Set your hearts on his kingdom first, and on his righteousness, and all these things will be given you as well. So do not worry about tomorrow: tomorrow will take care of itself. Each day has enough trouble of its own.'

I have always liked this passage dealing with trust in God. It is very simple and down to earth and colourful. Jesus was addressing hard-working people and he was not suggesting that they stop working but his emphasis was on trusting in God for the ultimately important things in their lives. Related to this it would be wrong for people to stop saving and planning for the future as the economy would collapse. We have to give time to both God and worldly things. How we balance these two in our life is important for a true disciple. In regard to the 'cubit' mentioned, the metaphor seems to be mixed as a cubit is a measurement of about 18–20 inches. We are inclined to worry too much about the future and we do not know if we will be alive tomorrow. Jesus ends with a nice statement, 'Each day has enough trouble of its own' and leave the past and the future to take care of themselves. It is worth comparing this with what Jesus has to say in Luke 12:22–32 on the same theme. Also Luke 12:18–23 where we have the parable of the rich man who built bigger barns to store his grain and when he had done so he died.

Any comment on this section which deals with trust in God. Who is a rich person? Where do you spend most of your thinking time – past, present or future?

Relations with one's neighbour (Mt 7:1–12)

a) Do not judge (Mt 7:1–5)

'Do not judge; and you will not be judged; because the judgements you give are the judgements you will get, and the amount you measure out is the amount you will be given. Why do you observe the splinter in your brother's eye and never notice the plank in your own? How dare you say to your brother, "Let me take the splinter out of your eye", when all the time there is a plank in your own? Hypocrite! Take the plank out of your own eye first, and then you will see clearly enough to take the splinter out of your brother's eye.'

Some people say that this whole Chapter 7 is a series of scattered sayings of Jesus that could have been uttered on different occasions. To judge is to take a harsh critical attitude about another person or their actions. It is a well-known fact that what irritates us most in others is our own faults that they display. It is like looking in a mirror at ourselves.

b) Do not profane sacred things (Mt 7:6)

'Do not give to dogs what is holy; and do not throw your pearls in front of pigs, or they may trample them and then turn on you and tear you to pieces.' Dogs should not be given meat that has been offered in sacrifice. Similarly sacred teaching of great worth must not be put before those who, incapable of receiving it with profit, may even abuse it. (cf. *Jerusalem Bible*) *The Jerome Commentary* says that it may refer to the Scribes and Pharisees who would be inclined to attack anybody proclaiming the gospel.

c) Effective prayer (Mt 7:7–11)

'Ask, and it will be given to you; search, and you will find; knock, and the door will be opened to you. For the one who asks receives; the one who searches always finds; the one who knocks will always have the door opened to him. Is there a man among you who would hand his son a stone when he asked for bread? Or would hand him a snake when he asked for a fish? If you, then, who are evil, know how to give your children what is good, how much more will your Father in heaven give good things to those who ask him?'

This is about prayer and since many of our prayers are prayers of petition we are encouraged to continue with such prayers by the use of the threefold approach of ask-receive, search-find, knock-opened. Basically we are encouraged to pray no matter how bleak things may be. The second part encourages us to think of God as our Father in heaven and his friendly disposition towards us at all times. We always face the problem of judging God by human attitudes rather than by God's way of acting.

d) The Golden rule (Mt 7:12)

'So always treat others as you would like them to treat you; that is the meaning of the Law and the Prophets.'

This has always been recognised as an essential part of Christianity. Sometimes we might say, 'Love God with all your heart and soul and mind and others as you love yourself.' I have always liked what the Rabbi Hillel is supposed to have told a pupil, 'That which displeases you do not do to another. That is the whole law. The rest is commentary.' As in Matthew's quotation the Law and the Prophets are very often linked together in scripture.

Any comments on dealing with other people?

The decisive act of choice must be made – and the practical consequences must be accepted – in order to enter the kingdom.

a) The two ways (Mt 7:13–14)

'Enter by the narrow gate, since the road that leads to perdition is wide and spacious, and many take it; but it is a narrow gate and a hard road that leads to life, and only a few find it.'

This same saying in Luke is given in answer to the question as to whether many get to heaven – Luke 13:22–30. There it is said that many Gentiles may get into heaven before many Jews. What it does point out to us is that we are challenged to choose God and life, and that the following of that choice may not be easy at times. Greek word for 'spacious' is obscure but this translation is probably correct. (*Jerusalem Bible*)

b) False prophets (Mt 7:15–20)

'Beware of false prophets who come to you disguised as sheep but underneath are ravenous wolves. You will be able to tell them by their fruits. Can people pick grapes from thorns, or figs from thistles? In the same way, a sound tree produces good fruit but a rotten tree bad fruit. A sound tree cannot bear bad fruit, nor a rotten tree good fruit. Any tree that does not produce good fruit is cut down and thrown on the fire. I repeat, you will be able to tell them by their fruits.'

There is no shortage of false prophets around in our time and they are experts in using the mass media. They can be found both outside and inside the church. It always surprises me the way people can be swept up by some new devotion or so-called message. Jesus gives us the litmus test for all such people: 'You will be able to tell them by their fruits.'

c) The true disciple (Mt 7:21–27)

'It is not those who say to me, "Lord, Lord, who will enter the kingdom of heaven", but the person who does the will of my Father in heaven. When the day comes many will say to me, "Lord, Lord, did we not prophesy in your name, cast out demons in your name, work many miracles in your name?" Then I shall tell them to their faces: "I have never known you; away from me, you evil people!"

Therefore, everyone who listens to these words of mine and acts on them will be like a sensible man who built his house on rock. Rain came down, floods rose, gales blew and hurled themselves against that house, and it did not fall: it was founded on rock. But everyone who listens to these words of mine and does not act on them will be like a stupid man who built his house on sand. Rain came down, floods rose, gales blew and struck that house, and it fell; and what a fall it had.'

'When the day comes' in the second sentence means the day of the final judgement. The simple story about the two types of houses is a challenge to us to make sure that our relationship to God, church and others is on a solid foundation.

Conclusion: the amazement of the crowd (Mt 7:28–29)
'Jesus had now finished what he wanted to say, and his teaching made a deep impression on the people because he taught them with authority, and not like their own scribes.' Their own scribes would be quoting Rabbi A or Rabbi B but Jesus did not quote any of these authorities in support of what he was saying. It came directly from him on a take it or leave it basis.

Discussion
The Sermon on the Mount is not a complete code of Christian ethics or teachings. The sermon is a statement of those principles that Matthew and his collaborators considered basic for a Christian, and they do give us a good picture of the teachings of Jesus.

Final Prayer
Try out some general prayers from individuals with the ending 'Lord hear me' and the response 'Lord graciously hear us' just like before the Offertory of the Mass. They could be about the contents of the session, for sick people, peace etc. Prayers could be of petition or thanks or anything at all … Wait for some one to start or the Leader could start it all off … People should pray about things that concern them or the world/society that they live in. Just starting is the hard part.

Finish: We ask these prayers through Christ Our Lord. Amen.

Reflection
   A Psalm of life
   Art is long and Time is fleeting.
   And our hearts, though stout and brave,
   Still, like muffled drums, are beating,
   Funeral marches to the grave.

   In the world's broad field of battle,
   In the bivouac of Life,
   Be not dumb driven cattle!
   Be a hero in the strife!

   Trust no Future, however pleasant!
   Let the dead Past bury its dead!
   Act – act in the living Present!
   Hear within, and God o'erhead.

Lives of great men all remind us,
We can make our lives sublime,
And, departing leave behind us,
Footprints on the sands of time.

Footprints, that perhaps another,
Sailing o'er life's solemn main,
A forlorn and shipwrecked brother,
Seeing, shall take heart again.

Let us, then, be up and doing,
With a heart for any fate,
Still achieving. Still pursuing,
Learn to labour and to wait.
Henry Wadsworth Longfellow

Scripture Memos

1. The Temple in Jerusalem at the time of Jesus was a very big building measuring about 300 yards by 450 yards. Occasionally you can see a small remaining part of it on television in the Wailing Wall. It was split into three sections and the middle section was the most sacred. It was built after the Babylonian exile and as time went on it was only here that sacrifices were generally offered to God.
2. It had special meaning for the Jewish people because it was here that they believed that God resided among his people.

Jesus Meets People

Use any opening prayer that you like or wish to use.

Introduction

A person can say all kinds of inspiring things but the real test is how he/she treats other people. To go back to the beginning, Jesus, because he was truly human, had to learn things like the rest of us. As the most perfect human being ever born it may have been easier for him. He had to learn to read and write in the simple Jewish education system that used the synagogues. Many would not have been able to read and write very well, if at all. But Jesus read in the synagogue from a scroll of the prophet Isaiah:

> The spirit of the Lord has been given to me,
> for he has anointed me.
> He has sent me to bring the Good News to the poor,
> to proclaim liberty to captives
> and to the blind new sight,
> to set the downtrodden free,
> and to proclaim the Lord's year of favour.
> (Lk 4:18–19, cf. Isaiah 61:1–2)

This tells us how Jesus saw his mission and is well worth thinking about as his mission is our mission today. In regard to writing we see that happening in the case of the woman caught in adultery where the crowd wanted him to condemn her to death by stoning in accordance with the law of Moses. The scripture tells us that Jesus bent down and started writing on the ground with his finger and said to the crowd: 'If there is one of you who has not sinned, let him be the first to throw a stone at her.' Again we read of the amazement of the crowd: 'How did he learn to read?' (Jn 7:15)

Jesus and people

The police went back to the Pharisees who had sent them to arrest Jesus but they were afraid to try to do so because they feared the crowd and they said: 'There has never been anybody who has spoken like him.' (Jn 7:46) Nicodemus who came to him secretly at night sought to defend him. (Jn 3:1–21 & Jn 7:49–52) He would appear again at the burial of Jesus. (Jn 19:39) Again at the end of the Sermon on the Mount we read: 'His teaching made a deep impression on the people, because he taught with authority, and not like their own scribes.' (Mt

7:29) It is a very simple deduction that Jesus was a very good speaker and that people walked long distances to hear him and were very impressed by what he told them. Try and imagine what it was like at that time with no mass media but just word of mouth to pass on news. Many would have set out with no clear idea where he was located but just hoping to meet him and hear him. His teaching was very simple and he used examples from ordinary life, and told simple stories to explain and make concrete his teachings in what we call parables.

Scripture words that I often associate with Jesus are compassion or pity or feeling sorry for others. 'I feel sorry for these people; they have been with me for three days now and have nothing to eat.' (Mt 15:32) 'Jesus felt pity for them and touched their eyes, and immediately their sight returned and they followed him.' (Mt 20:34) The cure of the only son of the widow of Nain: 'When the Lord saw her he felt sorry for her …' 'And when he saw the crowds he felt sorry for them because they were harassed and dejected, like sheep without a shepherd.' (Mt 9:36) We read continually in the scripture about sick people coming to him or being brought to him and he cured them all. In this he shows great empathy for the sick or troubled. He also liked to use the image of the Good Shepherd for himself which is an image of caring, worrying about others and helping them in any way possible.

Another word that I associate with Jesus is 'gentle'. He always had time to listen to people and whatever problem that they had. I think of the man who brought his sick child to him and asked Jesus to cure him. (Mk 9:14–29) Jesus told him all that was necessary was to believe, and the man said: 'I do have faith. Help the little faith that I have.' Jesus cured the boy. It is interesting to note how often Jesus was looking for faith in those who came looking for cures. He praised the faith of the men who let the sick man down through the roof in front of him. He also crossed cultural and religious boundaries in healing the servant of the Roman centurion. 'I tell you, not even in Israel have I found faith like this.' (Lk 7:1–10). He also cured the daughter of the Syrophoenician woman who was a pagan and a foreigner. (Mk 7:24–30)

'Patient' is a word to describe his approach to training his disciples. It was very difficult to get them to look at things from a heavenly point of view rather than a worldly point of view. They did not want to hear from him about his coming suffering and death. We see ambition in the case of the mother of James and John who wanted them to sit on each side of him when he entered his king-dom. He was gentle in pointing out to them what this would involve. (Mt 20:20–28) The other disciples were indignant at the pair.

'Table sharing' is another trait associated with Jesus. He ate with all kinds of people, rich and poor, saints and sinners, men and women, there were no distinctions. We read of him eating with Pharisees when he was invited, and it took courage on the part of a Pharisee to invite him to a meal. We can only guess at the number of times that he ate with his disciples and it was probably during those times that he tried to instruct them in many future things.

Jesus liked children. We read an interesting account in Mk 10:13–16. 'People were bringing little children to him, for him to touch. The disciples turned them away, but when Jesus saw this he was indignant and said to them, 'Let the little children come to me; do not stop them; for it is to such as these that the kingdom of God belongs. I tell you solemnly, anyone who does not welcome the kingdom of God like a little child will never enter it.' He put his arms around them, laid his hands on them and gave them his blessing.

Jesus was very clever at avoiding the traps of his enemies. We saw how he dealt with them over the woman caught committing adultery. He bent down and wrote on the ground and said: 'If there is one of you who has not sinned, let him be the first to throw a stone at her.' Again there was the question of paying tribute to Caesar which had all kinds of political implications. He asked whose image was on the coin of tribute and when told Caesar's he said, 'Give back to Caesar what belongs to Caesar, and to God what belongs to God.' (Mt 22:21)

The only groups that he condemned were the Scribes and the Pharisees. What he condemned in them was their condescending attitudes to other people, and how they made life difficult for ordinary people. (Mt 23:13–32).

There are many other things that I could write about Jesus, and I will deal with some of them later but I think Mark sums up things well in 7:37: 'Their admiration was unbounded. 'He has done all things well,' they said, 'He makes the deaf hear and the dumb speak.'

Any comments or points that you would like to bring up?

An image that intrigues me is Jesus crying outside the tomb of Lazarus before raising him from the dead. He seemed to be overcome with the grief of his sisters and the crowd.

Jesus and women

The status of women at the time of Jesus was very low, but they are mentioned a good deal in the story of Jesus. First we meet Elizabeth, the wife of Zechariah and the mother of John the Baptist. Next of course comes Mary at the annunciation and her willing 'yes' to the angel Gabriel. Then we have the visitation where the two women share the good news of what has happened to them and probably tried to guess at what it could all mean.

The nativity has Mary as its central character and we often overlook the difficulties of the pregnancy that she had just gone through. Many people forget that the child Jesus had to be looked after like any other baby. He had to be fed, changed and washed and there were no throw-away nappies in those days. The flight into Egypt would have added to the difficulties of Mary. Jesus was just like any other baby and would have learned to walk with the help of Mary and Joseph. Mary would have taught him to pray and would have helped with the beginning of his ordinary studies. Joseph would have taught him all that was necessary to become a carpenter. Jesus had to learn these things just like any other human child because he was truly human. It is not written about in the scriptures and we often overlook the ordinary human growth of Jesus and the part played by his mother. Nazareth is a blank in scripture but in reality it was a hive of ordinary human activity.

The first miracle at Cana of Galilee is another illustration of the influence of a woman – his mother. The young couple would have been embarrassed to run out of wine, and even though Jesus told his mother: 'My hour has not come yet,' she said to the servants, 'Do whatever he tells you.' Jesus turned six water jars of water into wine because his mother asked him to do so. (Jn 2:1–12)

You are familiar with the story in Jn 4:1–42 of how Jesus revealed himself to the Samaritans through a woman at Jacob's well near Sychar. Most Jews disliked the Samaritans or even hated them. Sometimes to avoid meeting Samaritans they would cross the Jordan and travel on the far bank. The disciples of Jesus had gone into the nearby town to buy food which was unusual for Jews as it would be considered contaminated. For Jesus to speak to the woman was against the normal custom and his status, and to ask her for a drink and to plan to drink from her utensil was to do something unclean that should need purification. However, Jesus saw good in her and was not interested in such laws. The mention of her having five husbands was also probably meant to refer to the fact that the Samaritans had five principal pagan gods. As they talked she came to realise that Jesus was the Messiah. She immediately left her bucket there and went off to tell her people about him, one of the first witnesses to him as Messiah and she a woman. As a result of her missionary work many others came out to meet him and listen to him, and many believed in him. He and his disciples stayed there for two days. This is the only incident that we have of Jesus working among the Samaritans.

We are all familiar with the story of the raising from the dead of Lazarus, but at that time and earlier when he stayed at their house it is Martha and Mary who were the principal characters. They were all friends of Jesus but especially Martha and Mary. (cf. Jn 11:1–44 – the raising of Lazarus and Lk 10:38–42 – meal in the house of Martha and Mary.)

In Lk 7:36–50 we have the story of a woman who was known to be a sinner who came and we are told: 'She waited behind him at his feet, weeping, and her tears fell on his feet, and she wiped them away with her hair and anointed them with the ointment.' The Pharisee who had invited him to the meal failed to do the usual welcoming ceremonies and she did them instead. Jesus praised her and said her sins were forgiven because of her great love and finally: 'Your faith has saved you; go in peace.' This woman is usually considered to be different from Mary the sister of Lazarus who anointed Jesus before his passion and death. (Jn 12:1–6)

'Now after this he made his way through towns and villages proclaiming the Good News of the kingdom of God. With him went the twelve, as well as certain women who had been cured of evil spirits and ailments, Mary sur-named the Magdalene, from whom seven demons had gone out, Joanna the wife of Herod's steward, Susanna, and several others who provided for them out of their resources.' (Lk 8:1–3) It was quite a big crowd and we can presume that his mother was also there and maybe others from time to time, twenty to twenty-five probably. They might have been able to get some food by fishing the rivers and picking wild fruit and hospitality was more common in those days. We read elsewhere that Judas held the common purse. (Jn 13:29)

We have the strange incident where the wife of Pilate tried to save his life. Pilate was seated in the chair of judgement, his wife sent him a message, 'Have nothing to do with that man; I have been upset all day by a dream I had about him.' (Mt 27–19)

Luke tells us that on the way to Calvary, 'Large numbers of people followed him, and of women too, who mourned and lamented for him.' (Lk 22:27)

We also read that his apostles and male disciples ran away but at the foot of the cross we find his mother, and his mother's sister, Mary the wife of Clopas and Mary of Magdala, and the beloved disciple. (Several scholars would main-tain that his mother's sister was really her natural sister and the wife of Zebedee and the mother of James and John [cf. Mk 1:19–20].)

It was here at Calvary that Jesus said to his mother, 'Woman, this is your son.' Then to the disciple he said, 'This is your mother.' And from that moment the disciple made a place for her in his home.' (Jn 19:26–27)

At that moment as his final gift to us – the only thing that he had left – Jesus gave us his mother to be our heavenly mother.

When Jesus died, Joseph of Arimathaea asked Pilate for the body for burial. Nicodemus was also there and his mother Mary and other women and they buried him in a nearby tomb. It was all done in a hurry as it was the eve of a major Sabbath.

On the first day of the week, namely Sunday, some of the women went to the tomb to wash and prepare the body of Jesus. Two men in brilliant clothes appeared to them and told them that Jesus was not among the dead but among the living. (cf. Luke 24:1–11) John gives us more details of Mary of Magdala coming early to the tomb. She first thought somebody had taken the body out of the tomb and met Jesus and thought that he was the gardener until he called her by name. 'Jesus said to her, "Do not cling to me, because I have not yet as-cended to the Father. But go and find the brothers, and tell them: I am ascending to my Father and your Father, to my God and your God." So Mary of Magdala went and told the disciples that she had seen the Lord and that he had said these things to her.' In this way Mary – a woman – became the first witness of the resurrection.

There are several accounts of Jesus after his resurrection appearing to various groups of his disciples. The number present varies and also the places. Some were inside buildings and some were out in the open. There is no account of an appearance to his mother but we can be sure that it happened at least once.

We do not know who exactly were present at the Ascension but it is likely Mary and the other women were there. We do know that Mary was present at Pentecost along with other women. (Acts 1:12–14) Pentecost is the last mention that we have of Mary the mother of Jesus. We can well imagine that as she had served Jesus during his lifetime she also served his church in a quiet, supportive way.

When Jesus died he was probably about thirty-six years of age, and when Mary gave birth to him she was probably about seventeen years of age. That would mean that she was about fifty-three years of age at Pentecost. Life expectancy at that time was about forty years. We have no idea how much time passed until her assumption into heaven, but after the descent of the Holy Spirit she is not mentioned again.

Discussion
There was no way that I could deal with all the people that Jesus dealt with and which are written about in the four gospels. Is there anybody else that you would like to mention or some particular incident that appeals to you?

Final Prayer
Use some intercessory prayers about the material in the session or the needs of the community or anything else that you think we should pray for. Use the endings: 'Lord, hear us.' 'Lord, graciously hear us.'

Reflection
    John Henry Newman – A Prayer
    O Lord, support us
    all the day long,
    until the shadows lengthen
    and the evening comes,
    and the busy world is hushed,
    and the fever of life is over,
    and our work is done.
    Then, Lord in your mercy
    grant us a safe lodging,
    and a holy rest,
    and peace at last;
    through Jesus Christ our Lord. Amen.

John Fuellenbach, SVD, *Throw Fire*, p. 43: 'The way we enter the kingdom of God is not by grace but by accepting an invitation.'

Karl Rahner SJ in *The Spirituality of the Future:* 'The Christian of the future will be a mystic or will not exist … By mysticism we mean a genuine experience of God emerging from the heart of existence.'

The gospels tell us not so much about what Jesus *was* like but what Jesus *is* like today.

Homework
Readings from Luke

Day	1	2	3	4	5	6	7
Chapter	9	9	9	9	9	9	9
Verses	10–17	18–22	23–27	28–36	37–43	44–50	51–62

Scripture Memos
1. We need to be careful not to attribute knowledge to the Jews living at the time of Jesus that they did not possess. We know that Jesus was the Son of God but the Jews of his time had no such knowledge or expectation of such a Messiah. What they hoped for was someone like King David or one of the great prophets who would lead them out of captivity and domination to all kinds of glory. They were very down to earth in their hopes and expectations.
2. Most scholars assume that Jesus ascended into heaven on the day of his resurrection but that he appeared to his disciples over a period of forty days until the final formal ascension after forty days.

SESSION TWELVE

Jesus Goes to Jerusalem

John Fuellenbach, SVD, in his book *Throw Fire*, p. 104, writing about Mark's gospel says: 'The first part of being a disciple in Mark's handbook could also be called the springtime of the disciples' vocation, the time with the Master in Galilee. The disciples become important, they bathe in the success of the Master, they are honoured and considered lucky. There is coming and going, they don't even have time to eat, their expectations are lofty. But they still have a long way to go before they really become his disciples.'

Then comes the pivotal point of Mark's gospel, namely, Peter's confession of faith in Jesus. (Mk 8:27–30) Fuellenbach then goes on to describe what happens, on p. 106. 'After the confession of Peter, the time has come for the disciples to enter into a new phase of being followers of Jesus. In this second phase they were to follow the Master to Jerusalem with the prospect of being crucified with him. In Galilee, the place of his public life, Jesus was in total control. He was the active one. He called disciples, he healed the people and they responded to him, he cast out demons and battled with his opponents.

'In Jerusalem, the place of his passion, Jesus played the passive part, he was handed over. The gospels use the phrase 'He was handed over' twenty-two times. The basic meaning of the phrase is that in the life of Jesus there comes a moment when he is no longer the active subject, fully in control of his actions, but he has become the object on which others acted. Jesus moved from being active to being passive, from the role of subject to that of object, and from working in freedom to waiting for what others decided and accepting what others did.'

The opposition to him had been growing all the time. We read of many attempts to trap him in his words and that even his life was in danger at times. We read in the gospels in a few places that Jesus set his face towards Jerusalem, in other words it took determination to go there. He warned his disciples that suffering and death awaited him in Jerusalem.

John tells us in Jn 7:1: 'After this (the talk on the Eucharist in Chapter 6) Jesus stayed in Galilee; he could not stay in Judaea, because the Jews were out to kill him. John tells us also about Jesus going up for the Feast of Tabernacles in Jerusalem, but he went secretly and separately from his disciples.' (John 7:2–7, 24) We are also told that he did not stay in the Temple at night but went out to Bethany or elsewhere: 'With that he left them and went out of the city to Bethany where he spent the night.' (Mt 21:17)

In the daytime he would be in the Temple teaching, but would spend the night on the hill called the Mount of Olives. (Luke 21:37) The implication is that it was probably for safety reasons. There were all kinds of discussions going on about who he was. It is interesting to note that Jesus often used the phrase Son of Man to describe himself. The meaning of the title is not clear and he is never addressed by that name. It was probably a safe name to use but at the same time it hinted at a deeper meaning. To say directly that he was the Messiah would cause an uproar, and to say that he was the Son of God would be blasphemy and he could be condemned to death. Eventually he was put to death for treason by the Romans and blasphemy by the Jews, not that either side was too worried by the details of the condemnation.

He had friends among the Scribes and Pharisees and elders and no doubt they were warning him about the dangerous plans of others. Probably he could also sense the anger and frustration and hatred of his opponents. He was clearly in danger and he knew that they would like to kill him publicly and in as painful a manner as possible even if that meant getting the cooperation of the hated Romans. I would now like to cover briefly the main events of those last terrible times. Sometimes when we get an overview of the whole story we can understand the details better. When we read them they fit in better, and we can understand them better.

I will list some of the major events of the final few months. With each gospel compiler working to his own plan for his gospel, absolute accuracy is impossible. For instance John has the cleansing of the Temple at the beginning of his gospel (Jn 3:13–22) whereas Matthew and the others have it towards the end of their gospels. (Mt 21:12–13; 11:15–17; Lk 19:45–46) A good Bible will give you the references on the side of the page for other gospels and parts of scripture. I will follow the gospel of John to a large extent but I will also use the others:

1. Jesus gives a long talk on giving us his body and blood for our food and drink preceded by the miracle of the loaves and fishes. Many leave and refuse to accept it. (Jn 6:26–66)
2. Jesus cures a man born blind and this leads to a great deal of controversy. The cause of the man's blindness is discussed and the blindness of the Pharisees. (Jn 9:1–41)
3. Jesus compares himself to the Good Shepherd who gives his life for his flock. (Jn 10:1–21)
4. Jesus tells them to judge him by his works. (Jn 10:22–42) John has centred much of his gospel around Jerusalem and major Jewish feasts. Jn 10:37–39:

> If I am not doing my Father's work
> there is no need to believe me;
> but if I am doing it,
> then even if you refuse to believe in me,
> at least believe in the work I do;

> then you will know for sure
> that the Father is in me and I am in the Father.

5. The raising from the dead of Lazarus. The Jewish elders plan not only to kill Jesus but also Lazarus. (Jn 11:1–44)

6. The anointing at Bethany by Mary the sister of Lazarus. Judas complains about the waste of money. (Jn 12:1–11)

7. Jesus enters Jerusalem in triumph and the Pharisees are very angry and frustrated. (Jn 12:12–19)

8. The Last Supper and Jesus washes his disciples' feet. This action by Jesus was a manifestation of his love for them but it also turned upside down the whole social scene. He explained the reason to them. 'If I, then, the Lord and Master, have washed your feet, you should wash each other's feet. (Jn 13:14) (cf. Jn 13:1–20)

9. Treachery of Judas foretold and Judas leaves the gathering. Very sad words of scripture describe the scene after Judas had left the room: 'Night had fallen.' (John 13:30)

10. Farewell discourse of Jesus in John. There is no mention of the institution of the Eucharist in John, but this discourse of Jesus at the Last Supper in John is one of the most beautiful parts of the Bible. It also includes the promise to send the Holy Spirit to guide the church and individuals and the promise of preparing a place for us in heaven etc. (Jn 13:13–17, 26)

11. Institution of the Eucharist and the priesthood. (Mt 26:26–29)

12. The agony in the garden in Gethsemane. (Mt 26:36–46)

13. The arrest of Jesus, and the disciples all run away. (Mt 26:47–56)

14. Jesus before Annas, father in law of Caiphas, the high priest. (Jn 18:12–14)

15. Jesus before Caiphas, the high priest of that year, and Peter disowns him in the courtyard there. Jesus sent from there to the Praetorium and Pilate. (Mt 26:57–68)

16. Jesus before Pilate who sends him to Herod hoping to get rid of the problem.(Jn 18:28–40)

17. Jesus refuses to answer Herod and is treated with contempt and sent back to Pilate. (Lk 22:6–12)

18. Barabbas chosen before Jesus when Pilate offers the crowd the choice. (Mt 27:15–25)

19. Jesus is sentenced to be scourged and crucified. (Mt 27:26)

20. Jesus is scourged, crowned with thorns and mocked. (Jn 19:1–3)

21. Jesus walks to Calvary carrying his cross and wearing a crown of thorns. (Jn 19:17–22)

22. He is crucified between two thieves. In crucifixion the nails were driven through the wrist and not through the hands as is normally depicted. Otherwise the body would tear free.(Lk 23:23–24)

24. Jesus' last words:

'Father forgive them; they do not know what they are doing.' (Lk 23:34)

'Woman this is your son.' (Jn 19:26)

'This is your mother.' (Jn 19:26)

'Indeed, I promise you today you will be with me in paradise.' (Lk 23:43)

'Eli, Eli, lama sabachtani', that is, 'My God, My God, why have you deserted me?' (Mt 27:46 & Mk 15:34 & Psalm 22:1) Psalm 22 is a psalm of confidence in God.

'I am thirsty.' (Jn 19:28)

'Father into your hands I commit my spirit.' (Lk 23:46)

25. His mother and other women and the beloved disciple are present at Calvary. (Jn 19:25–27)

26. Jesus dies after about three hours. Normally as the person got tired the body sagged and fluid built up in the lungs to cause death by asphyxiation. Jesus would also have been weak and suffering from loss of blood and this probably hastened his death. That is why when the Jews wanted the two thieves to die quickly they arranged for their legs to be broken. Jesus was already dead and so a spear was thrust into his side and water and blood came out of his body. (Jn 19:28–30)

27. Joseph of Arimathaea got permission from Pilate to take down the Body and bury it. Another person to help was Nicodemus who came secretly previously, and now comes with myrrh and aloes. They wrapped him in linen cloths in accordance with Jewish custom and buried him hurriedly in a new tomb, in which nobody had been buried that was in a nearby garden. It had to be done in a hurry as the Sabbath was close at hand. His mother Mary and the other women and the beloved disciple were also there. (Jn 19:38–42 & Mt 27:57–61)

28. The Guard at the Tomb. (Mt 28:62–66) Note that it was Roman guards who were placed as guards on the tomb. The penalty for failing in their duty would have been death.

I do not expect you to read all of this now, but if you have time in the future read the different parts and keep in mind the overall picture. As you saw in regard to the cleansing of the Temple, one evangelist has it at the beginning of his gospel and another at the end. They were also writing for different people and influenced by different oral traditions. John has a good deal of his gospel in or around Jerusalem and around major feast days. You could spend a long time thinking and praying about the discourse of Jesus at the Last Supper in John's gospel.

Conclusion

a) The Second Vatican Council, *The Catechism of the Catholic Church* (See Nos 597, 598) and pronouncements of Popes John Paul II and Benedict XVI make it clear that the Jewish people were not responsible for the death of Jesus but the sins of all humankind were the cause.

b) It is paradoxical that it was also the will of the Father that Jesus should die such a cruel death on the cross. It seems far from the image of Abba Father that Jesus painted for us. Jesus set out to walk the path of love and peace and teach us how to live and that is very dangerous. Look at what happened to Gandhi and Martin Luther King. Helder Camara put it well when he said, 'If I build food feeding centers for the poor I am called a saint, but if I ask about the cause of the poverty of the poor I am denounced as an agitator and a communist.' When it came to the end of his life Jesus freely offered his Life for all of us in order that all our lives would be enriched. (cf. *Catechism of Catholic Church*, Nos 606, 611)

c) When exactly did Jesus die? At that time it was the Roman calendar A.U.C. (*ab urbe condita* – from the foundation of the city) that was in use. It was four hundred years later before our Gregorian calendar came into use and it had to be corrected in the sixteenth century. However allowing for all this, the experts are fairly well agreed that Jesus died on 7 April in the year AD 30. John 19:34 tells us that to prevent the bodies remaining on the cross during the Sabbath, since the Sabbath was a day of special solemnity, the Jews asked Pilate to have the legs broken. The 'Full Moon' Sabbath after the Spring Equinox was on 8 April in the year AD 30. It only occurred occasionally that the full moon fell exactly on the Sabbath for the Passover feast and was a feast of special solemnity. We also need to remember that Jesus was probably born about 6 BC. Jewish writers at the time of Jesus were careless about matters of time. Luke tells us 'When he started to teach, Jesus was *about* thirty years old.' (Lk 3:23)

Discussion
There are so many things that you could discuss that I leave it to a general discussion. It might be worth thinking about the effects of hatred, jealousy, pride and envy.

Final Prayer
Prayers of intercession would fit in well with the subject matter.

Reflection
Fr Anthony de Mello, a Jesuit from India, in one of his books called *The Song of the Bird* tells an interesting story on pp. 131–132. It is called *The Look of Jesus*. We do not know whether it is just a story or his own personal experience, but it can relate to any one of us. The Asian approach is to leave the conclusion to the reader or listener:

> In the gospel according to Luke, 22:60–62, we read: '"My friend", said Peter, "I do not know what you are talking about." At that instant while he was still speaking the cock crew, and the Lord turned and looked straight at Peter, and Peter remembered what the Lord had said to him.

"Before the cock crows today, you will have disowned me three times."
And he went out and wept bitterly.'

I related well with the Lord. I would converse with him, thank him,
ask for his help. But always I had this uneasy feeling that he wanted to
look at me ... And I would not. I would talk, but look away when I
sensed he was looking at me. I was afraid that I would find some accusation in his eyes or some unrepented sin. Or a demand: something that
he wanted from me. One day I summoned up courage and looked! There
was no accusation. No demand. The eyes just said, 'I love you.' And like
Peter, I went outside and wept.

Homework
Reading from Luke

Day	1	2	3	4	5	6	7
Chapter	10	10	10	11	11	11	11
Verses	1–20	21–28	29–42	1–13	14–26	27–36	37–54

Scripture Memos

1. John and the Beloved Disciple. We read of John the Apostle and John the
   Evangelist and also John the Beloved Disciple who is a very important
   person in the gospel of John. Were they all the same person? Difficult to
   maintain according to modern biblical scholars. The Beloved Disciple was
   able to get Peter into the High Priest's house which would be difficult for a
   fisherman from Galilee. Pope Benedict XVI proposes a possibility in his
   book *Jesus of Nazareth*, but makes it a conditional suggestion and it is that
   John's father Zebedee was a priest in the Temple who would do his rota
   time there each year, and was in the habit of bringing his son John along
   with him, and so the staff members were familiar with him. It still leaves
   many difficulties to explain if all three were the one person.
2. The name Jesus in Hebrew means 'Yahweh saves', and it was a common
   name at that time. Mt 1:21 puts it very well: 'She will give birth to a Son who
   is to save his people from their sins.'
3. The Divinity of Jesus was defined by the Council of Nicaea in AD 325. The
   Humanity of Jesus was defined by the Council of Chalcedon in AD 451. The
   Council of Constantinople in AD 553 reaffirmed that Jesus was both true God
   and true man. *The Catechism of the Catholic Church* states the same doctrine
   and goes into detail in No. 464 and the following sections.

Jesus is Risen

Introduction

What an awful Sabbath it was the day after Jesus died. The disciples gathered together because they were afraid to go outside in case they might be recognised and attacked. The people were celebrating the Passover and Exodus and receiving the Ten Commandments from God at Mount Sinai. It was a Sabbath of great solemnity as the full moon fell on the Sabbath. (Jn 9:31) It was an occasion of great joy for others, but for the disciples it was a day of great sadness and despair. All their dreams and hopes lay shattered and they were afraid that what had happened to Jesus might happen to them. The conversation was curtailed and disjointed as they felt very depressed. They would have travelled home but it was impossible as no one was allowed to make a journey on the Sabbath unless it was less than a kilometre in distance. Some of the women were making preparations to go and wash the body of Jesus the next morning and arrange it properly for burial according to Jewish custom with spices and ointments. (Lk 23:56) Strange as it may seem his enemies were more worried about him rising from the dead than the disciples, and arranged for a Roman guard at the tomb and even sealed it (Mt 27:66)

The Resurrection

We do not have a direct description of how the resurrection occurred. It is more or less impossible to reconcile the various descriptions of the resurrection appearances in regard to who was where and even how often they occurred. It was such an earth-shattering event and the evangelists were probably not too concerned at reconciling the appearances, even Matthew, Mark and Luke. The shock of the resurrection left them confused. It was too good to be true.

Matthew 28:1–8 tells us: 'After the Sabbath, and towards dawn on the first day of the week, Mary of Magdala and the other Mary went to visit the sepulchre. And all at once there was a violent earthquake, for the angel of the Lord, descending from heaven, came and rolled away the stone and sat on it. His face was like lighting, his robe white as snow. The guards were so shaken, so frightened of him, that they were like dead men. (My note: probably knocked unconscious) But the angel spoke, and he said to the women, "There is no need for you to be afraid. I know that you are looking for Jesus, who was crucified. He is not here, for he has risen, as he said he would. Come and see the place where he lay, then go quickly and tell his disciples. He has risen from the dead, and now he is going before you to Galilee; it is there you will see him. Now I have told you." Filled with awe and great joy the women came quickly away from the tomb and ran to tell the disciples.

And there coming to meet them, was Jesus. "Greetings," he said. And the women came up to him and falling down before him, clasped his feet. Then Jesus said to them, "Do not be afraid; go and tell my brothers that they must leave for Galilee; they will see me there."

The guard meanwhile went to the chief priests and elders and told them what had happened. They paid them a large sum of money and told them: "This is what you must say, 'His disciples came during the night and stole him away while we were asleep.'" (Mt 28:11–15)

1. This story is not even a good lie. As I mentioned earlier, for a Roman soldier to sleep on duty it would be the death penalty, but the chief priests told them that they would put things right with Pilate if necessary. Moreover if they were asleep how could they know that his disciples had stolen his body?
2. The disciples were so afraid that it is impossible to imagine them trying to steal a body from a guarded tomb.
3. Imagine the situation. There were thousands of pilgrims in Jerusalem. They would have been moving about and sleeping in the open. It would have been impossible for the disciples to carry the body anywhere and not be seen. We also need to remember that it was the full moon and in the moonlight they would have been more easily seen.
4. The four gospels tell us that the tomb was *empty*. To disprove the story of his resurrection all the authorities had to do was to produce his body, but they failed to do so for the obvious reason that it was not available.

Were these women, just mentioned earlier, the first to see Jesus or was it Mary of Magdala? I think that it may have been Mary of Magdala. We are told Jesus said to her, 'Do not cling to me because I have not yet ascended to the Father. But go and find the brothers, and tell them: I am ascending to my Father, and your Father, to my God and your God.' (Jn 20:1–18) Although Galilee is mentioned it would seem that Jesus appeared to at least the apostles, less Thomas, on that same Sunday in Jerusalem. That same day we have the appearance of Jesus to the two disciples who did not believe the women's story and left for Emmaus.

We know that Jesus died on a cross at Calvary. There were professionals there to make sure that he had died, and they made sure that he died by sticking a spear into his side. Everything would have ended there but he rose from the dead. His rising from the dead was different from that of Lazarus, or the son of the widow in Nain or the daughter of Jairus, the official at the synagogue. Their bodies were unchanged and they would die eventually. Jesus' body was changed. He could suddenly appear in a room even though the doors were closed and he would never die again. Another remarkable fact about Jesus after his resurrection was that those who knew him so well seem to have some difficulty in initially recognising him. They knew him but he was different in some way. Unfortunately they do not tell us how he was changed but of course he was now resurrected and glorified.

One of the proofs of the resurrection of Jesus for us is the reluctance of the disciples to believe in it. We have the incident of the apostle Thomas refusing to believe unless he saw the wounds in Jesus' body, and Jesus had to specially appear to him. (Jn 20:19–29) We have those consoling words of Jesus in verse 29: 'You believe because you see me. Happy are those who have not seen and yet believe.' We also have the account of the two disciples on the way to Emmaus which is about seven miles from Jerusalem. They recognised Jesus in the breaking of the bread, but they mention that the story of the women who had gone to the tomb only disturbed them and they did not believe them or check out their story.

It took time for the message that Jesus is risen and everything is changed to sink into the minds and hearts of the disciples. With time, St Paul would write in 1 Corinthians 15:55–57: 'Death, where is your victory? Death, where is your sting? Now the sting of death is sin, and sin gets its power from the Law. So, let us thank God for giving us the victory through our Lord Jesus Christ.'

With time it all became clear and St Peter in Acts 10:40–42 tells Cornelius: 'Three days afterwards God raised him from the dead … we are those witnesses, we have eaten and drunk with him after his resurrection from the dead, and he has ordered us to proclaim this to his people.'

I suppose that the greatest proof that we have of the resurrection of Jesus is that the apostles and disciples, who were such ordinary people, were prepared to suffer all kinds of deaths as witnesses of his resurrection. Their scepticism and lack of faith is the foundation of our faith. That Jesus Christ has risen from the dead has been the basic message of Christianity from the beginning of the church. If there is no resurrection then the church is a waste of time, or worse than that it is deceiving people. However, for almost two thousand years, millions (billions) of people, men and women, young and old, of many nationalities have followed Jesus with joy, making him the centre of their lives, and tried to share that joy with others. These followers of Jesus have changed the world in many ways and made society better through education, medicine, exploration and many other ways. In its own way this is one of the proofs of the resurrection.

St Paul is an interesting example. He was not a disciple of Jesus but on the contrary tried to destroy this new movement and was involved in the killing of St Stephen. Acts 8:3 tells us: 'Saul worked for the total destruction of the church; he went from house to house arresting both men and women and sending them to prison.'

This all changed when he had an encounter with the Risen Lord on his way to Damascus to persecute the Christians there. This encounter led him to become a zealous disciple of Jesus and the apostle of the gentiles. He travelled widely telling people about the Good News of Jesus, set up many churches, endured much suffering and hardship and finally gave his life for his witness to Jesus in Rome.

We have never met Jesus face to face as people of his time could. But we can encounter him by getting to know him, by meeting him in the Mass and in the Blessed Sacrament. We meet him where ever people gather in his name and in the poor and suffering in this world.

It is interesting that we read about Jesus appearing to all kinds of people, both individuals and groups. These appearances were both inside and outside which eliminates the possibility of deceit. It is also interesting to note that the apostles and disciples seem to have done little or nothing about spreading the teachings of Jesus after his resurrection. Instead they are back in Galilee and working as fishermen at one of his appearances. (cf Jn 21:1–23) It was here that Jesus once more confirmed Peter as head of his church.

Afterword

1. After the Resurrection, the apostles and disciples had great difficulty in recognising Jesus. He was changed, because it was *now* the resurrected and glorified Jesus that they met. He could suddenly appear in a room that had all the doors closed.

   This is an important point to remember as it is the resurrected and glorified Jesus that we have in the Blessed Sacrament.

2. There was a Jewish belief that after any resurrection from the dead there would be a general resurrection from the dead, followed by the end of the world. In the early church there was also a belief or a hope among some Christians that Jesus would soon return in glory, and so they were expecting the end of the world to be imminent because of the resurrection of Jesus.

3. Death on a cross was seen as a very disgraceful thing. How the Messiah could die in such a way was a problem for the early church. As St Paul says in Galatians, 'Christ redeemed us from the curse of the Law by being cursed for our sake, since scripture says: Cursed be anybody who is hanged on a tree.' This background thinking made it all the more difficult for the disciples to believe in the resurrection.

   The Jews considered anybody who died on a tree as cursed by God, reference to Deuteronomy 21:22–23: 'If a man guilty of a capital offence is put to death and you hang him on a tree, his body must not remain on the tree overnight; you must bury him the same day, for one who has been hanged is accursed of God, and you must not defile the land Yahweh your God gives you for an inheritance.'

   According to the *Jerome Biblical Commentary* this is not to do with the method of execution as hanging was unknown in the Old Testament. However, sometimes after the death penalty the exposure of the corpse on a tree or a stake was done as a deterrent to others. (In this part of the world the head of an executed person was often put on a spike outside a prominent building as a deterrent to others.) What is dealt with here is the disposal of the corpse which was considered to be ritually impure, and could make anybody that touched it, or even the land, ritually impure.

4. Pilate the Procurator was appointed to his position in AD 26. He had several clashes with various Jewish groups until his recall to Rome in AD 36. He was considered to be inflexible, merciless and corrupt but these judgements may be slightly biased. After his recall until his death he seems to have had very little influence.

There is a sentence in Jn 24:41 which sums up the reaction of the disciples for me: 'Their joy was so great that they still could not believe, and they stood there dumbfounded.'

Final Prayer
Intercessory prayers dealing with the subject matter and topical problems.

Reflection
Read an account of the resurrection in one or more of the gospels. They are as follows: Matthew 28:1–20; Mark 16:1–20; Luke 24:1–53; John 20:1–21, 25. St Paul says in 1 Corinthians 15:14: 'If there is no resurrection from the dead, Christ himself cannot have been raised, and if Christ has not been raised then our preaching is useless, and your believing is useless.' But it really happened and so there is new meaning in all of our lives and we are grateful to the disciples for being so slow to believe and act on that belief.

Homework
Readings from Luke

Day	1	2	3	4	5	6	7
Chapter	12	12	12	12	12	13	13
Verses	1–12	13–21	22–32	33–48	49–59	1–9	10–17

SESSION FOURTEEN

Ascension and Pentecost

Ascension

There is not much written in the Bible about the Ascension but Luke tells us in 24:50–53: 'Then he took them out as far as the outskirts of Bethany, and lifting up his hands he blessed them. Now as he blessed them, he withdrew from them and was carried up to heaven. They worshipped him and then went back to Jerusalem full of joy; and they were continually in the Temple praising God.' It is interesting that Luke, a gentile convert, describes the ascension and he does it twice as it appears again at the beginning of the Acts of the Apostles which he also wrote. Mark only refers briefly to it in Mk 16:19–20.

Luke, probably following a different oral tradition, writes a slightly more detailed version in Acts 1:1–14. He may have got more details as time went on: 'In my earlier work, Theophilus, I dealt with everything Jesus had done and taught from the beginning until the day he gave his instructions to the apostles he had chosen through the Holy Spirit, and was taken up to heaven. He had shown Himself alive to them after his passion by many demonstrations; for forty days he had continued to appear and tell them about the kingdom of God. When he had been at table with them, he had told them not to leave Jerusalem, but to wait there for what the Father had promised. 'It is,' he had said, 'what you have heard me speak about: John baptised with water but you, not many days from now, will be baptised with the Holy Spirit.'

'Now having met together, they asked him, 'Lord, has the time come? Are you going to restore the kingdom to Israel?' He replied, 'It is not for you to know times and dates that the Father has decided by his own authority, but you will receive power when the Holy Spirit comes on you, and then you will be my witnesses not only in Jerusalem but throughout Judaea and Samaria, and indeed to the ends of the earth.'

'As he said this he was lifted up while they looked on, and a cloud (My note: cloud is often a manifestation of God) took him from their sight. They were still staring into the sky when suddenly two men in white were standing near them and they said, "Why are you men from Galilee standing here looking into the sky? Jesus, who has been taken up from you into heaven, this same Jesus will come back in the same way as you have seen him go there."'

Luke in Acts tells us that after the ascension they went back from the Mount of Olives to Jerusalem to the upper room where they were staying in Jerusalem. 'They joined in continuous prayer, together with several women, including Mary the mother of Jesus and with his brothers.' (Acts 1:14) Mary was present at

Pentecost with the others and this is the last time Mary is mentioned. While they were waiting and praying they chose Matthias to take the place of Judas among the twelve apostles.

Pentecost

'When Pentecost day came round, they had all met in one room, when suddenly they heard what sounded like a powerful wind from heaven, the noise of which filled the entire house in which they were sitting; and something appeared to them that seemed like tongues of fire; these separated and came to rest on the head of each of them. They were all filled with the Holy Spirit, and began to speak foreign languages as the Spirit gave them the gift of speech.

Now there were devout men living in Jerusalem from every nation under heaven, and at this sound they all assembled, each one bewildered to hear these men speaking in his own language.'

Despite the resurrection and the appearances of Jesus to them and the ascension, the apostles and disciples had done nothing about preaching the Risen Jesus until the day of Pentecost when the Holy Spirit came upon them. Pentecost changed everything. Up to then they were afraid but after the descent of the Holy Spirit they went forth fearlessly to proclaim Jesus and his teaching. Pentecost was the day that the church came into existence, and we can call it the birthday of the church. Here in Acts 2:14–41 we read about Peter going out fearlessly and telling the crowd about Jesus and how he was necessary for salvation. At the end of Peter's speech we read in Acts 2:41 that on that day about three thousand were added to their number.

We read about life in the early community in Acts 2:42–47: 'They remained faithful to the teaching of the apostles, to the brotherhood, to the breaking of the bread and to the prayers … They went as a body to the Temple every day and they met in their houses for the breaking of bread.'

Jesus only speaks twice of the Church in the gospels, Mt 16:18 and Mt 18:17, and it is amazing how quickly they set up churches wherever they went, with elders in charge. We would probably call them house churches or Eucharistic communities.

At the beginning they concentrated their efforts on Jewish people. It took time for them to realise the immensity of the mission that they had received. For a while they seemed to think that their Jewish compatriots would all come into the church. There were a few tentative efforts in regard to both the Samaritans and non-Jews. Eventually, when Peter had a vision of a large sheet full of all kinds of animals and a voice telling him to rise and kill, he refused to do so as he said that he had never eaten impure meat. (Acts 10:9–16) Then a voice said to him: 'What God has made clean you have no right to call profane or unclean.' Peter then found visitors waiting for him and travelled with them to the house of a Roman centurion called Cornelius who was a good man. While

Peter was speaking to Cornelius and his friends, the Holy Spirit descended on his listeners and he decided that they should be baptised. In this way the church gradually began to look outside the Jewish community. This movement got a great impetus with the arrival of Paul on the scene.

Not everything was perfect in the Early Church. Problems had to be sorted out. We read of the attempted fraud of Ananias and Sapphira. They said that they were going to give *all* the money that they got for their land but only gave part of it. By claiming that they had given all the money they were putting the Christian community under the obligation of looking after them. We would say that they wanted to eat their loaf of bread and keep it. (Acts 5:1–11) In Acts 6:1–7 we read about a dispute in regard to how the Greek and Hebrew-speaking widows were being treated in the daily distribution of food. The twelve called a meeting and proposed choosing seven deacons to look after this work. This was agreed to and the problem was solved.

In Acts 5:12–16 we read of the general situation. The disciples generally met in the Portico of Solomon in the Temple, but other people did not join them as they were probably afraid. They did bring the sick to be cured and Peter and the others were held in much admiration. Acts 6:7 sums it up when it says: 'The word of the Lord continued to spread; the number of disciples in Jerusalem was greatly increased, and a large group of priests made their submission to the faith.' It was the calm before the storm. Soon many of the followers would be forced to flee from Jerusalem, but that dispersion would mean that the faith was brought to new places. There was some discrimination against them all the time but people could survive and carry on. In the early years it was not too bad. We need to remember that the martyrdom of St Stephen was in AD 36. A short time after that is the estimated time of the conversion of Paul. He went to Damascus and stayed there and in the neighbouring locality for a consider-able time, studying and praying. St Paul is such a central character in the Acts and has written so many of the Letters in the New Testament that we should know something about him.

St Paul

Who was Paul, the Apostle of the Gentiles, who started out persecuting the church and ended up the great propagator of Jesus to the Gentile world and also to the Jewish world? We do not know exactly when he was born but there is general agreement that it was ten to fifteen years after Jesus. We know that he was born in Tarsus in Cilicia which is in Asia Minor. It was a city of learning and a Roman city. His parents were Jewish and he would have had Jewish and Greek influences in his life. Acts 22:3 tells us: 'I am a Jew … and was born at Tarsus in Cilicia. I was brought up here in this city. I studied under Gamaliel and was taught the exact observance of the Law of our ancestors.' He was of Pharisee stock and may have been studying to be a Rabbi. We are told that at the stoning of Stephen: 'The witnesses put down their clothes at the feet of a young man called Saul.' (Acts 7:58)

The date of Paul's conversion is generally considered to be about AD 36. That would have been shortly after the stoning to death of Stephen. It was also the year of the change of Procurators in Jerusalem. There are a couple of accounts of his conversion but the one most people are familiar with it is in Acts 9:1–19. Afterwards he began to preach in Damascus and it is said that he spent about three years there. The revelation of Jesus to Paul on the road was a decisive moment in his life and as a result he regarded himself as 'the servant of Christ'. (Galatians 1:10) He associated the revelation with his apostolic commission: 'I, personally, am free: I am an apostle and I have seen Jesus our Lord. You are all my work in the Lord.' (1 Corinthians 9:1)

It seems that he left Damascus for a short while and went to Arabia, probably for prayer and mediation. When he returned, he continued teaching about Jesus. After about three years, he was forced to leave Damascus because of Jewish opposition. He went to Jerusalem at least once, maybe more, to meet Peter and probably some other of the apostles. On one occasion he seems to have been bringing money to help with a famine situation in Jerusalem.

Paul's First Mission was from AD 46–49. He was designated for it by the Holy Spirit along with Barnabas. The Council of Jerusalem took place in AD 49 and Paul played an important part in it. It was here that the Gentile church took on its own particular form. It was freed from its Jewish control. The Gentiles generally were not interested in Jewish Law or the Temple. Some Jewish converts were loyal to both, but many Jewish converts because of discrimination and so on were also not that interested in the old Jewish side of things.

The Second Mission was from AD 49–52 and the Third Mission was from AD 54–57. On his return to Jerusalem from the third he was imprisoned, and he appealed to Caesar as a Roman citizen born in the Roman city of Tarsus. He probably arrived in Rome in AD 61.

The ending of Acts is not very satisfactory. It just tells us that he spent two years in rented lodgings in Rome proclaiming the kingdom of God and teaching. That does not mean that he died shortly afterwards. In Roman Law if his case had not been heard in two years he had to be released. The Pastoral Letters seem to suggest that he visited the east again, and there is even a suggestion in tradition that he might have gone to Spain. There is a certain amount of agreement that he died in the persecution of Nero during the period AD 64 to AD 68. It is said that he was beheaded.

Besides his untiring work to spread the gospel, Paul was also a prolific writer, as the New Testament has much of his writings. Hebrews is usually not considered to have been written by Paul. Likewise, the Pastoral letters of 1 Timothy and also Titus are often questioned as coming from Paul, especially by non-Catholic sources.

Discussion

What struck you about the Ascension, Pentecost and St Paul that you had not thought much about up to the present? What does Pentecost mean to us today and how should we celebrate it?

Final Prayer

Intercessory prayers dealing with the matter that came up plus topical subjects.

Reflection

The Shroud of Turin

It would be very nice to have a photograph of Jesus. Some people would say that we do have it in the Shroud of Turin. What is this Shroud?

Matthew tells us what happened when Jesus died. Mt 27:57–60: 'When it was evening, there came a rich man of Arimathea called Joseph, who had become a disciple of Jesus. This man went to Pilate and asked for the Body of Jesus. Pilate thereupon ordered it to be handed over. So Joseph took the body, wrapped it in a clean shroud and put it in his own new tomb which he had hewn out of the rock. He then rolled a large stone across the entrance and went away.'

John tells us what happened after the resurrection. 'So Peter set out with the other disciple to go to the tomb. They ran together but the other disciple, running faster than Peter, reached the tomb first; he bent down and saw the linen cloths lying on the ground, but did not go in. Simon Peter who was following now came up, went right into the tomb, saw the linen cloths on the ground, and also the cloth that had been over his head; this was not with the other cloths but rolled up in a place by itself. Then the other disciple who had reached the tomb first also went in; he saw and he believed.'

Some people claim that the Shroud of Turin was the shroud that Jesus was buried in. It is about fourteen feet and three inches long and three feet and seven inches wide (Metres 4.34 x 1.09) The Jewish custom of burial would have the body placed on the cloth, and then covered by the other half. Some binding cloths would also be used, and over the face, on the outside, another cloth would be placed over the head. In Jn 11:46, in regard to the raising from the dead of Lazarus, we read: 'The dead man came out, his feet and hands bound with bands of stuff and a cloth around his face.' People try to connect the burial shroud of Jesus with a cloth found in a niche in the walls of Edessa, in south central Turkey in AD 525. It can be definitely traced back to AD 1357 to the provincial town of Lirey about one hundred miles southeast of Paris. Spores from forty nine different plants have been found in the shroud. Some of them are from France and Italy, but thirty-nine are found only in Palestine and Turkey.

A shroud that someone had been buried in would be ritually impure to touch in Jewish thinking, and they would have been anxious to get rid of it, but would not like to destroy it if it belonged to Jesus. The image in the shroud is that of a crucified man.

It is not painted on the cloth but burned into it, like a scorch mark. It is like a negative photo, and it was only when it was photographed in 1898 that people became fully aware of what it was. The image is that of a bearded man, approximately 5'11" in height and weighing about 170 pounds and in his thirties. The man is well built and muscular, a man accustomed to manual work. He died a brutal death and his wounds correspond to those of Jesus.

There was a big scientific study of the shroud done in 1978 by scientists from different parts of the world using all kinds of modern instruments and technology and the results are as follows: There are indications of blood flow from the wounds and the swelling of the abdomen suggests asphyxiation, the usual cause of death in crucifixion. The man has his hair in a pigtail which was the custom at the time of Jesus. There were two scourges used and he has more than 220 wounds on his body. The knees of the man have cuts and bruises which could have been caused by falling. There is a wound on the right-hand side of the body that could correspond to the spear wound that Jesus received after death. The wound is the size of the short Roman spear.

One wrist has a pierced wound, and that wrist overlies the other wrist, and the nail was driven through the wrist. There are wounds in the feet caused by nails. One nail was used on the feet. There are many bruises about the face and head and even some hair seems to have been plucked from his beard. Isaiah writes in Isaiah 50:6: 'I offered my back to those who struck me, my cheeks to those who tore at my beard; I did not cover my face against insult and spittle.' There are indications of blood flow from wounds in the head which would correspond to the crown of thorns. It is also clear that blood and water flowed from the wound in the side. The similarity of the wounds with those of Jesus is very striking.

There are Roman coins over the eyes and one has the year AD 29 on it. Coins would be placed on the eyes to keep them closed. The body is unwashed with the blood on it, and we know that there was little time for the burial before sunset. The women went with spices, and to wash the body of Jesus on the morning of the resurrection. The body is in a state of rigor mortis.

Carbon testing was used some years ago on it, and it put the shroud's existence in the eleventh or twelfth century. It was then claimed to be a fake but a few years later they wanted to do the carbon testing again, as they had used threads for the testing from the outside edges of the shroud. Repairs had been done there over the years, and this made the findings obviously wrong. It is very unlikely that the Vatican will allow threads to be taken from where the image actually is as carbon testing destroys almost a square inch, and where the burn marks are located it is very fragile.

The experts agree that the best explanation is some kind of scorch marks. However they have no explanation about *how* it happened, but in Matthew 28:2–5 there is mention of an earthquake and an angel with a face like lightening:

'And all at once there was a violent earthquake, for an angel of the Lord, descending from heaven, came and rolled the stone away and sat on it. His face was like lighting, his robe white as snow. The guards were so shaken, so frightened of him, that they were like dead men.' (knocked unconscious)

Possible Explanation

For the resurrection a great deal of energy was necessary. Jesus was really dead and rigor mortis has set in. Where you have energy used you generally have heat. There is also a mention of strong light in regard to the angel in Matthew and where you have light you also have heat, which could cause the scorch marks. Many electric bulbs use more energy for heat than for light. Unless we could find a picture of Jesus painted or carved while he was alive it is impossible to prove it 100 per cent but the amount of similarities is amazing. Moreover, with all our machines and gadgets today we are not able to make anything like it.

Aggermian, in 1935, painted a beautiful picture of the Face of Christ based on the measurements of the Shroud of Turin. He took poetic licence to give him free-flowing hair and a serene face. Such pictures of artists help us in our prayers.

Homework
Readings from Luke

Day	1	2	3	4	5	6	7
Chapter	13	13	14	14	14	15	15
Verses	18–30	31–35	1–14	15–27	28–35	1–10	11–32

SESSION FIFTEEN

The Holy Spirit

Introduction

When I first started studying theology there was a question doing the rounds which was as follows: 'If St Paul was to come back to earth, what is the first question that he would ask?' At that time the answer was: 'Where is the Holy Spirit?'

Before Jesus had a chance to tell us about the Holy Spirit or to promise the Spirit to us, the Holy Spirit was already at work in God's plan for our salvation. In Lk 1:26ff. we read of the Angel Gabriel being sent to Mary at the time of the annunciation. He tells her how she will become the mother of Jesus. 'The Holy Spirit will come upon you ... and the power of the Most High will cover you with its shadow. And so the child will be holy and will be called the Son of God.' (Jesus means 'God/Yahweh saves' and Christ means 'the anointed One' or the Messiah. Son of God here does not necessarily imply Divinity.)

Peter in Acts 10:38 tells us how the Spirit was involved in the ministry of Jesus: 'God had anointed him with the Holy Spirit and with power, and because God was with him, Jesus went about doing good and curing all those who had fallen into the power of the devil.' Here Peter shows that his thinking at the time about Jesus is not well articulated – anointed by God and with the Holy Spirit. After Pentecost it still took time for them to realise that Jesus was God. We need to remember that their belief was that the Messiah would be like a great king or prophet. The idea of God becoming man was far beyond their hopes or dreams.

In Jn 3:5 Jesus speaks of the work of the Holy Spirit: 'I tell you solemnly unless a man is born of water and the Holy Spirit he cannot enter the Kingdom of God.' He goes on to compare the work of the Holy Spirit to the wind: 'The wind blows wherever it pleases; you hear its sound, but you cannot tell where it comes from or where it is going. That is how it is with all who are born of the Spirit.' (Jn 3:8)

When you deal with catechumens you find that some people enter the church very easily. They want to be baptised as soon as possible. For others it is a long and tiring journey. They keep putting baptism off and then one day they tell you that they are now ready to be baptised. Others will come and study and drift away without asking for baptism. I once baptised a man who had done his studies thirty years previously in a different place and with a different priest. We always need to remember that faith is a free gift of grace from God coming to us through the Holy Spirit.

It was at the Last Supper that Jesus promised to send us the Holy Spirit. 'I will ask the Father and he will give you another Advocate to be with you for ever, the Spirit of truth whom the world can never receive since it neither sees nor knows him; but you know him, because he is with you, he is in you.' (Jn 14:16–17)

Moreover, he told them what the Holy Spirit would do for them. 'The Advocate, the Holy Spirit, whom the Father will send in my name, will teach you everything, and remind you of all that I said to you.' (Jn 14–26) That work of the Holy Spirit is ongoing in the church today. Jesus saw the coming of the Holy Spirit as the culmination of his mission

The following words of Jesus at the Last Supper are short and cryptic, but we have to imagine the tension that he was under at that time. Moreover, there was the sadness of parting with his disciples, and the fear and dread of what was to come. In Jn 16:4b–15 we read:

I did not tell you this from the outset,
because I was with you;
but now I am going to the One who sent me.
Not one of you has asked,
'Where are you going?'
Yet you are sad at heart because I have told you this.
Still, I must tell you the truth;
it is for your own good that I am going,
because unless I go,
the Advocate will not come to you;
but if I do go,
I will send him to you.
And when he comes,
he will show the world how wrong it was,
about sin,
and about who was in the right,
and about judgement:
about sin
proved by their refusal to believe in me;
about who was in the right
proved by my going to the Father
and your seeing me no more;
about judgement
proved by the prince of this world already condemned.
I still have many things to say to you
but they would be too much for you now.
But when the Spirit of Truth comes
he will lead you to the complete truth,

since he will not be speaking as from himself
but will say only what he has learned;
and he will tell you of the things to come.
He will glorify me
since all he tells you
will be taken from what is mine;
that is why I said:
'All he tells you
will be taken from what is mine.'

The Coming of the Holy Spirit at Pentecost
We have just seen in the previous chapter the remarkable change that occurred
with the coming of the Holy Spirit at Pentecost. The apostles and disciples were
transformed and went out fearlessly to proclaim the Lord Jesus and to die as
witnesses of his resurrection. The church was very active and energised by the
Holy Spirit. To look at things from a purely human point of view, the transfor-
mation in the life of the disciples seems unbelievable.

For St Paul the presence of the Holy Spirit was very important. Reading the
Acts of the Apostles one gets the impression of Paul being led at times by the
Holy Spirit. 'They travelled through Phrygia and Galatian country, having
being told by the Holy Spirit not to preach the word in Asia. When they reached
the frontier of Mysia they thought to cross into Bithynia, but the Spirit of Jesus
would not allow them, they went down through Mysia and came down to
Troas. One night Paul had a vision: a Macedonian appeared and appealed to
him in these words, 'Come across to Macedonia and help us.' Once he had seen
this vision we (My memo: Luke seems to have joined them here.) lost no time
in arranging a passage to Macedonia, convinced that God had called us to bring
them the Good News.' (Acts 16:6–10)

Other names that we find for the Holy Spirit in the New Testament are the
Spirit of the Promise (Galatians 3:14 & Ephesians 1:13), the Spirit of Adoption
(Romans 8:15 & Galatians 4:6), the Spirit of Christ (Romans 8:9), the Spirit of
the Lord (2 Corinthians 3:17), the Spirit of God (Romans 8:9:14 & 15, 19 & 1
Corinthians 6:11 & 7:40), and Peter speaks of the Spirit of Glory (1 Peter 4:14).
The letters of St Paul have many references to the Holy Spirit and how the Holy
Spirit works in our lives. One that I like very much is in 1 Corinthians 6:19–20:
'Your body you know, is the temple of the Holy Spirit, who is in you since you
received him from God. You are not your own property, you have been bought
and paid for. That is why you should use your body for the glory of God.'

Symbols of the Holy Spirit
The Bible often uses symbols that can tell us a great deal about something, and
have a deep meaning. They can be more powerful than words. In John 13:21–30

we read of the treachery of Judas. It concludes: 'As soon as Judas had taken the piece of bread he went out. Night had fallen.' Those three words, 'night had fallen' are so full of meaning in regard to the state of mind of Judas and the general situation involving the betrayal of Jesus, and the coming sufferings of Jesus. They also imply a state of fear and uneasiness. They tell us that evil is in the ascendency as darkness is often associated with evil.

In regard to symbols for the Holy Spirit we have:

a) *Water:* Linked to the water of baptism. Paul writes in 1 Corinthians 12:13: 'In the Spirit we were all baptised, Jews as well as Greeks, slaves as well as citizens and one Spirit was given us to drink.'

In Jn 19:34 we read: 'One of the soldiers pierced his side with a lance; and immediately there came out blood and water.' A biblical note in my *Jerusalem Bible* says: 'The blood shows that the lamb has been sacrificed for the world, the water, symbol of the Spirit, shows us that the sacrifice is a source of grace. Many of the Fathers, not without good reason, interpret the water and blood as symbols of Baptism and the Eucharist, and these two sacraments as signifying the church which is born like a second Eve from the side of Christ.'

The first forms of life, we are told, appeared in water. Moreover, our natural birth was from water and here the Spirit is seen as living water welling up from Christ. In Jn 4:13–14 Jesus speaks to the Samaritan woman of giving her living water that will spring up into eternal life: 'Whoever drinks this water will get thirsty again; but anyone who drinks the water that I shall give will never be thirsty again; the water that I shall give will turn into a spring inside him, welling up to eternal life.'

b) *Anointing:* The symbolism of anointing with oil signifies the Holy Spirit. St John tells us in 1 John 2:20: 'You have been anointed by the Holy One and have received all knowledge.' St Paul in 2 Corinthians 1:21–22 writes: 'Remember it is God himself who assures us all, and you, of our standing in Christ, and has anointed us with his seal and pledge, the Spirit, that we carry in our hearts.'

In the Old Testament we read of kings and priests being anointed when they assumed office. We have been anointed as Christians and disciples of Jesus.

Anoint = power / medicine

c) *Fire:* While water signifies birth and the fullness of life, fire signifies the transforming energy of the Holy Spirit. Fire had a magical quality for ancient people. John the Baptist spoke of Jesus: 'I baptize you with water. But someone is coming, someone who is more powerful than I am, and I am not fit to undo the strap of his sandal; he will baptise you with the Holy Spirit and with fire.' (Lk 3:16) Jesus himself speaking of the Holy Spirit in Lk 12:49 says: 'I have come to bring fire to the earth, and how I wish it was blazing already.'

d) *Cloud and Light:* We can read of this in the Old Testament account of the exodus in Exodus 40:36: 'At every stage of their journey, whenever the cloud rose from the tabernacle the sons of Israel would resume the march.'

Again in Lk 9:34–35 at the transfiguration: 'As he spoke a cloud came and covered them with shadow; and when they went into the cloud the disciples were afraid. And a voice came out of the cloud saying, 'This is my Son, the Chosen One. Listen to him.' In Acts 1:9 at the time of the ascension St Luke tells us: 'As he said this he was lifted up while they looked on, and a cloud took him from their sight.'

e) A Dove: When Jesus comes up from his baptism we read: 'As soon as Jesus was baptised he came up from the water, and suddenly the heavens opened and he saw the Spirit of God descending like a dove and coming down on him. And a voice spoke from heaven, "This is my Son, the Beloved, My favour rests on him."'

The Work of the Holy Spirit in the Church and our Lives Today
St Paul in 1 Corinthians 2:10–11 tells us: 'These are the very things that God has revealed to us through the Spirit, for the Spirit reaches to the depths of everything, even the depths of God. After all, the depths of a man can only be known by his own spirit, not by any other man, and in the same way the depths of God can only be known by the Spirit of God.' We can never fully know another person unless they reveal themselves to us. If we in our own lives, or the church in its mission to all peoples, wish to know the mind and heart of God, then we are dependent on the Holy Spirit making that known to us or to the church. In the Vatican II documents the work of the Holy Spirit is mentioned in many places.

The Church is a communion or fellowship living in the faith of the apostles and she transmits that faith to succeeding generations. It is there that we come in contact with the Holy Spirit:

— in the scriptures inspired by the Spirit;
— in the tradition, church fathers, liturgy and so on;
— in the church Magisterium or teaching authority protected by the Holy Spirit;
— in prayer, especially the prayer of the church, where the Spirit intercedes for us;
— charisms and ministries by which the church is built up;
— in the many signs of apostolic and missionary life;
— in the witness of saints through whom the Spirit manifests holiness and continues the work of salvation. This applies not just to the likes of Mother Teresa of Calcutta, but to many people leading very simple and ordinary lives.

The Holy Spirit is God's gift to each of us. 'The love of God has been poured into our hearts by the Holy Spirit which has been given to us.' (Rom 5:5) At our Baptism the Holy Spirit restores to the baptised the divine likeness lost through sin. We become the adopted children of God and as the pledge or first fruits of this new status we receive the Holy Spirit to guide, lead and enlighten us. 'Your body, you know is the temple of the Holy Spirit.' (1 Cor 6:19)

By the power of the Spirit all things are possible for us. We can bear much fruit as Jesus told us. Jesus is the tree and we are the branches. 'I am the vine, you are the branches. Whoever remains in Me, with Me in him, bears fruit in plenty.' (Jn 15:5)

When we realise that we have the Holy Spirit dwelling in us and that we are connected to Jesus, then we have the strength, courage and confidence to go out and do the work of God that he is calling us to do.

Discussion

Can you see the Holy Spirit working in your life or the world around you or in the church? It is happening but can we see it? Look for it in all kinds of places.

Final Prayer

Prayers of intercession to the Holy Spirit for various needs would be suitable.

Reflection

The Pilgrim Church

The church to which we are called in Christ Jesus, and in which by the grace of God we acquire holiness, will receive its perfection only in the glory of heaven, when will come the time of the renewal of all things. (Acts 3:21) At that time, together with the human race, the universe itself which is so closely related to humankind, and which attains its destiny through humanity, will be perfectly re-established in Christ. (cf. Ephesians 1:10; Colossians 1:20; 2 Peter 3:10–13)

Christ lifted up from the earth, has drawn all people to Himself (Jn 12:23). Rising from the dead (Romans 6:9), he sent his life-giving Spirit upon his disciples and through the Spirit set up his body which is the church as the universal sacrament of salvation. Sitting at the right hand of the Father he is continually active in the world in order to lead people to the church and through it, join them more closely to himself; and by nourishing them with his own body and blood, make them partakers of his glorious life. The promised and hoped for restoration, therefore, has already begun in Christ. It is carried forward in the sending of the Holy Spirit, and through him continues in the church in which, through our faith, we learn the meaning of our earthly life, while we bring to term, with hope of future good, the task allotted to us in this world by the Father, and so work out our salvation (Philippians 2:12)

Already the final age of the world is upon us (1 Corinthians 10:11), and the renewal of the world is irrevocably underway. It is even now anticipated in a certain way, for the church on earth is endowed already with a sanctity that is real though imperfect. However, until new heavens and a new earth in which justice dwells (2 Peter 3:13) the pilgrim church, in its sacraments and institutions, which belong to this present age, carries the mark of this world which will pass, and she herself takes her place among the creatures which groan and travail yet, and await the revelation of the children of God. (Rom 8:15–22) 'The

Spirit you received is not the spirit of slaves, bringing fear into your lives again; it is the Spirit of sons and daughters, and it makes us cry out, Abba Father! The Spirit himself and our spirit bear witness that we are children of God. And if we are children we are heirs as well: heirs of God and coheirs with Christ, sharing our sufferings so as to share his glory.'

So it is united with Christ in the church, and marked with the Holy Spirit who is the guarantee of our inheritance (Ephesians 1:14) that we are truly called and indeed are children of God (1 John 3:1), though we have not yet appeared with Christ in glory (Colossians 3:4) in which we will be like to God, for we will see him as he is (1 John 3:2). 'While we are at home in this body we are away from the Lord' (2 Cor 5:6), and having the first fruits of the Spirit we groan inwardly (Rom 8:23), and we desire to be with Christ (Phil 1:23). That same charity urges us to live more for him who died for us and rose again (2 Cor 5–15). We make it our aim, then, to please the Lord in all things (2 Cor 5:9), and we put on the armour of God that we may be able to stand against the wiles of the devil and resist in the evil day (Eph 6:11–13).

Since we know neither the day nor the hour we should follow the advice of the Lord and watch constantly so that, when the single course of our earthly life is completed (Heb 9:27), we may merit to enter into the marriage feast, and be numbered among the blessed (Mt 25:31–46), and not, like the wicked and slothful servants (Mt 25:26), to be ordered to depart into the eternal fire, into the outer darkness where people will weep and gnash their teeth (Mt 22:13 & 25:30).

Before we reign with Christ in glory we must all appear 'before the judgement seat of Christ, so that each one may receive good or evil, according to what he/she has done in the body' (2 Cor 5:10), and at the end of the world 'they will come forth, those who have done good, to the resurrection of life, and those who have done evil, to the resurrection of judgement.' (John 5:29, cf. Mt 25:46) We reckon that the 'sufferings of this present time are not worth comparing with the glory that is to be revealed to us' (Rom 8:18:2; Timothy 11:12), and strong in faith 'we look for the blessed hope, the appearing of the glory of Our Lord Jesus Christ' (Titus 2:13), 'who will change our lowly body to be like his glorious body' (Philippians 3:21), and 'who will come to be glorified in his saints, and to be marvelled at in all who have believed.' (2 Tim 1:10) (From Vatican II *Dogmatic Constitution on the Church* No. 48.)

Homework
Readings from St Luke

Day	1	2	3	4	5	6	7
Chapter	16	16	16	17	17	17	18
Verses	1–8	9–18	19–31	1–10	11–21	22–37	1–17

Profession of Faith
Nicene Creed

I believe in One God, the Father Almighty, maker of heaven and earth, of all things visible and invisible. I believe in One Lord Jesus Christ, the Only Begotten Son of God, born of the Father before all ages, God from God, Light from Light, true God from true God, begotten, not made, consubstantial with the Father; through him all things were made. For us and for our salvation he came down from heaven: and by the Holy Spirit was incarnate of the Virgin Mary, and became man. For our sake he was crucified under Pontius Pilate, he suffered death and was buried, and rose again on the third day in accordance with the scriptures. He ascended into heaven and is seated at the right hand of the Father. He will come again in glory to judge the living and the dead, and his kingdom will have no end. I believe in the Holy Spirit, the Lord, the giver of life, who proceeds from the Father and the Son. Who with the Father and the Son is adored and glorified, who has spoken through the prophets. I believe in one, holy, catholic and apostolic church. I confess one baptism for the forgiveness of sins and I look for the resurrection of the dead, and the life of the world to come. Amen.

BOOK TWO

The Father

We have dealt with Jesus and the Holy Spirit and we should now deal with the Father. Trinity or Three Persons in One God must have been a very difficult concept for the Jews in the early church to grasp and accept. Their concept of God throughout their history was that there was only one God, and to any imagined diminution of that teaching, as they would see it, they would raise objections. 'I am Yahweh your God who brought you out of the land of Egypt, out of the house of slavery. You shall have no gods except me.' (Deut 5:6–7) The Trinity is not a diminution of that teaching, more an expansion of it, but it could be a problem for them. On the other hand, for the Gentiles the idea of only One God would be a problem for them as they were used to having many gods.

We need to look at the relationship of Jesus and the Father to know what our relationship should be to God. We often think of our relationship with Jesus and the Holy Spirit, but we can overlook our relationship with the Father. The relationship of Jesus and the Father should be the model for our relationships with each of the Three Persons of the Trinity.

The unique oneness of Jesus and the Father is shown in the extremely intimate and beautiful relationship which Jesus maintained with the Father at all times. The gospels show us how close Jesus was to the Father, and how conscious he was at all times in prayer and actions to do the Father's will. 'My food is to do the will of the One who sent me and to complete his work.' (Jn 4:34) Again Jesus tells us about his mission: 'I have come from heaven, not to do my own will, but to do the will of the One who sent me. Now the will of him who sent me is that I should lose nothing of all that he has given me, but that I should raise it up on the last day. Yes, it is my Father's will that whoever sees the Son and believes in him shall have eternal life, and that I shall raise him up on the last day.' (Jn 6:38–40)

A question we could ask ourselves here is what is our relationship with the Father at the present moment. What is his will or plan for me at the present time? Am I conscious of it?

In the gospels Jesus speaks many times of his and our heavenly Father. As just mentioned, he was very conscious of fulfilling the will of the Father at all times. He spoke of him as Abba which is an Aramaic word that a child would use towards his/her father. In the beautiful parable of the Prodigal Son it is the father who is the dominant person, and who is tolerant and forgiving in acts beyond our human understanding. The incomprehensible love of the Father for each and every one of us is central to the Good News that Jesus came to announce. Jesus also liked, before making a big decision and also at other times, to go into the mountains or a quiet place, and spend a long time in prayer with the Father. He found peace, quiet, guidance and strength there.

In the garden of Gethsemane at the Mount of Olives, Jesus prayed: 'Father, if you are willing, take this cup away from me. Nevertheless, let your will be done, not mine.' (Lk 22:42)

The *will* of the Father was all-important for Jesus. Even when he was only twelve years old and lost in the Temple he said to his parents when they found him: 'Why are you looking for me? Did you not know that I must be about My Father's affairs?'

We do not have many spoken words from the Father in the scriptures and so we must rely on Jesus to tell us about him. Jesus tells us that we need to be aware of the will of the Father in our lives just as he was aware of the will of the Father in his life: 'It is not those who say to me "Lord, Lord" who will enter the kingdom of heaven, but the person who does the will of my Father in heaven.'

Again in Mt 12:50 we have the words of Jesus: 'Anyone who does the will of my Father in heaven is my brother, and sister and mother.' Jesus here spells out the new and beautiful relationship we can have with him if we follow the will of his Father. A simple answer to what is the will of the Father is to say that we need to be conscious of the Father in our lives and in obedience to his will, walk the path of loving God and other people.

In Mt 5:43–45 we read: 'You have learnt how it was said: You must love your neighbour and hate your enemy. But I say to you: love your enemies and pray for those who persecute you, in this way you will be children of your Father in heaven, for he causes his sun to rise on bad people as well as good, and his rain to fall on honest and dishonest people alike.' It can be a help for us in dealing with a difficult person to remember that the Father loves that person and wishes that person good.

We also need to think and pray about the fact that each one of us has a special value in the eyes of the Father. No matter what happens or has happened each one of us has been loved from eternity by the Father and is still loved. The Father's love for each one of us is without limits or conditions. We are never alone but the Father is always at our side ready to help and support us. We may forget about him but he never forgets about us. St Teresa of Avila has a very nice prayer that applies to all the Persons of the Blessed Trinity but especially the Father:

Let nothing trouble you. Let nothing frighten you.
Everything passes. God never changes.
Patience obtains all.
Whoever has God wants for nothing.
God alone is enough.

There was a time when I would have tried to explain the Trinity to catechumens but I quickly realised that this was a bad idea. There is no way that I as a human being could find words or material examples to explain the spiritual mystery that is God. Still I can believe in a Trinitarian God because my source for that belief is the God-Man Jesus. He told us about it but he did not try to explain it to us. If an electrician tells me a wire is live I do not test it with my hand but I believe him. The big question is why did Jesus tell us. One reason is that each Person in the Trinity has a role to play in our lives, and knowing the Person and the role enables us to cooperate. The Trinity, which could be called a mystery of love, shows us the greatness of our God. We feel thankful for having someone who is so greatly concerned about us, and we realise our true dignity. Also to tell someone an intimate family secret like the Trinity shows trust in that person and puts the person informed on a different level of relationship.

Some words of Jesus that I like are his last words to his disciples in Matthew 28:18–19: 'Go therefore make disciples of all the nations; baptise them in the *name* of the Father and of the Son and of the Holy Spirit, and teach them to observe all the commands that I gave you. And know that I am with you always; yes to the end of time.'

I have put *name* in italics to emphasise that Jesus used the singular *name* and not *names*. Our Trinitarian God is One God. Also in regard to the matter of the personal name of God we were told it through Moses to be Yahweh (YHWH). It is in some ways a mysterious name meaning 'I am who am' or 'I am who I am', but telling the Jews and us this personal name is a sign of trust and love and friendship.

The scripture tells us several things about God. These are true of all the Persons but especially relevant to the Father. God is our creator and the creator of our world. In John 1:5 we read: 'God is light; there is no darkness in him.' In 1 John 4:8 we also hear that 'God is love.' These and other statements about God (Father) are not abstract statements, but they also mean that we share in an appropriate way in them. You could make other statements that God is truth, God is justice, God is hope and so on and they are all true.

It might be good at this point to state briefly the Church's teaching on the Trinity as put forward in *The Catechism of the Catholic Church.*

The Trinity is One. We do not confess three Gods but one God in Three Persons, the 'consubstantial trinity' (Council of Constantinople 11 [AD 553]) The divine persons do not share the one divinity among themselves but each of them is God whole and entire …

The divine Persons are really distinct from one another. God is one but not solitary. Father, Son and Holy Spirit are not simply names designating modalities of the divine being, for they are really distinct from one another … The divine unity is triune.

The divine Persons are relative to one another. Because it does not divide the divine unity, the real distinction of the persons from one another resides in the relationships which relate them to one another …

The whole divine economy is the common work of the three divine persons. For as the Trinity has only one and the same nature, so too does it have only one and the same operation. 'The Father, the Son and the Holy Spirit are not three principles of creation but one principle. However, each divine person performs the common work according to his unique personal property. Thus the church confesses, following the New Testament, one God and Father *from* whom all things are, and one Lord Jesus Christ *through* whom all things are, and one Holy Spirit *in* whom all things are. It is above all the divine missions of the Son's incarnation and the gift of the Holy Spirit that show forth the properties of the divine person.' (*Catechism of the Catholic Church,* Nos 253, 254, 255, 258. There is much more starting with No. 199 to No. 324 if you wish to read it. (Emphasis added)

To return to more ordinary things and more ordinary language I would like to quote Jesus on the concern of the Father for each and every one of us as he spoke of it in Mt 6:25–34. As the words of Jesus it is simpler and has more impact for us. 'This is why I am telling you not to worry about your life, and what you are to eat, nor about your body and how you are to clothe it. Surely life means more than food, and the body more than clothing! Look at the birds in the sky. They do not sow or reap or gather into barns; yet your heavenly Father feeds them. Are you not worth much more than they are? Can any of you, for all his/her worrying, add one cubit to his/her span of life? And why worry about clothing? Think of the flowers growing in the fields; they never have to work or spin; yet I assure you that not even Solomon in all his regalia was robed like one of these. Now if that is how God clothes the grass in the field which is there today and thrown into the furnace tomorrow, will he not much more look after you, you people of little faith? So do not worry: do not say, "What are we to eat? What are we to drink? How are we to be clothed?" It is the pagans who set their hearts on these things. Your Heavenly Father knows that you need them all. Set your hearts on the kingdom first, and on his righteousness, and all these things will be given to you as well. So do not worry about tomorrow, tomorrow will take care of itself. Each day has enough trouble of its own.'

In the Mass which is our principal prayer and worship of God, the Opening Prayer sets out the main purpose/petition of each particular Mass. We start it often by addressing it to the Father and at other times to 'God' or to 'Lord' and we always conclude it by invoking the Blessed Trinity. 'We ask this through Our Lord Jesus Christ, your Son, who lives and reigns with you and the Holy Spirit, one God, for ever and ever. Amen.' Moreover each of the four Canons of the Mass starts by invoking the Father, and also after the Consecration we again invoke the Father. He is also mentioned at times in other places in some of the Canons. Finally at the start of the Communion section we have the Lord's Prayer which is so aptly known as the Our Father.

It was customary at the time of Jesus for a religious leader to teach his disciples to pray, and when his disciples asked Jesus to teach them to pray we read in Mt 6:7–15 that Jesus taught them as follows:

> In your prayers do not babble as the pagans do, for they think that by using many words they will make themselves heard. Do not be like them; your Father knows what you need before you ask him. So you should pray like this:
>
> Our Father in heaven,
> (Shows our relationship to God)
> may your name be held holy,
> (Seeks recognition of God by all people)
> your kingdom come,
> (God's plans for our world to be actualised)
> your will be done,
> (Linked to the one above)
> on earth as it is in heaven.
> (Actualisation of the will of God on earth as in heaven)
> Give us today our daily bread
> (Usually linked to daily sustenance but the Fathers linked it to the Eucharist)
> And forgive us our debts,
> (Prayer for forgiveness)
> as we have forgiven those who are in debt to us.
> (Condition for forgiveness)
> And do not put us to the test,
> (Asking for God's help when confronted with evil)
> but save us from the evil one
> (Asking for God's help in trouble)
> Yes, if you forgive others their failings, your heavenly Father will forgive yours; but if you do not forgive others, your Father will not forgive your failings either.

Discussion
Discuss the role of the Father in the church and in your personal life. Discuss the different parts of the Our Father as set forth by Matthew.

Final Prayer
Prayers of intercession and end with the Our Father in the way you are familiar with it.

Reflection

Psalm 23: The Good Shepherd

> The Lord is my shepherd;
> there is nothing I shall want.
> Fresh and green are the pastures
> where he gives me repose.
> Near restful waters he leads me,
> to revive my drooping spirit.
> He guides me along the right path;
> He is true to his name.
> If I should walk in the valley of darkness
> no evil would I fear.
> You are there with your crook and your staff;
> with these you give me comfort.
> You have prepared a banquet for me
> in the sight of my foes.
> My head you have anointed with oil;
> my cup is overflowing.
> Surely goodness and kindness shall follow me
> all the days of my life.
> In the Lord's own house shall I dwell
> for ever and ever.

Homework

Readings from Luke

Day	1	2	3	4	5	6	7
Chapter	18	18	19	19	19	20	20
Verses	18–30	31–43	1–10	11–27	28–48	1–19	20–40

Prayer

Jesus said: 'Ask, and it will be given to you; search and you will find; knock and the door will be opened to you.'

When we are separated from a friend we try to keep in touch with that person by letter, e-mail, telephone, send messages in various ways, try to visit and so on. God is more important in our lives than any friend, and so it is only natural for us to try to keep in touch with God. It is easier than with a friend because God is always close at hand. God can help us in many ways and always has a loving concern for us that is much greater than that of any friend. You could say that God is the greatest, most powerful and most loving friend that we have, and he can help us when and where no human friend can help us. We maintain and build up our relationship with God through prayer which can be both private or common prayer with others.

Jesus gave us an example of prayer in his life. When he was faced with a difficult situation like choosing his apostles or facing danger in the garden of Gethsemane he prayed. At other times as we have seen he liked to go to some quiet or lonely place and pray at length to his and our heavenly Father. We can say that his whole life was a prayer because he was always conscious of and actually doing his Father's will. We read about the practice of the early church in Acts 2:42: 'They remained faithful to the teaching of the apostles, to the brotherhood, to the breaking of the bread, and to the prayers.' The breaking of the bread is the Mass which is the greatest prayer of all, and we will deal with it later.

Jesus spoke of prayer many times: 'According to scripture my house shall be called a house of prayer but you are turning it into a robbers den.' (Mt 21:1, cf. Mk 11:17) – Cleansing of the Temple: 'Zechariah, do not be afraid, your prayer has been heard.' (Luke 1:13) – Promise of birth of John the Baptist: 'I tell you solemnly, if you have faith and do not doubt at all, not only will you do what I have done to the fig tree, but even if you say to this mountain "Get up and throw yourself into the sea" it will be done. And if you have faith, everything you ask for in prayer you will receive.' (Mt 21:21–22) 'Now it was about this time that he went into the hills to pray; and he spent the whole night in prayer to God. (Lk 6:12) – The choice of the twelve: 'And when you pray, do not imitate the hypocrites: they love to say their prayers standing up in the synagogues and at the street corners for people to see them. I tell you solemnly, they have had their reward. But when you pray, go to your private room, and when you have shut your door, pray to your Father who is in that secret place, and your Father who sees all that is done in secret will reward you. (Mt 6:5–6) Where and how to pray. In the discourse at the Last Supper in John's gospel Jesus prays several times for his disciples and for us who would be his disciples at a later time. We also have those wonderful words of Jesus on the Cross: 'Father, forgive them; they do not know what they are doing.' (Lk 23:34)

One of the most beautiful parables that Jesus gave us is about a Pharisee and a publican in Lk 18:9–14: 'He spoke this parable to some people who prided themselves on being virtuous and despised everyone else. Two men went up to the Temple to pray, one a Pharisee, the other a tax collector. The Pharisee stood there and said this prayer to himself, "I thank you, God, that I am not grasping, unjust, adulterous like the rest of mankind, and particularly that I am not like this tax collector here. I fast twice a week; I pay tithes on all I get." The tax collector stood some distance away, not daring to raise his eyes to heaven, but he beat his breast and said, "God, be merciful to me a sinner." This man, I tell you, went home again at rights with God; the other did not. For everyone who exalts himself will be humbled, but the man who humbles himself will be exalted.'

There are many other sayings in the scripture about prayer, but these give us a sense about prayer and I have limited the quotations to what Jesus said, even though he said more than this. We also read about prayer in the Old Testament, especially the Psalms, and also in Acts and the rest of the New Testament.

Sometimes people will say that prayer is an encounter or a dialogue with God. This is certainly true but it is more than that. It has got to do with our relationship with God and God is very close to us. 'Your body, you know, is the Temple of the Holy Spirit, who is in you since you received him from God.' (1 Cor 6:19) Just as everything that Jesus did, whether it was travelling, or working as a carpenter or praying or preaching, was a prayer as it was the will of the Father for him, so everything we do in our daily life, even sleeping, is the will of God for us and is likewise a prayer. For me a good definition of prayer is *the living relationship of the children of God with their Abba Father who is good and loving beyond measure or imagining, with his Son Jesus Christ, and with the Holy Spirit.* A living relationship is always changing and needs to be attended to at regular intervals.

The prayer of Jesus in the gospels is shown as a continual inter-communion between Jesus and the Father. 'I am in the Father and the Father is in me.' (Jn 14:11) For Jesus prayer was essential. Whether he was in the mountains or the marketplace, the Temple or on the Cross, working or walking, his prayer, or if you like his communion with the Father was constant. Prayer was a frame of mind for Jesus. It is important to remember that when Jesus was making a chair as a carpenter he was concentrating on making that chair as St Joseph had taught him how to do it. We need to remember that fact as we go about our ordinary work and realise that the work we are doing is the will of God for us at that time and hence a prayer. It would be wrong to be trying to say prayers when we should be concentrating on driving a car.

Thérèse of Lisieux defined prayer as 'a surge of the heart; it is a simple look turned toward heaven; it is a cry of recognition and of love, embracing both trial and joy.' St Augustine said: 'Man/woman is a beggar before God.' St John Damascene said: 'Prayer is the raising of one's mind and heart to God or the requesting of good things from God. *The Catechism of the Catholic Church* in No. 2564 defines prayer: 'Christian prayer is a covenant relationship between God and man/woman in Christ. It is the action of God and of man/woman, springing forth from both the Holy Spirit and ourselves, wholly directed to the Father, in union with the human will of the Son of God made man.' We need to think about these words and the relationship to the New Covenant. In the Old Covenant the Jewish people were the People of God, but in the New Covenant we are the Children of God. In the Old Testament era God dwelt among his people in the Temple in Jerusalem and people tried to go there at least three times a year. The first was Passover or Exodus (our Easter), the second was First Fruits – our Pentecost, and the third was the Feast of Tabernacles (or Tents) which was a harvest thanksgiving feast and supposed to have been the most popular. They had to go to Jerusalem to come into contact with the living God, but for us God dwells in the smallest chapel that we have. The Columban Mission song says it all:

> For this is the dream that the young men dream,
> the vision the old men see,
> to march in the glory of Pentecost,
> to bring to the nations the sweet white Host,
> and the truth to make them free.

Jesus would have attended the synagogue for prayers on the Sabbath. This would have been a service of readings from the Old Testament, hymns, a talk of some kind if there was somebody competent present, and intercessory prayers. It would have been somewhat like the first part of our Mass and the early Christians attended it and then went to one of their homes for the breaking of the bread ceremony or our Mass. The early Christians did not take any part in the sacrifices and ceremonies of the temple – only prayed there.

How exactly did Jesus pray? We have two recorded examples of Jesus at prayer. *Both start with a prayer of thanksgiving*, and this is an important message for us about how to start our prayers. In the *first*, Jesus confesses the Father, acknowledges and blesses him because he has hidden the mysteries of the kingdom from those who think themselves learned and has revealed them to children or the unlearned. Luke 10:21–22 tells us: 'It was then that, filled with joy by the Holy Spirit, he said, 'I bless (thank) you, Father, Lord of heaven and earth, for hiding these things from the learned and clever and revealing them to mere children. Yes, Father, for that is what it pleases you to do. Everything has been entrusted to me by my Father; for no one knows who the Son is except the Father, and who the Father is except the Son and those to whom the Son chooses to reveal him.'

The *second* prayer, before the raising of Lazarus from the dead is recorded in John 11:41–43. Again thanksgiving precedes the event of raising Lazarus: 'Then Jesus lifted his eyes and said: Father, I thank you for hearing my prayer. I knew indeed that you always hear me, but I speak for the sake of those who stand around me, so that they may believe it was you who sent me.' When he had said this, he cried out in a loud voice, 'Lazarus here! Come out.'

There are so many things in our lives that we can thank God for, starting with our life, and the fact that in God's plan we are children of God with an eternal destiny in heaven. We may have problems but we also have many blessings. As humans we tend to count our crosses rather than our blessings. We need to continually remind ourselves that God loves each and every one of us as individuals. That love of God for us is unconditional and unchanging. No matter what our failings may have been the love of God for each of us is unchanged, and cannot be changed. This unchanging personal love of God for each of us is something that many people find hard to grasp. It is too good to be true and they feel that they should earn God's love, which in reality is impossible. Look at the beauty in the natural world around you as the guarantee of God's love for you. He made it for your enjoyment.

Besides Thanksgiving there are other kinds of prayer:

Blessing and Adoration: Blessing is an encounter between God and us. God blesses us with his gifts, and we bless God in return for his gifts. It is close to thanksgiving and praise.

Adoration is to acknowledge that God is the Creator and we are the creature. It exalts the greatness of God as the Creator who made us, and the loving power of the Saviour who set us free from sin. Adoration is the homage of the creature for God, the King of Glory. Adoration of the sovereign God of love blends with humility and gives assurance to our petitions.

Petition: We know that we are sinners but that God's love for us is greater than our sinfulness. Our prayers of petition express our relationship to God. Our petitions are always a turning towards God and a recognition of his greatness and his goodness. We start by asking for forgiveness like the publican in Lk 18:9–14. We need forgiveness to participate in the Mass or to pray. We pray for the kingdom of God on earth, for its coming and for what is necessary for its coming. Any need can become a petition. St Paul tells us in Philippians 4:6: 'There is no need to worry, but if there is anything you need, pray for it, asking God for it with prayer and thanksgiving.'

Intercession: This is to join in the prayer of Jesus. From the time of Abraham we read of prayers of intercession or of praying for someone else to God, or for something else like peace. It may be for someone close to us or it could be for the leaders of the country or the world, there are no boundaries. It is also tied into the Communion of Saints.

Praise means that we honour God as God and praise him for what He does and has done, and also for who and what he is. The Mass has all these different elements in it and we will do it later as it is the perfect prayer.

We can say that we pray to the Father through Jesus and with the help of the Holy Spirit. For personal prayer we need some suitable place. We saw how Jesus sought out quiet places for prayer, but we also need to remember that he also prayed in the synagogues and the Temple in Jerusalem. He prayed both with others and by himself. There is so much noise in our world today that it is hard to find a quiet place. People have radios and other devices on from morning to night. They almost seem to be afraid of silence. It is only in silence that we can hear God speaking to us. A quiet place or a church are good, and pilgrimages are part of all religions when we get away from our normal surroundings, and they remind us that we are on a journey to heaven.

Kinds of Prayer

It is interesting to note that when Jesus responded to the request of his disciples to teach them to pray he taught them a vocal prayer in the form of the Our Father. Vocal prayers are very common as they can be said in all kinds of places and at all kinds of times. They can also become common prayers like the Rosary. There are prayers that we learned as children and there are all kinds of prayer books. For children, vocal prayers are probably the most suitable. Many of us learned the Memorare as children; pick whatever prayer you like.

Meditation: Someone once described it as a search to find out what the meaning of life is and what God wants from us. Usually people use a book especially the gospels, moving from the written word to reality, and finding out what God wants from us and developing a closer relationship with God. We use our intellect, imagination, will and feelings and so on. We may be reading a piece of scripture and we try to enter the scene or situation. As a result of living in Japan and knowing about Zen meditation, I am inclined nowadays to just wait in silence on God. Before, I was too active and it was hard for the Lord to enter in, but now I am happy just to sit and wait. I think that instead of just sitting quietly there is an inclination in the West to be too pro-active. It is good to have a spiritual director of some kind.

Contemplation: This prayer is very closely related to God. We are acutely and immediately aware of God. St Teresa of Avila said that 'Contemplative prayer in my opinion is nothing more than a close sharing between friends, it means taking time frequently to be alone with him who we know loves us.'

Very often in such a situation there is not much need for words. I always think of the man who spent much time each evening before the Blessed Sacrament in the Church of St John Vianney, and when asked by the Curé what prayers he used he said that he used none. He just said, 'I look at him and he looks at me.' Contemplative prayer is the prayer of the child of God who is confident of the forgiveness and personal unconditional love of God. Contemplative prayer is hearing the word of God in silence and with faith and keeping vigil with God. *The Catechism of the Catholic Church* defines it as 'the simple expression of the mystery of prayer. It is a gaze of faith fixed on Jesus, an attentiveness to the Word of God, a silent love. It achieves real union with the prayer of Jesus to the extent that it makes us share in his mystery.' (No. 2724)

Mary the mother of Jesus often has prayers directed to her. Mary can intercede for us with her Son. We saw how it happened at the marriage feast of Cana, and Jesus gave her to us as our mother from the Cross on Calvary when he had nothing else left to give. In ordinary life if we are looking for something and we know someone who can put in a good word for us we do not hesitate to ask them. Because Mary was a full human being we also feel a closeness to her, and we are inspired and encouraged by her faith and trust in God. Likewise we can be inspired by the example of some of the saints and ask them also to intercede for us.

However, Jesus is the all important person in our prayer life and St Augustine sums it up well: 'He prays for us as our priest, prays in us as our Head, and is prayed to by us as our God. Therefore let us acknowledge our voice in him and his in us.'

Prayer is sometimes easy and it can, at times, be hard and dry. People often worry about distractions. Do not fight them, just ignore them. Start your prayer with some picture in your mind from the scriptures and go back to it. Do not under any circumstances regard distractions as sins. In the same way do not regard missing prayers as sins. Many good people worry about sin in prayers. Put it out of your mind. Another thing is that if you find yourself falling asleep, go and have a sleep. God is telling you through your body that you need to sleep.

Sometimes we feel that our prayers are not answered. How do you know? God has many ways of answering our prayers. We are seldom in a position to see the overall picture. We need faith in prayer to realise that God has a master plan for us and others and all his creation. To pray we need the grace or help of God, but there is also an effort needed on our part. Someone once said to me, 'We pray as we live, because we live as we pray.' Time and time again we need to remind ourselves that God is Abba, our all-loving, all-forgiving, all-understanding Father. St Paul told the Ephesians in 5:19–20: 'Sing the words and tunes of the psalms and hymns when you are together, and go on singing and chanting to the Lord in your hearts, so that always and everywhere you are giving thanks to God who is our Father in the name of the Lord Jesus.'

We must always remember that Jesus insisted on conversion of heart before praying. 'When you stand in prayer, forgive whatever you have against anybody, so that your Father in heaven may forgive your failings too.' (Mt 11:25)

For prayer we also need faith. When Jesus was performing one of his signs or miracles he was always looking for faith in people. He praised it when he found it as in the case of the Canaanite woman – a foreigner – whose daughter he cured, 'Woman, you have great faith. Let your wish be granted.' (Mt 15:28)

For prayer we need the *boldness* of children who ask expecting to get what they are asking for. Children do not easily take no for an answer but just approach the problem from a different angle. 'I tell you, therefore; everything you ask and pray for, believe that you have it already, and it will be yours.' (Mk 11:24)

Prayer is *keeping watch* with the Lord. When we pray we are keeping vigil with the Lord. Moreover in our prayers we are working for the coming of his kingdom that Jesus spoke so much about, and invited us to work with him for its coming. 'The harvest is rich but the labourers are few, so ask the Lord of the harvest to send labourers into his harvest.' (Mt 9:37) In various ways we can do our part to cooperate with God's plan for all peoples.

For prayer we need *purity of heart*. In other words we seek the growth of the kingdom of God rather than our own selfish needs. 'Where your treasure is, there will be your heart.' (Mt 6:21) 'Set your heart on his kingdom first, and on his righteousness, and all other things will be given to you.' (Mt 6:21)

In Hebrews 5:7–9 we read about how Jesus brought about our salvation. 'During his life on earth he offered up prayers and entreaty, aloud and in silent tears, to the One who had the power to save him out of death, and he submitted so humbly that his prayer was heard. Although he was Son, he learnt to obey through suffering, but having been made perfect, he became for all who obey him the source of eternal salvation.'

Discussion
What did you learn or find useful? You may find the reflection useful for discussion. This session is on prayer and you may wish to make it into two sessions.

Final Prayer
Make it one of intercessions.

Reflection
1. The liturgy of the church is most important, especially the Mass and the sacraments. The use of the Prayer of the Church, the Breviary, is becoming more widespread, like having Morning Prayer before Mass.

2. Verbal prayer vs meditation or contemplative prayer. It can vary greatly depending on all kinds of circumstances. Time causes us to make changes. Probably a mixture is best. Our tastes will vary with time and place.

3. Private vs community. Again there can be various circumstances and situations, but community prayer does have a special meaning. Jesus said in Mt 18:19-20: 'I tell you solemnly once again, if two of you on earth agree to ask for anything at all, it will be granted to you by my Father in heaven. For where two or three meet in my name, I shall be there with them.'

4. Places favourable for prayer. A church can be very suitable but also someplace that is quiet. It can be outside as we saw Jesus liked to pray outside, especially in quiet places. Of course he needed to get away from the crowds and get some rest. In your home you might like to light a candle, or burn incense or play soft music. Whatever helps you to pray is alright and any posture is okay. We have the cathedral of the great outdoors. A beautiful sunrise or sunset or beautiful scenery or even some flowers can help us feel the presence of God.

5. Material for prayer. The scriptures, especially the New Testament, provide us with unlimited material. Just read a little and then think about it and it will lead to prayer. Any aspect of God's dealings with you or others could be used. A poem, a book or just looking at God's creation in the world around you can move you to wonder and prayer. Different things appeal to different people, and you can keep using the same material time and time again. Any part of the Bible can appeal to different people. Be prepared to just sit and wait in silence. Do not be afraid of silence or inactivity.

6. How much time? We normally need some time to settle our minds down and breathing exercises can help. Sometimes we may only have time to enter a church and more or less say hello and goodbye to Jesus. If possible it is good to have a fixed time and start with a short time but …

7. Composition of place. Just look at some scene in the New Testament as we did and enter into it, and look at the people in it and what they are doing or saying. It is good to have some place to return to if you are distracted. Have some special scenes, for distractions, like Jesus sitting by the lakeside on his own and just sit with him, or in Bethlehem, or on the Cross and ones that you like. If you are very sleepy the best thing you can do is have a sleep, and come back to your personal prayers when you are fresh.

8. Our ordinary life is a prayer. If our life is orientated towards God in a general way, the ordinary things of our life are God's will or plan for us and doing them is a prayer in itself.

9. Prayer groups can be helpful. If you have the chance to join one, try it out or maybe you could start one on your own. You could start a scripture class and use one of the gospels and share a chapter or part of a chapter, and then discuss its meaning and application and pray about it using prayers

of intercession. Sing a hymn and be free to let the Spirit lead you into new ways. If it does not work out for you do not hesitate to move on to something else.

10. Pilgrimages as mentioned earlier have always been a part of all religions. You do not have to travel long distances or even with a group. Getting away from our usual surroundings helps us to pray.

11. A final thought. Prayer is a constructive way of wasting time, and life is not a problem to be solved, a question to be answered.

Life is a mystery to be contemplated, wondered at and savoured.

Homework
Readings from Luke

Day	1	2	3	4	5	6	7
Chapter	20	21	21	22	22	22	23
Verses	20:41–21:4	5–24	25–38	1–30	31–53	54–71	1–25

SESSION THREE

God's Plans for Humankind

When I read that our universe is almost fourteen billion years old I am amazed at God's preparations for us human beings and our existence. Furthermore when I read about the size of our universe (or universes) I am moved to wonder at the greatness of our God. If you were to put a timeframe on how long human beings have been on this earth it would be just a matter of seconds. The Bible does not set out to give us a history of the universe, or how our world came into existence, but to tell us about God's dealings with human beings and God's plans for us and our destiny. In *The Catechism of the Catholic Church*, No. 761 we read: 'The Gathering together of the People of God began at the moment when sin destroyed the communion of people with God, and that of people among themselves.'

God gave Adam hope after the Fall when he said to the serpent: 'I will make you enemies of each other; you and the woman, your offspring and her offspring. It will crush your head and you will strike its heel.' (Genesis 3:15) Here we have the promise of a saviour even though the idea of what a saviour would do is not clear. We must always remember that God was dealing with a very simple and primitive people and only by degrees would they be able to understand his plans for them.

Then God chose Abram and he believed God's command to him, and left for a distant country and travelled to Canaan, later called Palestine. 'Yahweh said to Abram, 'Leave your country, your family and your father's house for the land that I will show you. I will make you a great nation; I will bless you and make your name so famous that it will be used as a blessing.' (Gen 12:1–2) Abram believed God's words to him and set forth with his family and servants and his nephew Lot. Abram is always seen as an example of faith in God's promises.

Many people make contracts of different kinds. It might be for a loan or for a mortgage and so on. You do this by signing some kind of legal agreement. A Covenant is like a contract but it is with God and not a fellow human being or some kind of institution. Abram followed the custom of his time in Genesis 15. He killed some animals and cut them in half and then walked between the parts. The meaning was that if he did not keep his promise he could be killed as the animals and birds had been killed. We read in verse 17 how God fulfilled his side of the agreement: 'When the sun had set and darkness had fallen, there appeared a smoking furnace and a firebrand that went between the halves.' It was God pledging himself to the Covenant with his chosen people.

In Genesis 17 we read more about God's Covenant with Abram and how God changed his name to Abraham and told him that all his males were to be circumcised. Later on, God promised him the land of Canaan, later Palestine, as the land of his people. Land was very precious to people at that time and gave them an identity. God did many other things to help Abraham and his descendants. They on their part were to worship the one true God and no other. In Genesis 9:12–13 we read: 'Here is the sign of the Covenant I make between myself and you and every living creature with you for all generations. I set my bow in the clouds, and it shall be a sign of the Covenant between me and the earth.' The bow in the clouds or the rainbow reminded the Jews of God's Covenant with them, and it should call to mind for us the greater manifestation of God's love for us through Jesus in the New Covenant.

Later Moses led the descendants of Abraham from the slavery of Egypt to the freedom of their own land. They also received from God at Mount Sinai the Ten Commandments. There was a gap of several hundred years between the making of the Covenant with Abraham and the giving of the Ten Command- ments to Moses. There was then a solemn ceremony by which the Israelites pledged to become the People of God, and to worship only the One True God and to keep his commandments, and it is described in Exodus 24:3–8: 'Moses went and told the people all the commands of Yahweh and all the ordinances. In answer, all the people said with one voice, 'We will observe all the command- ments that Yahweh has decreed.' Moses put all the commandments into writ- ing, and early next morning he built an altar at the foot of the mountain, with twelve standing-stones for the twelve tribes of Israel. Then he directed certain young Israelites to offer holocausts and to immolate bullocks to Yahweh as communion sacrifices. Half of the blood, Moses took up and put into basins, the other half, he cast on the altar. And taking the Book of the Covenant he read it to the listening people, and they said. 'We will observe all that Yahweh has decreed; we will obey. Then Moses took the blood and cast it towards the people. 'This,' he said, 'is the blood of the Covenant that Yahweh had made with you, containing all these rules.' Blood was very sacred at that time as it was considered the source of life. Moses cast half of the blood of the holocaust on the altar which represented God, and the other half on the people which bound them to the Covenant. It also bound them to God and God to them, and made them the People of God. At that time, blood and not the brain was seen as the source of life.

We read that it was 'communion sacrifices' that were offered. The ritual of communion sacrifices is described in Leviticus 3 and its characteristic feature lies in the fact that the sacrificial victim is shared or eaten, with portions going to God, to the priest and to those who wished to offer the sacrifice. Yahweh's portion was burned on the altar, completely destroyed, and that meant that it belonged to God alone. For the Israelites and other people of that time and place, sharing food together with God or others had a deep significance of friendship and trust and love.

The Catechism of the Catholic Church in No. 762 tells us: 'The remote preparation for this gathering of the People of God begins when he calls Abraham and promises that he will become the father of a great people. Its immediate preparation begins with Israel's election as the People of God. By this election, Israel is to be the sign of the future gathering of all nations. But the prophets accuse Israel of breaking the Covenant and behaving like a prostitute.' They announce a new and eternal Covenant. Jesus instituted this New Covenant.

God gave his chosen people various leaders to govern them and also lead them in religious matters. One group that we read a good deal about are prophets. From the name we often think of them as foretelling things about the future. They certainly did this at times but their main role was that of teachers. The Israelites often tended to forget about Yahweh and to follow foreign idols and immoral ways of behaviour. They needed to be warned about their conduct, and led back to the correct practice of worshipping God and proper behaviour. On the other hand, the prophets were not clear about what the Messiah would be like, but they kept reminding the people about this hope and their destiny and their relationship with God. Even when they were slaves or oppressed the prophets could remind them of their great destiny in the future, and this was a consolation and a source of hope.

The Covenant between God and Israel was something like that between a strong and a weak country. God promised to defend Israel as his own country and people, while Israel repeated the promise of Abraham to worship the One True God and no other god or idol.

'I will be your God and you shall be my people.' (Leviticus 26:12) At various times this Covenant would be repeated and reaffirmed in the religious life of the people, and it gave them their own special identity.

We speak of the Covenant between God and the Israelites as it appears in the books of the Old Testament. It was not a frozen, eternal reality. It was the preparatory step towards the more glorious Covenant which God was to enter into with all human beings through Jesus Christ. That Covenant we call the New Covenant of the New Testament.

The New Covenant is complete, perfect and unchanging and we will deal with it later. One thing that we need to remind ourselves of is that it is thanks to the Israelites that we have the Old Testament which is a great treasure for us. There are various themes in it, history, God's plans for humankind, exhortation, poetry, prayers and prophecy amongst others. To sum it up very simply it shows that God had a plan from eternity for the human race and we are now part of that plan.

It shows that God is prepared to enter into human history to help us but he likes to use other human beings. The story of Moses and the Exodus from Egypt is interesting. Moses was not very happy to get involved in freeing the Israelites from Egypt, and made various excuses but God persuaded him to cooperate. In Exodus 3:7 we read: 'I have seen the miserable state of my people. I have heard their appeal to be free of their slave-drivers. Yes, I am well aware of their suffering. I mean to deliver them out of the hand of the Egyptians and bring them to a land rich and broad where milk and honey flow.'

Moses was the person chosen by God even if he was not very enthusiastic about the whole project. The central theme of the Old Testament is the involvement of God in the history of the chosen people, and his faithfulness that he had promised to Abraham and his successors. The Israelites failed many times but God was always faithful to his promise. I am reminded of the dying words of Jacob to his sons: 'The sceptre shall not pass from Judah, nor the mace from between his feet, until he comes to whom it belongs, to whom the peoples shall render obedience.'

Over the years the prophets added to the knowledge of the coming Messiah as it was made known to them, but it must have been hard for the listeners to hear about a suffering servant of God when their hopes were on an all conquering king or warrior. However their faith may have failed at times but they always returned to God: 'For Yahweh your God is a merciful God and will not desert or destroy you or forget the Covenant he made on oath with your fathers.' (Deut 4:31)

Just a limited comparison of the Old and New Covenants and we will deal with the latter later in more detail:

Old Covenant	New Covenant
Israelites only	All humankind
Ten commandments	Twofold commandments of love
Earthly reward e.g. own land	Eternal happiness of heaven
Israelites were People of God	We are the children of God
Many sacrifices	One eternal sacrifice of Calvary

These are some of the principal differences between the two Covenants.

Some people would like to have God interfere more in worldly matters. The problem is that God has given us *free will,* and that is why there is meaning and value in our actions. We are the children of an all-loving God who respects our freedom. If we think of the parable of the Prodigal Son the father probably foresaw that the younger son would get into trouble and lose his money, but he respected his freedom and let him go on his way. It is sometimes harder to do that than to interfere.

The evil in our world generally comes from human beings. If there was genuine love instead of greed and selfishness much suffering would be avoided. There is much more money spent on military armaments than there is on food for poor hungry people. In the recent nuclear disaster in Fukushima in Japan we need to ask the question of why anybody would build nuclear reactors in a country which is very prone to earthquakes, typhoons and tsunamis. Also why were the sea barriers not higher and so could have kept the tsunami at bay? The land is low lying in from the sea in that particular area, and that made it easy for the waters to come in quite a distance. Again people are causing climate change and some known and also unknown problems are caused as a result of this carelessness.

I like the story about God walking in his garden in the evening. A man approached him and started giving out to him. He wanted to know what God was doing about all the problems in the world. He listed them for God as wars, famine, climate change, disease, accidents of all kinds and so on. God told him that he had already done something about these problems and when the man asked what had he done God answered, 'I created you.' Just as in the case of Moses, God saw a problem and he chose Moses to rectify it, and so he calls us to help him in helping others and also his/our world in general.

Discussion

Discuss what parts of the Old Testament appeal to you. Do you find any particular parts that appeal to you or any parts that you do not like?

What do you think of the Old Covenant and especially the way God chose the Israelites?

Final Prayer

Prayers of intercession or any prayer or psalm that you like.

Reflection
The Old Covenant

When God chose to reveal himself to humankind, he began with the Israelites, who are known to us as the chosen people. Why he did so is a mystery of Love. The outstanding point in their history is their Covenant with God. In general we can say that a Covenant is a commitment or promise between God and some person or persons. Both sides promise to do something for each other. In a Covenant, God is the biggest giver.

Unlike an ordinary contract which is based on legal obligations, God's Covenant with the Israelites was based on his freely given love to them. In the Covenant, God promised to make them into a great nation and to give them their own land, and that from them would come a great leader. God made and extended his Covenant with different leaders, such as Abraham, Moses, and David. He also expounded about a great leader and his promises through the prophets e.g. he would be born of a virgin, in Bethlehem and be a descendant of David.

In return for God's many and great blessings, the Jews were to obey God's law which is summarised in the Ten Commandments. The law gave the Israelites an identity distinct from their neighbours and gave them a special task, a mission to witness to the One True God.

The most important aspect of the Israelites' response was to worship Yahweh, and to witness to him as the One True God who keeps everything and everybody in existence. All other gods were false and powerless; only Yahweh was the true, living, unique God. Old Testament history is full of the sad story of how the Israelites were unfaithful to God, and how they continually fell back into the worship of false gods – especially the gods of the people that they came into contact with. But the Old Testament also has a happy story for us. It is that of God's continuous love for his people, and how time and time again he forgave them and received them back as his chosen people. His faithfulness was greater than their leaving him and falling into sin. They remained the chosen people.

What Kind of Being is God?

God is essentially a mystery. Human words cannot describe or express all that God is. He reveals himself as One who is *transcendent,* that is, totally separate from his creation; he is at the same time totally concerned about his creation. He is above it and beyond it and at the same time part of it. He is also *immanent,* that is, present to and joined to his creation and concerned about it. These may be technical words but they do give us some ideas about God. Certain traits emphasise his majesty and beyondness as far as we are concerned, and other characteristics stress his nearness and concern for us. If we could really fully comprehend God he would no longer really be God: but we can get to know something about him from his Son who became man and also from his creation.

Transcendent: God is unique, omnipotent, eternal, immense, omniscient, contains all things, beyond human understanding, keeps all things in existence, is due our love and praise and homage as his creatures and creation.

Immanent: God is near to us and not far away, as people thought in the Old Testament era. God chose a people – the Israelites – for his chosen people. He led them and guided them to the promised land of Canaan. He gave them judges, kings and prophets as guides. He was always concerned about them even when they forgot about him. The same is true of our present situation. He is concerned about us and our welfare.

Now he has chosen us as his adopted children. He leads us and guides us through his church which he established, and sustains us through his sacraments. He has an eternal destiny for us in heaven, which is our promised land. He is concerned both about our present and eternal welfare.

Homework
Readings from Luke and Acts of the Apostles

Day	1	2	3	4	5	6	7
Chapter	23	24	24	ACTS 1	1	2	2
Verses	26–56	1–35	36–53	1–11	10–26	1–13	14–47

SESSION FOUR

The Mass as Sacrifice

The Last Supper occurred at the time of the Jewish feast of Passover which celebrated their escape from the slavery of Egypt, and also the whole Exodus story before they arrived in their own land and freedom, and was and still is a most important feast in the Jewish calendar. It was a feast to commemorate and *re-present* the astonishing actions and the love of God in leading the Israelites out of the slavery of Egypt to the freedom of their own land, and also the Covenant with God at Mount Sinai and the receiving of the Ten Commandments, and the formal ritual by which they became the People of God.

In accordance with ritual it was celebrated in conjunction with the full moon after the spring equinox, in families or groups. The meal centred on the eating of a one-year-old male lamb that was roasted, together with unleavened bread and bitter herbs. The people eating it would be dressed ready to leave on a journey. There were readings from the Old Testament about the Passover and the escape from Egypt. Also psalms and prayers. Blood from the lamb was sprinkled on the doorposts and lintel at the entrance to the house or room. Along with the unleavened bread, toasts of wine were drunk at various intervals during the meal. (The Passover meal could be eaten over a number of days before the Sabbath after the full moon after the Spring equinox.) The Passover fell on the Sabbath the year that Jesus died – John 19:31. Usually the Last Supper pictures show us Jesus at a table with his disciples. However, it is much more likely that they were lying on their sides on cushions with low tables in front of them. (cf. John 13:21–26)

People often use signs and symbols to express themselves. They help us at times to express feelings that are beyond words. They can also show us and others what we value or wish to celebrate or thank other people or God for in our lives. We use symbols at birthdays, baptisms, marriages, funerals, celebrations and so on to express something that is greater and more profound than mere words. It could be a special meal at Christmas or a wedding ring. However, signs and symbols can easily degenerate like words into mere charades or empty tokens. A party can be most enjoyable or it can be a bore. But if something means a great deal to us or we find it hard to express it or our feelings in words, then signs and ceremonies can express that feeling or thought within us. Words are not enough but the proper sign or symbol is unforgettable and beyond words.

In Exodus 12:26–27 we read: 'And when your children ask you, "What does this ritual mean?", you will tell them, "It is the sacrifice of the Passover in honour of Yahweh who passed over the houses of the sons of Israel in Egypt, and struck Egypt but spared our houses."' If you would like to read more about this incident then read Exodus 12:1–28. When Jesus and his disciples re-enacted the deeds of their ancestors, they recalled the Covenant entered into between God and the Israelites and God's special love for them. They promised to be faithful to the Covenant which Moses and their ancestors had made on their behalf. On this particular Passover of the Last Supper, Jesus would change all this by establishing a New Covenant. The feast of the Passover was an occasion of great joy for the Jewish people. It recalled them to an awareness of (1) God's loving kindness for them and (2) their special relationship with God.

'Moses said to the people, "Keep this day in remembrance, the day that you came out of Egypt, from the house of slavery, for it was by sheer power that Yahweh brought you out of … You will observe this ordinance each year at its appointed time."' (Ex 13:3, 13) In Deuteronomy 7:6, 8–9 Moses offers a further explanation: 'You are a people consecrated to Yahweh your God; it is you that Yahweh has chosen to be his very own people out of all the peoples of the earth … It was for love of you and to keep the oath that he swore to your fathers that Yahweh brought you out with his mighty hand and redeemed you from the house of slavery, from the power of Pharaoh King of Egypt. Know then that Yahweh your God is God indeed, the faithful God who is true to his Covenant and his graciousness for a thousand generations towards those who love him and keep his commandments.' These words of Moses can have meaning for us today even though they have been superseded by a greater Covenant with God by which we are the adopted children of God.

The disciples would have looked forward to this meal with Jesus with a mixture of hope and apprehension. Matthew 26:17–19 tells us how it was arranged: 'Now on the first day of Unleavened Bread the disciples came to Jesus to say, "Where do you want us to make the preparations for you to eat the Passover?" "Go to so-and-so in the city," he replied "and say to him, The Master says: My time is near. It is at your house that I am keeping the Passover with my disciples." The disciples did what Jesus told them and prepared the Passover.'

When Jesus and his disciples came together to eat the Passover meal, Jesus said: 'I have longed to eat this Passover with you before I suffer; because I tell you, I shall not eat it again until it is fulfilled in the kingdom of God.' (Lk 22:15) (*Jerusalem Bible* explanation of 'fulfilled' – The first stage of fulfilment is the Eucharist itself, the centre of spiritual life in the kingdom founded by Jesus: the final stage will be at the end of time when the Passover is to be fulfilled perfectly and in a manner no longer veiled – at the *parousia* or the end of world.)

The disciples did not understand the full meaning of the words of Jesus. This Last Supper/Passover was a prefiguring of the Passion – Death – Resurrection of Jesus. It was a sign of greater things to come. The average Jewish believer observed the feast in gratitude for what God had done in the *past*. Jesus saw the past as the *beginning* of God's gracious mercy about to be extended and enriched in a *new* way.

At the time of the first Passover in Egypt the Jewish people were saved from possible extinction and freed from slavery. The blood of the sacrificial lamb in the past was the *model* of the greater reality of the blood which Jesus was to shed at Calvary. John the Baptist had said in John 1:29: 'Look, there is the Lamb of God that takes away the sins of the world.' *Jerusalem Bible* notes: This is one of the most significant of John's symbols for Christ. It blends the idea of the 'servant' (Isaiah 53) who takes on himself the sins of humankind, and offers himself as a 'lamb of expiation' (Leviticus 14) with that of the 'Passover lamb' (Exodus 12, cf. John 19:36 and Genesis 22) whose ritual symbolises Israel's redemption. (cf. Acts 8:31-35, 1 Corinthians 5:7 and 1 Peter 1:18–20

At Mount Sinai the Israelites made a Covenant with God, and became the People of God. The Covenant was ratified by the blood of sacrificial bullocks. For the Israelites and other people of that time blood signified life, and had a close relationship with God. It is for this reason that the Jewish people eat kosher meat or meat that has had all the blood drained out of it.

In Genesis we read in 9:4: 'I give you everything, you must not eat flesh with life, that is to say, with blood in it.' Again in Leviticus 17:11–12 it is written: 'The life of the flesh is in the blood. This blood I myself have given you to perform the rite of atonement for your lives at the altar; for it is blood that atones for a life. This is why I have said to the sons of Israel; none of you nor any stranger living among you shall eat blood.'

Life belongs to God and to God only. Blood – signifying life – belongs to God and to God only. To pour out blood on the altar of God – in other words to return life to God from whom it comes – is the only suitable way to acknowledge the gift of life which we have received.

When Moses ratified the Covenant on Mount Sinai, he first poured the blood on the altar and then sprinkled it on the people and said: 'This is the blood of the Covenant that Yahweh has made with you …' (Exodus 24:8) Note that the sacrifice at Mount Sinai was a *communion* sacrifice, as the people eat part of the sacrifice that was offered.

The Last Supper

The Mosaic Covenant was a *preliminary* Covenant, the blood of the sacrificial bullocks a preparatory sign. The Mosaic Covenant was to find its fulfilment in and through Jesus Christ. The Last Supper was the actualisation of an ancient promise. It was the beginning of a new era – the prelude of a new age. The time had now come, through the mediation of Jesus, for the making of a *new* Covenant between God and humankind. The New Covenant, like the Old, would be ratified in blood. But the blood would not be the blood of some sacrificial animal, but rather the blood of the Son of God, Jesus Christ, poured out on Calvary. Matthew gives us the words of Jesus in 26:27–28: 'Then he took the cup and when he had returned thanks he gave it to them. "Drink all of you from this", he said, "for this is my Blood, the blood of the Covenant which is to be poured out for many for the forgiveness of sins".'

It was in this way that the Last Supper differed from the usual ritual of the Passover. It signified at the highest level of *grace* all that was signified at the lower level of the geographical and physical deliverance of the Israelites from Egyptian slavery. It was a Passover from sin to grace, from estrangement to friendship, from death to eternal life. It was a Passover not for a small group or a small nation but for all human beings. We are joined to this New Covenant when we share in faith in the Sacrifice of the Covenant. For this reason the Last Supper and the Sacrifice of Calvary come together as two phases of the one Passover, namely, Covenant and Sacrifice.

In 1 Corinthians 11:23–26, St Paul tells us what happened at the Last Supper as it had been told to him as he was not present. 'For this is what I received from the Lord, and in turn passed to you; that on the same night that he was betrayed, the Lord Jesus took some bread, and thanked God for it and broke it, and he said, "This is My Body, which is for you; do this as a memorial for me." In the same way he took the cup after supper, and said, "This cup is the New Covenant in my blood. Whenever you drink it, do this as a memorial for me." Until the Lord comes, therefore, every time you eat this bread and drink this cup you are proclaiming his death …' Until the end of the world the church must proclaim the Lord's redemptive death when celebrating the Eucharist. It is the sacrament of the unseen Presence, recalling the past death and pledging the future triumph. In the previous short passage the apostle (Paul) stresses the sacrificial aspect of the sacrament as memorial and symbol of the Lord's death. Just as the Passover celebration commemorated the deliverance of Israel from Egyptian bondage, so the Eucharist commemorates the deliverance from sin and death for us brought about by Jesus. The Eucharist is the proclamation of the Lord's redemptive death that the church makes until his coming, when there will no longer be a need of his sacramental presence. (*Jerome Biblical Commentary*, pp. 270–271)

The ritual of Jesus at the Last Supper was just one small part of the Passover meal. However, by the words of Jesus, bread and wine became his body and blood. This was a prior manifestation of what he was to actualise the next day on the Cross at Calvary through the shedding of his blood and the giving up of his life. Taking the cup of wine – and there had probably been other cups of wine offered during the meal – Jesus pronounced the words of the New Covenant. 'This cup is the New Covenant in my blood. Whenever you drink it, do this as a memorial of me.' (1 Corinthians 11:25) Jesus has left this thanksgiving meal to us his followers. We know it as the thanksgiving meal, the

Eucharist, or simply as the Mass. The next session will deal in more detail with the Mass. (St Paul wrote about the Last Supper before the gospel accounts.) After the meal Jesus went with his disciples to the garden of Gethsemane where he was betrayed by Judas and arrested. His disciples ran away and he was alone except for the Father to face his death.

Sacrifices

We find many accounts of sacrifices among all kinds of people all over the world and not just among the Israelites. The basic idea was that people recognised some kind of deity or deities. They also recognised some kind of relationship with the deity, and wished to perform some kind of ceremony of homage, thanks, petition and so on. When a sacrificial offering was made to a deity they normally felt that it could not be used again by humans as it belonged to the deity, and so it was destroyed in some way by killing and burning or pouring out wine on an altar or the ground. The usual name for this kind of sacrifice is a holocaust. In a *communion* sacrifice, part of the animal was eaten by those who offered it to show communion with their deity. Even in human sacrifices the people were offering something, namely a human life, that they considered very precious to their deity. Common elements in a sacrifice were:

1. Some kind of offering, e.g. an animal.
2. An altar of some kind.
3. A priest who offered the sacrifice.
4. Worshippers.

In the Old Testament we read of many sacrifices of animals and birds. Wheat and other cereals were offered and burned. Wine was poured out on the altar or the ground. However, the offering of animals or birds was the main one. In this way the people acknowledged their indebtedness to God, their sinfulness and their desire to make amends. In many of the sacrifices of the Old Testament, there was the aspect of renewing the Covenant between God and Israel, of rededicating themselves as the People of God. There were also sin sacrifices where the animal was seen as bearing the guilt of the nation or of an individual. Of course internal repentance was recognised as a pre-condition for pardon and forgiveness. The sacrifices of the Old Testament were endless.

However, all the sacrifices of the Old Testament and its priesthood were prefigures of the one unique, perfect and complete sacrifice of Jesus, which was offered for all humanity at Calvary.

The perfect sacrifice for the sins of the world was offered on Calvary by Jesus. The Passover Lamb of the New Covenant, Jesus Christ, bore the sins of the world and expiated them in his body at Calvary.

An interesting question to ask yourself is how you could adequately worship God other than by sacrifice – strange as sacrifice may seem in our era.

Final Prayer

   Prayer to Our Redeemer
   Soul of Christ, make me holy.
   Body of Christ, be my salvation.
   Blood of Christ, let me drink your wine.
   Water flowing from the side of Christ, wash me clean.
   Passion of Christ, strengthen me.
   Kind Jesus, hear my prayer;
   hide me within your wounds
   and keep me close to you.
   Defend me from the evil enemy.
   Call me at my death
   to the fellowship of your saints,
   that I may sing your praise with them
   through all eternity. Amen.

Reflection

Vatican II: Constitution on the Church, No. 9

At all times and in every race, anyone who fears God and does what is right is acceptable to him (cf. Acts 10:33). He has, however, willed to make people holy and save them, *not as individuals* without any bond or link between them, but rather to make them into a People who might acknowledge him and serve him in holiness.

He therefore chose the Israelite race to be his own People, and established a Covenant with it. He gradually instructed this People – in its history manifesting both himself and the decrees of his will – and made it holy unto himself. All these things, however, happened as a preparation and figure of that new and perfect Covenant which was to be ratified in Christ, and of the fuller revelation which was to be given through the Word of God made flesh. 'Behold the days are coming, says the Lord, when I will make a new Covenant with the house of Israel and the house of Judah ... I will put my law within them, and I will write it upon their hearts, and they shall be my people ... For they shall all know me from the least of them to the greatest, says the Lord.' (Jeremiah 31:31–34)

Christ instituted this New Covenant, namely the New Covenant in His Blood (cf. 1 Corinthians 11:25): He called a race made up of Jews and Gentiles, which would be *one*, not according to the flesh, but in the Spirit, and this race would be the New People of God. For those who believe in Christ, who are reborn, not from a corruptible seed, but from an incorruptible one through the word of the living God (cf. 1 Peter 1:23), not from flesh, but from water and the Holy Spirit (cf. John 3:5–6), and are finally established as a 'chosen race, a royal priesthood, a holy nation ... who in times past were not a people, but are now the People of God.' (1 Peter 2:9–10)

The Messianic people has as its Head Christ, 'Who was delivered up for our sins and rose again for our justification' (Romans 4:25), and now having acquired the name which is above all names, reigns gloriously in heaven. The state of this people is that of the dignity and freedom of the children of God, in whose hearts the Holy Spirit dwells as in a temple. Its law is the New Commandment to love as God has loved us. Its destiny is the kingdom of God which has been begun by God himself on earth, and which must be further extended until it is brought to perfection by him at the end of time when Christ our life (cf. Colossians 3:4) will appear and 'creation itself also will be delivered from its slavery to corruption into the freedom of the glory of the children of God' (Romans 8:21).

Hence the Messianic People, although it does not actually include all people, and at times may appear as a small flock, is, however, a most sure seed of unity, hope and salvation for the whole human race. Established by Christ as a communion of life, love and truth, it is taken up by him also as the instrument for the salvation of all; as the light of the world and the salt of the earth (cf. Mt 5:13–16) and it is sent forth into the whole world.

As Israel according to the flesh which wandered in the desert was already called the church of God (Nehemiah 13:1, cf. Numbers 20:4; Deuteronomy 23:1ff.), so too, the New Israel, which advances in this present era in search of a future and permanent city (cf. Hebrews 13:14), is called the church of Christ (cf. Matthew 16:18). It is Christ indeed who has purchased it with his own blood (cf. Acts 20:28); he has filled it with his Spirit. He has provided means adapted to its visible and social union. All those, who in faith look towards Jesus, the author of salvation and the principle of unity and peace, God has gathered together and established as the church, that it may be for each and every one the visible sacrament of this saving unity.

Destined to extend to all regions of the earth, it enters into human history, though it transcends at once all times and racial boundaries. Advancing through trials and tribulations, the church is strengthened by God's grace, promised to her by the Lord, so that she may not waver from perfect fidelity, but remain the worthy bride of Lord, *until, through the Cross, she may attain to that light which knows no setting.* (Emphasis added)

Homework
Readings from the Acts of the Apostles

Day	1	2	3	4	5	6	7
Chapter	3	4	4	5	5	6	7
Verses	1–26	1–22	23–37	1–21	22–42	1–15	1–43

Scripture memos

1. *Bible* is derived from a Greek word meaning book. The Old Testament is *a collection of books* written over 900 years. The Protestant version has 39 books and the Catholic version has 46 books. The Protestant version only recognises books that were written in Hebrew, whereas the Catholic version also recognises books that were written in Aramaic and/or Greek. The Septuagint was a translation from Hebrew and Aramaic into Greek. The Israelites stopped speaking Hebrew and started using Aramaic from the time of the Babylonian exile 587–538 BC. Greek became a spoken language within the Roman Empire. The extra seven books that the Catholic Church recognises are Tobit, Judith, Wisdom, Sirach, Baruch and 1 and 2 Maccabees, plus additions in Esther and Daniel. In the New Testament there are 27 books and they were written over a period of about 50 years starting AD 50–51 during the second journey of St Paul with his First Letter to the Thessalonians. They were all written in Greek which was the common language of the day in the Roman Empire. The book that caused the most discussion about whether it should be in the canon of scripture was Revelation. The Hebrew Bible has only twenty four books but they have amalgamated several books into one at times.

2. *Sacrifice.* Previously when people regarded blood as the source of life and directly connected with God they considered that by offering the blood of a bullock in sacrifice they were offering themselves to the deity. As we saw earlier, when they partook of the sacrifice they were seeking union with the deity.

SESSION FIVE

The Mass as Sacrament

Introduction

Mass: The word comes from the Latin words at the end of Mass, *Ite missa est*, meaning 'You are sent forth.' Eucharist – the Greek word *eucharistein* recalls the Jewish blessings that proclaim, especially during a meal, God's works of creation, redemption and sanctification. Whatever you like to call it, it's the central act of worship in the Catholic Church.

The wonderful works of God for the Israelites were just a *prelude* for the wonderful works of Jesus – the God-Man – on our behalf which resulted in our salvation through his passion–death–resurrection. From our baptism and confirmation we can participate in this ongoing plan of *salvation* by God in the liturgy. Through the liturgy we can participate in the prayer of Jesus to the Father in the Holy Spirit. Vatican II in *The Constitution on the Sacred Liturgy* says that 'it is the liturgy through which, especially in the divine sacrifice of the Eucharist, the work of our redemption is accomplished.' (Article 2) Again in Article 10 we read: 'The liturgy is the summit towards which the activity of the church is directed; it is also the fount from which all her power flows. For the goal of apostolic endeavour is that all who are made children of God by faith and baptism should come together to praise God in the midst of his church, to take part in the sacrifice and to eat the Lord's Supper.'

St Paul tells us in Ephesians 1:3–7 of God's plan for us: 'Blessed be God the Father of our Lord Jesus Christ, who has blessed us with all the spiritual blessings of heaven in Christ.

1. Before the world was made he chose us, chose us in Christ, to be holy and spotless, and
2. to live through love in his presence, determining that
3. we should become his adopted children, through Jesus Christ, for his own kind purpose, to make us praise the glory of his grace, his free gift to us in the Beloved,
4. in whom, through his blood, we gain our freedom, the forgiveness of our sins.' (My numbering)

Old and New Covenants

We will make a brief comparison of the two Covenants.

Old Covenant	*New Covenant*
1. Applied only to the Israelites.	1. Applies to all human beings.
2. God is seen as a strict monarch.	2. God is Abba Daddy God.

3. God punishes, also pardons.
4. God promises the Israelites
   their own land.
5. God is distant – transcendent.

6. Ten Commandments.
7. Many sacrifices.
8. Many priests.
9. Israelites are people of God.
10. Leaders are both political
    and religious.
11. God sends prophets.
    from time to time.

3. God forgives and is merciful.
4. God promises the happiness
   of heaven.
5. God is both transcendent and
   immanent.
6. Two commandments of love.
7. One eternal sacrifice.
8. One priest in Jesus.
9. We are all children of God.
10. Jesus sets up a Church to
    lead/guide.
11. Holy Spirit always present
    to guide.

The Old Covenant was a history of sin, bondage, fear and darkness and the New Covenant is a history of grace, freedom, love, light and compassion. Jesus said: 'I am the way, the truth and the life.' (John 14:6) and again he said: 'I am ascending to my Father and to your Father, to my God and to your God.' (John 20:17)

Discussion – What parts of the New Covenant appeal most to you?

It is very easy for us to overlook how much more we *now* know about God than the Israelites of old from the words, life and actions, and the passion–death–resurrection of Jesus, and from the history of the church, and the work of the Holy Spirit both in the past and in the present. In the Old Testament era their knowledge of God was very basic at the beginning, even though it did grow with time, it still was very much lacking in depth. Even at the time of Christ most were still simple people with not very much education.

The Israelites by their many sacrifices and especially at the Passover and other big feasts were reminded of their Covenant with God. The sacrifice of the Mass does the same for us, but goes much further by making the sacrifice of Calvary once more present to us. The sacrifice of Calvary was offered *once* for us by Jesus and is now the *one* and *eternal* sacrifice of the New Covenant. In trying to explain this matter to catechumens I often used an illustration that is deficient in many ways but which they found useful. It is as follows: I can watch a football game on television from a distance of thousands of miles. I am present in some way at the game thanks to miles of cables, satellites, cameras and a television set. The Mass is something like that but much more than that because it really makes me present at Calvary, and I can offer the sacrifice of Jesus with him and his mother and the other women and the Beloved Disciple. Through the Mass we are really present at Calvary. The Priest is the same, and the sacrifice is the same, namely Jesus, and the only addition or difference is that we are now really present and can join in the offering.

The Mass as Sacrifice or an Offering to God

The Mass is the *sacrifice* of the New People of God, who are also the adopted children of God. In the early church we read of it as the 'ceremony of the breaking of the bread'. In Acts 2:46: 'They went to the Temple every day, but met in their houses for the breaking of the bread.' In the Mass we have two parts namely:

1. The Liturgy of the Word.
2. The Liturgy of the Eucharist.

The first is based on the prayers and readings in the Temple or synagogue, and the second on the ceremony of the 'breaking of the bread' in their houses or our Eucharist.

   To understand the Mass it is good to think of offering a *present* to God. Presents are common in our daily life and they can have many meanings. For instance, there are presents to commemorate various anniversaries, to say thanks for something, to petition for something, to apologise, to congratulate someone, to express love or friendship and so on. In Japan there were books on giving presents and what was suitable for different occasions, and to show how to wrap them. Never offer *four* of anything in Japan as it has the meaning of death. Let us look at what happens when Person A offers a present to Person B. It could have one of several meanings. For instance, a man has a disagreement with his girlfriend. He could go along and apologise, but if he is smart he will bring a present. (You can imagine other kinds of scenarios.)

1. Man buys a present to give to his girlfriend with whom he has had a disagreement. The *first* thing that will happen when he goes to her place is that they will greet one another and engage in some small talk. Now apply this to the Mass.
   a) When we go to Mass, at the beginning we do the talking. There may be an entrance hymn followed by greetings and apologies on our part, and a plea for forgiveness at the 'Lord have mercy ...'
   b) This is followed up by praising God at the 'Glory to God in the highest.'
   c) We then make a special petition for the Mass in the Opening Prayer.
   d) Then God speaks to us through the readings from scripture. God always likes to act indirectly and he then uses the priest to speak through the homily.
   e) We then profess our faith in the Creed followed by more particular petitions in the Bidding Prayers.
   This ends the Liturgy of the Word which in many ways resembles the prayers in the Temple of the early church.

2. Back to the man with the present for his girlfriend.
   a) He has made preparations in buying his present. We now make preparations by preparing bread and wine.

b) After talking to his girlfriend for a while, he offers her a nicely wrapped gift of expensive chocolates. Hopefully she takes them, opens them and samples one and then suggests that he help her eat them. If that happens all is well and the previous disagreement is forgotten. Now let us apply this to the Mass.

c) We have now moved into the Liturgy of the Eucharist which means thanking God for his great works of *creation, redemption* and *sanctification*, and in Jewish tradition it is associated with a meal.

d) Our problem is, *what* kind of present can we offer to God?

* Like Jesus did at the Last Supper we offer up some bread and wine.
* They are not worth very much in themselves, but just as Jesus put meaning into them so we can do the same.
* The bread and wine – which are food and drink and symbolise life – are symbols of our lives, our hopes, our fears, of what we are and what we hope to be. Through the bread and wine we offer our past, our present and our future lives to God.
* You can take a piece of cloth and it is worth very little, but if you dye it with some colours it becomes a tricolour, and it symbolises Ireland and its people, and has new and great value and a special meaning.
* There are no spectators at Mass. Each person must make a personal offering of his/her life to God together with the priest.
* If you say that we are not offering God very much as he is our Creator, and all we are offering back is what he created, then you need to remember that all God wants from you is your love and yourself. It is often easier to give money than to give yourself and your time.
* I remember once being at the birthday party for the father of a family. The older children had presents for their father, but the youngest who was about three had nothing. She went outside and brought back some dandelions and daises and gave them to her father, and he was just as pleased with her present as he was with any of the other presents because it was a symbol of her love and trust.

3. This is as much that we as human beings can offer God, namely, our lives and our love.

Consecration of the Mass. This is where everything changes.
Jesus working through the priest changes our gifts of bread and wine into his body and blood. We now join Jesus in offering himself and ourselves – his gift and our gift – to the Father. His life and our lives. We now have the perfect and eternal sacrifice or present to offer to God. It is eternal because it is the same sacrifice as at Calvary. In the Old Covenant there were many sacrifices but in the New Covenant there is only one. In the Epistle to the Hebrews we read: 'It

follows that it is a greater Covenant for which Jesus has become our guarantee. Then there used to be a great number of those other priests, because death put an end to each one of them; but this One, because he remains for ever, can never lose his priesthood. It follows, then, that his power to save is utterly certain, since he is living to intercede for all who come to God through him.

'To suit us the ideal High Priest would have to be holy, innocent and un-contaminated, beyond the influence of sinners, and raised up above the heavens; One who would not need to offer sacrifices every day, as the other High Priests do for their own sins, and then for those of the people, because he has done this once and for all by offering himself.'(Hebrews 7:22–28)

Jesus, the perfect and eternal priest, offers the perfect and once only eternal sacrifice, together with the New People of God, who are the adopted children of God, to the heavenly Father. The Mass is the same sacrifice as Calvary as we read in the Letter to the Hebrews: 'But now Christ has come, as the High Priest of all the blessings that were to come … He has entered the sanctuary once and for all, taking with him not the blood of goats and bull calves, but his own blood, having won an eternal redemption for us … how much more effectively the Blood of Christ, Who offered Himself as the Perfect Sacrifice through the eternal Spirit, can purify our inner self from dead actions so that we do our service to the Living God … He does not have to offer himself again and again like the High Priest going into the sanctuary year after year … Instead of that, he has made his appearance once and for all, now at the end of the last age, to do away with sin by sacrificing himself.' (Hebrews 9:11–27)

We need to Remember that the Mass is a Sacrifice – the One and Eternal Sacrifice of Calvary.
All are called to participate in the Mass *from their baptism and confirmation.* 1 Peter 2:9–10: 'But you are a chosen race, a royal priesthood, a consecrated nation, a people set apart to sing the praises of God who called you out of darkness into his wonderful light. Once you were not a people at all and now you are the People of God; once you were outside the mercy and now you have been given mercy.'

4. To return to the man who gave his girlfriend a present of an expensive box of chocolates, what would you expect to happen when she accepts them?
*   Naturally what we would hope would happen would be that she would open the wrapping of the box and sample the chocolates with great delight.
*   Then she would offer the box to him and ask him to sample one. He would take one and eat it and in a small way they would share together in a meal.
*   This is what happens in the communion of the Mass and we will go into it in the next session.

Afterword

Did Jesus know that he was God? Many decades ago when I first heard this question my immediate reaction was: 'Of course he did.' The answer of the professor was that if he knew that he was God then he would have known of his ultimate triumph, and he would not have been truly human. As humans we have to live with all kinds of worries and apprehensions and doubts, and uncertainty about the future. Jesus because he was truly human had to live in the same state as we do. In that way we can identify with him on his human journey. The scripture mentions him reading and writing, just like the rest of us he had to learn to do so. Like the rest of us he had to seek out God, but because he was the perfect human being it was clearer for him. Hebrews 4:15 tells us: 'For it was not as if we had a High Priest who was incapable of feeling our weakness with us; but we have one who was tempted in every way that we are, though he is without sin.'

He gradually began to realise that he was a prophet like other prophets before him. Being a prophet basically means being a teacher, and eventually he set out to fulfil that role. Then he probably began to realise that he was the Messiah, but in Jewish thinking the Messiah would be someone like King David or one of the great prophets or a mixture of both. There was no knowledge of a Triune God and hence the idea of God becoming man would not be considered. In his role as prophet or teacher he taught a new concept of God as a kind, compassionate, all-loving Father. His teaching was in many ways different from the other teachers of his day and this led him into conflict with them. He was a teacher who was different from other teachers of his time as the scripture tells us that 'He taught them with authority, and not like their own scribes'. (Mt 7:29) He knew that he had a special relationship with God, but it is not clear how he understood that relationship, but he did give the people new insights into God as Abba Daddy God who was compassionate and loving. On the other hand he told his disciples that he did not know when the end of the world would happen as only the Father knew that time. (Mk 12:32)

It is not clear when he knew that he was divine or somebody special. He did not need any special knowledge to know that the Jewish authorities were planning to kill him. He was meeting with opposition all the time, and he had friends like Nicodemus among the Pharisees. They were also continually trying to set traps for him. We also saw in the earlier book how he went up secretly to Jerusalem for fear of the Jews and also how he did not stay in the Temple at night as it would have been dangerous. It would seem likely that at least at the Last Supper and on Calvary that he knew that he was in some way divine or special.

A question that follows from this is, after his resurrection when did his disciples realise that he was divine? It is not clear and the answer probably differed from person to person. After his resurrection, the disciples realised that he was the Messiah, but by dying and rising from the dead he did not follow their pre-conceived ideas of what the Messiah would do. At one of his post-resurrection appearances to them they are back in Galilee and working as fisherman. (Jn 21:1–14) In a book by Fr Raymond Brown, the great American biblical scholar, titled *An Introduction to New Testament Christology* (1994) he deals with this problem. He does not give a definite answer but points out that we need to allow some time for the development of Christian thought. We also need to remember that something can be so taken for granted that it is not mentioned. In those early days it was all oral tradition and we cannot hope to get written material except in so far as it was recorded later in the scriptures. However, the decisive moment in the history of the early church was the coming of the Holy Spirit at Pentecost. Not only did the disciples receive courage to go out and preach but they were also enlightened by the Holy Spirit. At the Last Supper, Jesus had made a promise to his disciples in Jn 14:26, 'The Advocate, the Holy Spirit, whom the Father will send in my name, will teach you everything, and remind you of all I have said to you.'

Final Prayer
Prayers of intercession or any other prayer that you wish to use.

Reflection and Review
Passover in Egypt. It was not a sacrifice but a meal.
Altar was a table of some kind.
Priest was the head of the family or the father.
Sacrifice – none, but blood of the lamb was scattered on the door or its lintels.
Meal was the roasted lamb, unleavened bread and bitter herbs.

The First Passover in Egypt was eaten as the Israelites waited for word to start their escape from Egypt. Later it commemorated that escape, and the saving of the first-born children. It celebrated God's love and protection and the deliverance of the Chosen People. (Exodus 12:1–12)

The Old Covenant. This was made at Mount Sinai and it was a *communion* sacrifice. It occurred three months or more after escaping from Egypt – Exodus 19:1.
Altar was made of twelve standing stones.
Priest was Moses.
Sacrifice was of bullocks. They were killed and some of the blood was poured on the altar, as representing God, and the rest was sprinkled on the people to establish the Covenant.
Meal was part of the burned bullocks that had been offered in sacrifice, and so a communion sacrifice.

Last Supper and New Covenant
It was the thanksgiving meal of the Passover, but what Jesus did during it by changing bread and wine into his body and blood, and instituting holy communion was to change everything. This would provide the *communion* for the

sacrifice of Calvary. It was here that Jesus proclaimed and established the New Covenant just like Moses had proclaimed the Old Covenant before the sacrifice at Mount Sinai. It was the last Passover meal. What was symbolically fore-shown at the Last Supper was done at Calvary. Jesus, a priest, offered himself as a sacrificial victim for humankind. Jesus was both priest and victim. As a sacrifice he had to die. The Last Supper was the fulfilment of the Passover and the beginning of the New Covenant.

Calvary
Altar was the Cross.
Priest was/is Jesus.
Sacrifice was/is Jesus – the 'Lamb of God'.
Meal was the last Supper. 1 Peter 1:19. 'Remember the ransom that was paid to set you free from the useless way of life your ancestors handed down was not paid in anything corruptible, neither in silver nor gold, but in the precious blood of a lamb without spot or stain, namely Christ.'

The Mass
Altar is the altar or a table.
Priest is the Risen Christ working through a priest.
Sacrifice is Christ under the form of bread and wine.
Meal is the Holy Communion.

On the Cross at Calvary, Jesus offered himself to the Father on behalf of humankind. In the Mass we have the opportunity to offer ourselves with Jesus to the Father on our own behalf and on behalf of all humankind. We should never make the mistake of saying that it was the will of the Father that Jesus should die such a cruel death on the Cross at Calvary. If we say that we make the Father very cruel and heartless and far from the Father that Jesus spoke of many times. It was the will of the Father and of Jesus to walk the path of love to the bitter end. This is very dangerous as we have seen in the case of Gandhi, Martin Luther King, Archbishop Romero and many others. It is all right to help the poor and those discriminated against, but if you condemn the causes of poverty, discrimination and so forth, then you will be in trouble with the authorities and those with power and vested interests.

Vatican II Constitution on the Liturgy
No. 10: 'The liturgy is the summit towards which the activity of the church is directed; it is also the fount from which all her power flows. For the goal of apostolic endeavour is that all who are made children of God by faith and baptism should come together to praise God in the midst of his church, to take part in the sacrifice and eat the Lord's Supper.'

No. 47: 'At the Last Supper, on the night he was betrayed, our Saviour instituted the eucharistic *sacrifice* of his body and blood. This he did in order to perpetuate the sacrifice of the Cross throughout the ages until he should come again, and so to entrust to his beloved spouse, the church, a memorial of his death and resurrection: a sacrament of love, a sign of unity, a bond of charity, a paschal banquet in which Christ is consumed, the mind is filled with grace, and a pledge of future glory is given to us.'

No. 48: 'The church, therefore, earnestly desires that Christ's faithful, when present in this mystery of faith, *should not be there as strangers or silent spectators.* On the contrary, through a good understanding of the rites and prayers they should take part in the sacred action, conscious of what they are doing, with devotion and full collaboration. *They should be instructed by God's word, and nourished at the table of the Lord's body.* They should give thanks to God. *Offering the immaculate victim, not only through the hands of the priest, but also together with him, they should learn to offer themselves.* Through Christ the Mediator, they should be drawn day by day into ever more perfect union with God and each other, so that finally God may be all in all.'

Homework
Readings from the Acts of the Apostle

Day	1	2	3	4	5	6	7
Chapter	8	8	9	9	10	10	11
Verses	1–25	26–40	1–25	26–43	1–33	34–48	1–30

SESSION SIX

Holy Communion

There have been many changes in our modern lifestyle, but one thing that has remained constant is the custom of having a meal together. It is a custom that is very meaningful and satisfying. To dine with friends in a leisurely manner can be a wonderful experience. To eat together with friends deepens our mutual understanding and appreciation of one another, and helps us relax and enjoy life, and appreciate life. Eating together with other people can occur for many and varied reasons, friendship, love, anniversaries and other occasions both sad and happy. With our modern awareness of famine and shortage of food in many places, we also thank God for the food that we have to eat.

To eat and drink together in a happy atmosphere is a sign, if you like, of sharing life with one another. When we eat the food that supports our lives, and share our food with others, we are rejoicing in and sharing life itself with one another. We form bonds with people we may not have known, and deepen the bonds we already have with our friends.

Since ancient times eating together has been a sign of friendship, and a uniquely powerful way of making friends. The Israelites and many other peoples and tribes were nomadic. Such people meeting others by chance would be wary and fearful of one another. However, there was a custom and understanding that if they had a meal together, then they would not attack or harm the other people, and everybody could relax and feel safe. In our modern society, if people have a misunderstanding and can be persuaded to talk it out, and share even a cup of tea or coffee, then in many cases the problem is solved.

A problem in modern life is that families often do not eat together and so talk and communication are reduced. Moreover, very often when they do eat together they have the television on and that puts an end to communication. People are afraid of silence.

This pattern of eating together has entered religions. According to Bernard Haring CSsR in *Free and Faithful in Christ*, Vol. 2, p. 132: 'It seems that in all historically known cultures, the chief meaning of the feast (meal) is worship and rejoicing before God.' We saw that despite the fact that there were many kinds of sacrifices offered, the most important ones were *communion sacrifices*. This happened when those offering the sacrifice partook of part of what was offered. It was a kind of union or communion with a deity, and an occasion of thankfulness, peace and joy. Even at its most basic level, food is a gift from God to be received with thanks.

> To fully rejoice in a meal or feast presuppose a basic trust in God, and in
> the goodness of life, and in the final victory of good over evil … The
> believer not only rejoices for having received wonderful gifts, but he is
> assured of God's Covenant, of his love, of his fidelity, and thus he keeps
> his response of gratitude and fidelity alive. (Häring, ibid., pp. 132–133)

We see this kind of attitude in the history of the Israelites as in the case of Abraham. Genesis 18:1–8: 'Yahweh appeared to him at the oak of Mamre while he was sitting at the entrance to his tent during the hottest part of the day. He looked up and there he saw three men standing near him. As soon as he saw them he ran from the entrance of the tent to meet them, and bowed to the ground. "My lord", he said, "I beg you, if I find favour with you, kindly do not pass your servant by. A little water shall be brought; you shall wash your feet and lie down under the tree. Let me fetch a little bread and you shall refresh yourselves before going further. This is why you have come in your servant's direction." They replied, "Do as you say."

Abraham hastened to the tent to find Sarah. "Hurry," he said "knead three bushels of flour and make loaves." Then running to the cattle Abraham took a fine and tender calf and gave it to the servants, who hurried to prepare it. Then taking cream, milk and the calf he had prepared, he laid it all before them, and they ate while he remained standing near them under the tree.'

One of the men then told Abraham that his wife Sarah would have a child before they returned at the same time the next year. Sarah was not inclined to believe them because of her age, but it happened and Isaac was born to carry on the line of Abraham, and the Promise of God to Abraham that he would be the father of a great nation was fulfilled. (Some scripture scholars see a reference to the Trinity in this apparition of God in the form of three men to Abraham at Mamre.)

In the gospels we read of Jesus being invited to meals from time to time and attending them. For example, to the house of Martha and Mary (Lk 10:38–42); to the marriage feast at Cana (Jn 2:1–11); to the house of Simon a Pharisee (Lk 7:37ff.); to the house of Matthew or Levi (Lk 5:27–32); to the house of Zacchaeus (Lk 19:1–10). We also read of Jesus feeding a great number of people with just five loaves and two fish (Mt 14:15–21). When Jesus wants to paint a picture of heaven or the world to come it is often in the form of a wedding feast or a great banquet (Mt 22:1–14 or Lk 14:15–24).

The Promise of Communion

At the beginning of John 6, verses 1–15, we read of Jesus feeding a large crowd with five barley loaves and two fish. Next day the crowds again came looking for Jesus. He tells them that they should not be seeking him out in order to get earthly food, but should be seeking for what he called 'food that endures to eternal life'. It is good to read all of Chapter 6 in John's gospel and meditate about it. Even when the Jews complained about his teaching on Holy Communion, he did not withdraw it or soften it, but repeated it and reaffirmed it. Many left and Jesus asked his disciples if they wanted to go with the others who were leaving because of his teaching about giving them his flesh and blood for food and drink. Peter replied: 'Lord, who shall we go to? You have the message of eternal life, and we believe; we know that you are the Holy One of God.' (Jn 6:68)

Let us look at a few of the things Jesus told us about Holy Communion and himself in Chapter 6 of John's gospel:

Jn 35: 'I am the bread of life. He who comes to me will never be hungry; he who believes in me will never thirst.'

Jn 53–58: 'I tell you most solemnly, if you do not eat the flesh of the Son of Man and drink his blood, you will not have life in you. Anyone who does eat my flesh and drink my blood has eternal life, and I shall raise him up on the last day. For my flesh is real food and my blood is real drink. He who eats my flesh and drinks my blood lives in me and I live in him.'

Jesus fulfilled his promise at the Last Supper. 'Now as they were eating, Jesus took some bread, and when he had given the blessing he broke it and gave it to his disciples, "Take it and eat," he said, "This is my body." Then he took a cup and when he had returned thanks he gave it to them. "Drink all of you of this", he said, "For this is my blood, the blood of the Covenant, which is poured out for many for the forgiveness of sins."' (Mt 26:26–28)

Holy Communion is the communion of the sacrifice of Calvary by which the New Covenant was established. It is the communion of that sacrifice by which we establish union or communion with God. It is also participating in the meal of thanksgiving of Jesus with our brothers and sisters. It is an opportunity to praise and thank God. From our baptism we are the adopted children of God, and as such carry the supernatural life of God within us. Holy Communion provides supernatural food and drink for our supernatural life as adopted children of God. We also celebrate the Eucharist as a memorial of the passion, death and resurrection of Christ, and we do so in union with the Risen Christ. As we read earlier in the Vatican II decree on the *Constitution on the Sacred Liturgy*: 'The goal of apostolic endeavour is that all who are made children of God by faith and baptism should come together to praise God in the midst of the church, to take part in the sacrifice and to eat the Lord's Supper.' (Article 10) In the Mass we have the sacrifice of Calvary, and also we have the Lord's Supper which we share together with our brothers and sisters. As we share together with our brothers and sisters we have to be also concerned about our brothers and sisters who are sick, suffering, downtrodden or discriminated against in any way. 'It is impossible to celebrate feasts with the Eucharist as centre if we are neglecting our suffering and downtrodden brothers and sisters. We can give thanks to the Lord and celebrate feasts only if we are using our God-given energies to cooperate for justice and peace.' (Häring, ibid., p. 133)

Jesus in Holy Communion

When you think about Jesus present in Holy Communion, who exactly do you think about? Is it the Baby Jesus in Bethlehem? Jesus as a young boy – Jesus as an adult – Jesus as a carpenter – Jesus in his role as teacher and Messiah – Jesus in his suffering and death – Jesus in his resurrection? Any opinions? What appeals to you?

Jesus was the God-Man. As God, *time* had no meaning for Jesus. He is from eternity to eternity. Jesus as man is different. Jesus as man was born at a particular time and in a particular place. Time applies to the humanity of Jesus. To a certain extent you can say that the child and youth experiences continue in all of us.

The humanity of Jesus can be dated from just over two thousand years ago when he was born in a stable in Bethlehem. *That humanity is now resurrected and glorified*, and that is the only Jesus that now lives, and we have the glorified and resurrected Jesus in Holy Communion. After the resurrection we find that the disciples had difficulty in recognising Jesus. Mary of Magdala in the garden thought he was the gardener until he spoke to her. (Jn 20:11–18) Again in the case of the two disciples on their way to Emmaus, they walked with Jesus on the way but did not recognise him until the 'breaking of the bread'. (Lk 24:13–35) Even the apostles had difficulty when he appeared to them, and he had to eat with them to prove that it really was himself. (Lk 24:36–43) Thomas would not believe until he saw his wounds. (Jn 20:19–29) He was changed in his resurrected and glorified humanity but unfortunately they do not give us any details of how he was changed.

After his resurrection Jesus could suddenly appear in a room even though the doors and windows were closed. This was because he was resurrected and glorified. Because he is resurrected and glorified he can be in a billion places or more like in Holy Communion. There are no spatial limits for the resurrected and glorified Jesus. It also helps us to remember that through the resurrected and glorified Jesus we are directly connected with all the saints and our own beloved dead in heaven.

Holy Communion brings to mind for us the sacrifice of Jesus at Calvary, and the Last Supper and the New Covenant by which we are the children of God. It brings us into union with Jesus, and with one another, and with all the faithful departed. It is also the guarantee of our eternal destiny in heaven. John 6:54: 'Anyone who does eat my flesh and drink my blood has eternal life, and I shall raise him up on the last day.' When we think of the Mass or the Eucharist it is good to think of three things:

1. The New Covenant of the New People of God which applies to us.
2. The sacrifice of Jesus at Calvary which is the same as the sacrifice of the Mass.
3. The thanksgiving meal of the Last Supper and how it applies to us at Holy Communion.

If it is possible it would be good to have a Mass with the group wherever you meet.

Final Prayer
If Mass is not possible then you could have prayers of intercession of whatever kind appeal to the participants.

History
St Justin (AD 100–165 approximately) who died a martyr's death wrote an interesting description of the Mass to the Emperor Antonius Pius (AD 131–161) about AD 155. His feast day is 1st June.

> On the day we call the day of the sun, all who dwell in the city or the country gather in the same place. The memoirs of the apostles and the prophets are read, as much as time permits. When the reader has finished, he who presides over those gathered admonishes and challenges them to imitate these beautiful things. Then we all rise together and offer prayers for ourselves, and for all others, wherever they may be, so that we may be found righteous by our life and actions, and faithful to the commandments, so as to obtain eternal salvation. When the prayers are concluded we exchange the kiss of peace.
>
> Then someone brings bread and a cup of water and wine mixed together to him who presides over the brethren. He takes them and offers praise and glory to the Father of the universe, through the name of the Son and of the Holy Spirit, and for a considerable time he gives thanks that we have been judged worthy of these gifts. When he has concluded the prayers and thanksgiving, all present give voice to an acclamation by saying 'Amen'.
>
> When he who presides has given thanks and the people have responded, those whom we call deacons give to those present the 'eucharisted' bread, wine and water and take them to those who are absent.

Reference material: *The Catechism of the Catholic Church*, pp. 297–319

Reflection
Table Fellowship Movement
There were many movements in the time of Jesus which proclaimed the nearness of God's kingdom, and told people to get ready for its coming. One of the most distinctive traits that set Jesus and his followers apart from other movements was Jesus' habit of expressing the meaning and goal of his Mission by sitting at table with people, particularly with the outcasts and the marginalised. This 'sitting at table' became the symbol of what he stood for. Some scholars regard it as the most distinctive feature of Jesus' behaviour. Others even hold that Jesus' regular table-fellowship with the outcasts and sinners in the name of the kingdom was the decisive factor which led to his violent death on the

Cross. Jesus was well aware of what his enemies were saying about him: 'For John the Baptist comes, not eating bread, not drinking wine, and you say "He is possessed," The Son of Man comes and you say, "Look, a glutton and a drunkard, a friend of tax collectors and sinners." Yet wisdom has been proved right by all her children.' (Lk 7:33–35) Other factors were his view regarding the Sabbath – 'The Sabbath was made for man, not man for the Sabbath' (Mk 2:27–28), and his stance towards women, where he disregarded the traditional taboos, and made them his friends and followers, his criticism of the Scribes and Pharisees and their way of life.

'Like the miracles (which are not just works of individual healings, but signs of a radical structural change which put Satan's rule at an end, and ushered in a new social order, namely God's rule) the table fellowship of Jesus is more than a form of pastoral care. It is an expression of a radically new (and therefore thoroughly disturbing) theological vision, rooted in a new experience of God, and calling for a new kind of society.' (G. Soares-Prabhu, *The Table Fellowship of Jesus*, p. 144)

The gospels report many occasions where Jesus eats and drinks and enjoys meals in the company of all kinds of people – both good and bad. After the resurrection these meals gain a new significance. The Lord's Supper becomes *the* celebration of Jesus' resurrection. The disciples recognised that the Risen Christ was calling them to the kingdom-anticipating meals, but this time with a stunning new revelatory meaning. Now the meal with the Risen Christ was an anticipation of the great end-of-the-world banquet that he had spoken about. When the Early Christians celebrated the 'breaking of the bread with joy and gladness' (Acts 2:46), they experienced above all, the Risen Christ present in their midst, as the apostles had experienced him in the meals they shared with him after the resurrection.

There are two memorials celebrated during the Eucharist. First, the joyful eating and drinking with each other in a meal that the Risen Lord had recommended in his doing so, before and after his resurrection. Secondly, the memorial of his passion and suffering and death for our sakes.

The death of Jesus needs to be understood in the light of the table community. The body of Jesus is food that is shared, and his blood is wine that is drunk in community. This does not mean that upon the death of Jesus, the meaning of the table community is weakened, but rather, that Jesus himself becomes incarnated in the table community movement. Jesus' death must be understood in the light of his life, and this movement.

In a way Jesus died as a result of this movement, and becomes incarnated in this movement through his death. Jesus loved a life of total sharing with others which culminated in his death. He shared himself even to the point of sharing his body and his blood. His death is the perfect realisation of the table community movement. The Last Supper shows that Jesus, even after his death, is resurrected as and in the table community of his church.

Sharing in the Eucharist – in the table community of the Lord – we are strengthened and challenged to go forth to work on behalf of our brothers and sisters in the building of the kingdom of God. His death is our life: 'For the Son of Man himself did not come to be served but to serve, and to give his Life for many.' (Mk 10:45)

(Based on *Throw Fire* by John Fuellenbach, SVD, pp. 183–188 plus personal material.)

Homework

Readings from the Acts of the Apostles

Day	1	2	3	4	5	6	7
Chapter	12	13	13	14	15	15	16
Verses	1–25	1–16	17–52	1–28	1–29	30–41	1–40

Scripture memos

1. It was a Jewish custom to add a little water to wine before drinking it. The same custom was/is here in Ireland of adding a little water to whiskey before drinking it.
2. Jesus refers to himself here as Son of Man in regard to John the Baptist. It is a name that he often uses in regard to himself in other places. He is never addressed directly by that name. The meaning is unclear but scholars think that it refers to the Book of Daniel 7:13–14: 'I gazed into the vision of the night. And I saw coming on the clouds of heaven, one like a son of man. He came to the one of great age and was led into his presence. On him was conferred sovereignty, glory and kingship, and people of all nations and languages became his servants.' The book of Daniel has the last of the Messianic prophecies of the Old Testament. 'Son of Man' could be the equivalent of the pronoun 'I', or the Son of Man coming in the clouds of Heaven (Mt 24:30), or the suffering Son of Man (Mk 8:31). These are three uses and the meaning depends on the context. It could mean Messiah which would be too dangerous to use.

Memo: Have some holy water for the next Session.

SESSION SEVEN

Baptism

Christ instituted the seven sacraments of the new law. The seven sacraments touch all the stages, and all the important moments of our Christian life. They give birth and increase of life, healing and mission to the Christian life of faith. There is thus a certain resemblance between the stages of natural life and the stages of the supernatural life. (cf. *The Catechism of the Catholic Church*, No. 1210ff.) I have already dealt with the Eucharist as it is so important and linked with the sacrifice of Christ and is the basis of our salvation.

We can divide the sacraments as follows:

1. Sacraments of Christian Initiation: baptism, confirmation and the Eucharist. As we saw the Eucharist is linked with the Mass and the new Covenant. Among the sacraments, the Eucharist occupies a unique place. St Thomas Aquinas refers to it as the 'sacrament of sacraments' and says 'all other sacraments are ordered to it as to their end'. (*Summa Theologiae*, 111, 65, 3)
2. Sacraments of Healing: Reconciliation and Healing of the sick.
3. Sacraments of the service of communion and mission of the faithful: holy orders and matrimony.

Background
We are all familiar with the baptism practice of John the Baptist (Lk 3:1–18). It was not something unique to John but was practised by others before John's baptism. Baptism meant renouncing your sins and pledging to lead a better life in the future. On the other hand, a sacrament is a sign that does what if signifies and hence is greater. It is difficult for us to appreciate the importance and significance of water for people who lived in ancient times. We take it, unfortunately, for granted as being always available to us from a tap. For a nomadic people, water was the difference between death and life for them and their flocks. We forget that a large part of our bodies is water, and that a child before birth is nurtured in water. We also know nowadays from scientists that the first signs of life on our earth were in the oceans. Water can turn a desert into fertile land and it is necessary for growth, and we can only live for a few days without water. There are all kinds of irrigation schemes nowadays, and it is possible that the next war could be about the supply and use of water. The amount of water in the Jordan river and other rivers has greatly decreased because of irrigation. Bottled water can almost cost as much as petrol! Water as a *sign* is very powerful and meaningful.

Wells are mentioned several times in the Old Testament as significant places. In the New Testament Jesus spoke to the Samaritan about giving her 'living water'. (John 4:10) Again we have an invitation from Jesus in John 7:37–38: 'If anybody is thirsty let that person come to me! Let that person come and drink who believes in me. As scripture says: From his breast shall flow fountains of living water.'

The *Jerusalem Bible*, on page 163, reference 'R', speaks of the Feast of Tabernacles which was a feast of thanksgiving in the autumn. It says that it formed the background for these words as the feast included prayers for rain, and rites which commemorated the Mosaic water miracle in the desert. The Blessing of Baptismal Water on Holy Saturday night gives us the church's thinking about the water of baptism and also baptism itself:

> Father, you give us grace through sacramental signs,
> which tell us of the wonder of your unseen power.
> In baptism we use your gift of water,
> which you have made a rich symbol
> of the grace you give us in this sacrament.
> At the very dawn of creation
> your Spirit breathed on the waters,
> making them the wellspring of all holiness.
> The waters of the great flood
> you made a sign of the waters of baptism,
> that make an end of sin and a new beginning of goodness.
> Through the waters of the Red Sea,
> you led Israel out of slavery,
> to be an image of God's holy people,
> (*Crossed Red Sea into freedom*)
> set free from sin by baptism.
> (*Crossed Jordan into Promised Land*)
> In the waters of the Jordan
> your son was baptised by John
> and anointed with the Spirit.
> Your Son willed that water and blood
> (*Some Fathers of the Church write that Water = Baptism*
> *Blood = Sacrifice = Eucharist*)
> should flow from his side
> as he hung upon the Cross.
> After his resurrection he told his disciples:
> 'Go out and teach the nations,
> baptising them in the *name* of the Father,
> and of the Son and of the Holy Spirit.'
> Father, look now with love upon your church,
> and unseal for her the fountain of baptism.

By the power of the Spirit,
give to the water of this font
the grace of your Son.
You created man in your own likeness:
cleanse him from sin in a new birth of innocence
by water and the Holy Spirit.
We ask you, Father, with your Son
to send the Holy Spirit upon the waters of this font.
May all who are buried with Christ
in the death of baptism
rise also with him to newness of life.
We ask this through Christ Our Lord. Amen.

Can you get any new meaning or understanding about baptism from these words and references in the blessing of baptismal water?

Baptism: The Sacrament
In Mt 28:18–20 just before his ascension Jesus gave his final instructions to his disciples: 'All authority in heaven and on earth has been given to me. Go, therefore, make disciples of all the nations; baptise them in the *name* of the Father, and of the Son and of the Holy Spirit, and teach them to observe all the commands that I gave you. And know that I am with you always; yes, to the end of time.' From the very first day of Pentecost the church has celebrated and administered baptism to those who wished to join it. After Peter had spoken to the people on Pentecost Day, they asked him what they should do. He replied: 'You must repent, and every one of you must be baptised in the name of Jesus Christ for the forgiveness of your sins, and you will receive the gift of the Holy Spirit.' (Acts 2:38) We read what happened: 'They accepted what he said and were baptised. That very day three thousand were added to their number.'(Acts 2:41)

The meaning and grace of the sacrament of baptism are clearly seen in the rites of its celebration. This is in a baptism that takes place during Mass. I have always had baptisms during Mass as baptism is not a private matter but by baptism a person joins the Christian community, and I consider that the Mass is when this can be best done. It is not a name calling ceremony but a special sacrament.

1. The sign of the cross on the forehead of the person to receive baptism at the beginning of the ceremony marks him/her with the imprint of Christ and as belonging to Christ, and signifies the grace of redemption Christ won for us by his Cross.
2. The proclamation of the word of God enlightens the candidate and the assembly with the revealed truth, and elicits the response in the Creed, which is inseparable from baptism. Indeed baptism is the sacrament of faith in a special way, since it is the sacramental entry into the life of faith, and the other sacraments.

3. Since baptism signifies liberation from sin and from its instigator, the devil, one or more exorcisms are pronounced over the candidate. The celebrant anoints him/her with the oil of catechumens, and may also lay hands on the candidate.

4. The candidate renounces the devil and all his works, and is able to profess the faith of the church.

5. The essential rite of the sacrament then follows. Baptism, properly speaking, signifies and actually brings about death to sin, and entry into the life of the Most Holy Trinity through configuration to the paschal mystery of Christ. (*Catechism*, No. 1239) As St Paul said in Romans 6:3–4: 'You have been taught that when we were baptised in Christ Jesus we were baptised into his death: in other words when we were baptised we went into the tomb with him and joined him in death, so that as Christ was raised from the dead by the Father's glory, we might live a new life.' Again in *The Catechism of the Catholic Church* No. 1262 we read: 'Immersion in water symbolises not only death and purification, but also regeneration as well. Thus the two principal effects are purification from sins and new birth in the Holy Spirit.' It is important to remember that in the case of adults any actual sins committed are forgiven by the sacrament of baptism.

6. The anointing with chrism signifies the gift of the Holy Spirit to the newly–baptised who has become a Christian, that is, one 'anointed' by the Holy Spirit, one who is anointed priest, prophet and king. (*Rite of Baptism for Children*, 62) The baptised person can now address God as Father, and also take a full part in the offering of the Mass.

7. The white garment symbolises that the person baptised has 'put on Christ' (Galatians 3:27), and has risen with Christ. St Paul wrote to the Galatians in 3:26-27: 'All of you are children of God, through faith in Christ Jesus, since every one of you that has been baptised has been clothed in Christ.'

8. The candle, lit from the paschal candle signifies that Christ has enlightened the newly-baptised person so that the newly-baptised are the light of the world as Jesus said in Mt 5:14: 'You are the light of the world.' (*The Catechism of the Catholic Church*, Nos 1234–1243)

There are slight differences between baptism for children and adults. In my experience working in Japan the baptism of children was done on one single occasion. In the case of adults we had some ceremonies along the way. There was a ceremony by which they became candidates to study, and another by which they became catechumens. Adults also normally received confirmation after baptism. In the Orthodox Church, normally, children receive confirmation immediately after baptism. After coming back to Ireland I have found it very strange to have children's baptism outside of Mass. After all, by baptism a child joins the Christian *community* and should be welcomed into it.

Baptism: Its Effects

Baptism is the sacrament of faith and the entrance door to the other sacraments. By it we become children of God, and are entitled to say 'Our Father' to God. Any sin that we may have committed is forgiven. We are the temples of the Holy Spirit and we share in the priestly, prophetic and missionary work of Christ Jesus. We are heirs of the kingdom of God.

Sometimes there is too much emphasis on the forgiveness of sin. Baptism is much more positive in helping us to share in the life of God, and in the ongoing ministry of Christ on earth. It is often associated with 'original sin'. What is original sin? At the beginning of the world there was harmony between God and his creatures. However, Adam by his sin of rebellion wanted to become like God, and he broke this harmony. 'By his sin Adam, as the first man, lost the original holiness and justice he had received from God, not only for himself but for all human beings. Adam and Eve transmitted to their descendants human nature wounded by their own first sin, and hence deprived of original holiness and justice: this *deprivation* is called "original sin". As a result of orig- inal sin, human nature is weakened in its powers, subject to ignorance, suffer- ing and the domination of death, and inclined to sin (this inclination is called 'concupiscence'). *The Catechism of the Catholic Church,* Nos 416–418. Original sin means that there is something lacking in our lives, namely sharing in the life of God as children of God. We are also suffering from weakness of intellect and will because of the original sin of Adam. It is not something positive but some- thing negative. We are not children of God or heirs of heaven because of orig- inal sin. We get something positive from baptism rather than have something negative removed.

To summarize the effects of baptism:

1. All sins actual or 'original' are forgiven.
2. We become the adopted children of God – a partaker in the divine nature. St Paul tells the Galatians in 4:5–7: 'God sent his Son, born of a woman, born a subject of the law, to redeem the subjects of the law, so that we would receive adoption as children. The proof that you are children is that God has sent the Spirit of his Son into our hearts; the Spirit that cries "Abba, Father".'
3. We become members of Christ's body as St Paul said in 1 Corinthians 6:15: 'You know surely, that your bodies are members making up the body of Christ.'
4. We become temples of the Holy Spirit. 1 Corinthians 6:19: 'Your body, you know, is the temple of the Holy Spirit, who is in you since you received him from God.'
5. We receive sanctifying grace and with it the virtues of faith, hope and charity.
6. By baptism we share in the priesthood of Christ, and in his prophetic, and royal mission. St Peter tells us in 1 Peter 2:9: 'You are a chosen race, a con- secrated nation, a people set apart to sing the praises of God who called you out of darkness into his wonderful light.'

7. By baptism we are members of the church and this includes rights and obligations: 'Reborn as children of God, (the baptised) must profess before people the faith they have received from God through the church.' (Vatican II: *Dogmatic Constitution the Church*, No. 11).

8. Baptism constitutes the foundation of communion among all Christians, including those who are not yet in full communion with the Catholic Church. Baptism constitutes the sacramental bond existing among all those who are reborn in Christ.

9. Baptism seals us with an indelible mark (character) of belonging to Christ. St Irenaeus says: 'Baptism is indeed the seal of eternal life.' The faithful Christian who has 'kept the seal' until the end, will be able to depart this life 'marked with the sign of faith', with his/her baptismal faith, in expectation of the blessed vision of God – the consummation of faith – and in the hope of resurrection. (cf. *The Catechism of the Catholic Church*, Nos 1262–1284)

Afterword

a) The church has always held the firm conviction that those who suffer death for the sake of the faith without having received baptism are baptised by their death for and with Christ. This baptism of blood, like the baptism of desire, brings about the fruits of baptism without being a sacrament. (*Catechism*, No. 1258)

b) Since the earliest times, baptism has been administered to children, for it is a grace and gift of God that does not presume any human merit; children are baptised in the faith of the church. Entry into Christian life gives access to true freedom. (*Catechism*, No. 1282) Some experts argue that this practice is linked to the words of Jesus: 'Let the little children come to me; do not stop them; for it is to such as these that the kingdom of God belongs.'(Mk 10:14 and Mt 18:3 and *Catechism*, No. 1252) 'There is explicit testimony to this practice from the second century, and it is quite possible that, from the beginning of the apostolic preaching, when whole 'households' received baptism, infants may also have been baptised.' (*Catechism*, No. 1252)

c) Children who have died without baptism the church entrusts to the mercy of God, as she does in her funeral rites for them. (*Catechism*, No. 1261)

Baptism is the formal ratification of the Covenant of life between God and the baptised person.

'I tell you, most solemnly, unless the wheat grain falls on the ground and dies, it remains only a single grain; but if it dies it bears much fruit.' (Jn 12:24)

God's pattern of intervention in salvation history

Life	Death	New life
Grain of wheat	Dies in the earth	Sprouts new life
Abram's old life	Leaves his old life, friends etc.	Father of a new nation

Slavery in Egypt	The Exodus	New life, new land
The man Jesus	Death on the Cross	Resurrection, eternal life
Our human lives	Baptism	New life in Christ

Final Prayer

The Renewal of Baptismal Promises (NB Have small container of Holy Water)

> Father, you give us grace through sacramental signs,
> which tell us of the wonder of your unseen power.
> In baptism you use your gift of water,
> which you have made a rich symbol of the grace
> you give us in this sacrament.
> At the very dawn of creation
> your Spirit breathed on the waters,
> making them the wellspring of all holiness.
> The waters of the great flood you made
> a sign of the waters of baptism,
> that make an end of sin and a new beginning of holiness.
> Through the water of the Red Sea,
> You led Israel out of slavery,
> to be an image of God's holy people,
> set free from sin by baptism.
> In the waters of the Jordan
> your Son was baptised by John
> and anointed with the Spirit.
> Your Son willed that water and blood
> should flow from his side as he hung upon the Cross.
> After his resurrection he told his disciples,
> 'Go out and teach the nations,
> baptising them in the name of the Father
> and of the Son and of the Holy Spirit.'
> Father, look now with love upon your church,
> and unseal for her the fountain of baptism.
> By the power of the Spirit
> give to this water the grace of your Son.
> You created us in your own likeness;
> cleanse us from sin in a new birth of innocence,
> by water and the Spirit.
> We ask you, Father, with your Son
> to send the Holy Spirit upon this water.
> May all who are buried with Christ in the death of baptism,
> rise also with him to newness of life.
> We ask this through Christ Our Lord. Amen.

Acclamation: Sing or recite three times.
Springs of water, bless the Lord.
Give Him glory and praise for ever.

Leader: Do you reject Satan? *All:* I do.
Leader: And all his works? *All:* I do.
Leader: And all his empty promises? *All:* I do.
Leader: Do you reject sin so as to live in the freedom of
God's children? *All:* I do.
Leader: Do you reject the glamour of evil,
and refuse to be mastered by sin? *All:* I do.
Leader: Do you reject Satan, father of sin
and prince of darkness? *All:* I do.
Leader: Do you believe in God, the Father almighty,
creator of heaven and earth? *All:* I do.
Leader: Do you believe in Jesus Christ, His only Son,
Our Lord, who was born of the virgin Mary, was crucified,
died and was buried, rose from the dead, and is now seated
at the right hand of the Father? *All:* I do.
Leader: Do you believe in the Holy Spirit, the Holy Catholic
Church, the communion of saints, the forgiveness of sins,
the resurrection of the body, and life everlasting? *All:* I do.
Let each person in turn make the sign of the Cross on the forehead of the person sitting on their right-hand side with the holy water.
All: God, the all-powerful Father of Our Lord Jesus Christ,
has given us a new birth by water and the Holy Spirit,
and forgiven all our sins. May He also keep us faithful to
Our Lord Jesus Christ for ever and ever. Amen.

Reflection
A Reading to the Newly-Baptised at Jerusalem
Now that you have been baptised into Christ and have put on Christ, you have become conformed to the Son of God. For God destined us to be his children, so he has made us like to the glorious body of Christ. Hence since you share in Christ, it is right to call you 'Christs' or anointed ones. As God said, referring to you 'Touch not my anointed ones'.

You have become 'Christs' by receiving the sign of the Holy Spirit. Since you are images of Christ, all the rites carried out over you have a symbolic meaning. Christ bathed in the river Jordan, and having imparted to the waters the divine touch of his body, he emerged from them, and the Holy Spirit descended upon him in substantial form.

In the same way when you emerged from the pool of sacred waters you were anointed in a manner corresponding to Christ's anointing. That anointing is the Holy Spirit, of whom the blessed Isaiah spoke when he prophesied to the person of the Lord: 'The Spirit of the Lord is upon me, because he has anointed me; he has sent me to bring good tidings to the poor.'

For Christ was not anointed by human hand with any tangible oil. No, the Father chose him to be Saviour of the whole world, and anointed him with the Holy Spirit. As Peter says, 'Jesus of Nazareth whom God anointed with the Holy Spirit.' Again the prophet Daniel cried out: 'Your throne, O God, endures for ever and ever; your royal sceptre is a sceptre of equity. You love righteousness and hate wickedness; therefore God, your God, has anointed you with the oil of gladness above your fellows.'

Christ was anointed with the spiritual oil of gladness, that is with the Holy Spirit, who is called the oil of gladness because he is the author of spiritual joy; and you have been anointed with chrism because you have become fellows and sharers of Christ.

But be sure not to regard the chrism merely as an ointment. Just as the bread of the Eucharist after the invocation of the Holy Spirit is no longer just bread, but the body of Christ, so when the Holy Spirit has been invoked on the holy chrism, it is no longer mere or holy ointment; it is the gift of Christ, which through the presence of the Holy Spirit instils his divinity into us. It is applied to your forehead and organs of sense with symbolic meaning; the body is anointed with visible ointment, and the soul is sanctified by the holy, hidden Spirit.

(Reading from the Breviary of Easter Friday, Myst 3:1–3)

Homework
Readings from the Acts of the Apostles

Day	1	2	3	4	5	6	7
Chapter	17	17	18	19	19	20	20
Verses	1–22	23–34	1–28	1–20	21–41	1–16	17–38

SESSION EIGHT

Confirmation

We already dealt with the Holy Spirit but it was in a general way, and also with the role of the Holy Spirit in the church. Here in the sacrament of confirmation we are dealing with the role of the Holy Spirit in the life of an individual. Jesus had promised the Holy Spirit several times to his disciples. 'When they take you before synagogues and magistrates and authorities, do not worry about how to defend yourselves or what to say, because when the time comes, the Holy Spirit will teach you what you must say.' (Lk 12:12) Jesus said to Nicodemus in John 3:5: 'I tell you most solemnly, unless a man is born again through water and the Holy Spirit, he cannot enter the kingdom of God.' At the Last Supper Jesus told his disciples: 'It is for your own good that I am going, because unless I go, the Advocate will not come to you; but if I do go, I will send him to you.' (Jn 16:7)

Confirmation is a separate sacrament from baptism. With Baptism and the Eucharist, as we saw previously, it is one of the three sacraments of initiation. *The Catechism of the Catholic Church* tells us in No. 1285: 'It must be explained to the faithful that the reception of the sacrament of confirmation is necessary for the *completion* of baptismal grace. For by the sacrament of confirmation, (the baptised) are more perfectly bound to the church, and are enriched with a special strength of the Holy Spirit. Hence they are, as true witnesses of Christ, more strictly obliged to spread and defend the faith by word and deed.' (Emphasis added) By confirmation the believer shares more fully in the priesthood of Christ, and in the missionary work of the church of bringing the Good News to all people.

Confirmation is normally administered after baptism in the case of adults, and in the case of all, including infants, in the Orthodox Church. It is conferred through the imposition of hands and the anointing with oil. 'Laying on of hands' is an extremely old ritual, frequently mentioned in the Old Testament. Laying one's hands on the head of another person, one prays that the blessings of God will descend on that person; that the person will receive health or strength or forgiveness or have a safe journey or whatever that person needs spiritually or physically. Laying on of hands also occurs in the sacraments of the sick and of ordination, and may occur in the sacrament of reconciliation.

The Catechism of the Catholic Church, No. 1288 quoting an address of Pope Paul VI says: 'From that time on (Pentecost) the apostles, in fulfilment of Christ's will, imparted to the newly-baptised by the laying on of hands, the gift of the Holy Spirit that completes the grace of baptism. For this reason in the

Letter to the Hebrews the doctrine concerning baptism and the laying on of hands, is listed among the first elements of Christian instruction. The imposition of hands is rightly recognised by the Catholic tradition as the origin of the sacrament of confirmation, which in a certain way perpetuates the grace of Pentecost in the church.' For all of us our confirmation is our own personal Pentecost, when the Holy Spirit descends on us in a special way. Confirmation as 'our own personal pentecost' is something worth thinking and praying about.

We read about the practice of confirmation in the early church in Acts 8:14–17: 'When the apostles in Jerusalem heard that Samaria had accepted the word of God, they sent Peter and John to them, and they went down there, and prayed for the Samaritans to receive the Holy Spirit, for as yet he had not come down on any of them: they had only been baptised in the name of the Lord Jesus. Then they laid hands on them, and they received the Holy Spirit.' It is good to remember that the Samaritans were despised and normally ignored by the Jews, but here we read about the fact that the early church had obviously been working among them, and was open to receiving them into the church. In Acts 12:4–8 we read of Philip leaving Jerusalem because of persecution and going to work in Samaria.

The signs and rite of confirmation
Besides the laying on of hands, the anointing with oil in biblical and other ancient traditions is rich in meaning. (cf. *Catechism* No. 1294 for some of this material)

1. It is a sign of abundance and joy. Deuteronomy 11:14 reads: 'I will give your land rain in season, autumn rain and spring, so that you may harvest your corn, your wine, your oil.'
2. Anointing the head was also a sign of welcome. (cf Lk 7:44–46.) Jesus tells the Pharisee that he did not anoint his head with oil in welcome, but that the sinner woman anointed his feet.
3. It limbers one up and hence was often used by athletes and wrestlers.
4. It cleanses and hence there was anointing before and after a bath.
5. Oil was used for curing bruises and wounds. In Luke 10:34 in regard to the Good Samaritan we read: 'He went up and bandaged his wounds, pouring oil and wine on them.'
6. It makes a person radiant with beauty, health and strength. Hence it was often used like modern make-up and perfumes.
7. Oil was something strange and mysterious for ancient people. It was a mysterious source of fire and light, and because they could not explain this it was seen as mysterious and a source of power and energy. Kings and priests were anointed with oil on taking up office.

The Catechism No. 1294 tells us: 'Anointing with oil has all these meanings in the sacramental life. The pre-baptismal anointing with the oil of catechumens signifies cleansing and strengthening; the anointing of the sick expresses healing and comfort. The post-baptismal anointing with sacred chrism in confirmation and ordination is the sign of consecration. By confirmation Christians, that is, those who are anointed, share more completely in the mission of Jesus Christ and the fullness of the Holy Spirit with which he is filled, so that their lives may give off the "aroma of Christ".' (2 Corinthians 2:15)

The rite of confirmation on Holy Saturday night
It is good to read the prayers of the rite of confirmation as they tell us what happened when we received confirmation. The prayers can change from place to place but the essentials are the same.

NN:
1) Born again in Christ by baptism,
2) you have become a member of Christ and of his priestly people.
3) Now you are to share in the outpouring of the Holy Spirit among us, the Spirit sent by the Lord upon his apostles at Pentecost, and given by them and their successors to the baptised.
4) The promised strength of the Holy Spirit which you are to receive will make you more like Christ, and
5) help you to be a witness to his suffering, death and resurrection.
6) It will strengthen you to be an active member of the church, and
7) to build up the body of Christ in faith and love. (Numbering added)

Let us pray, dear friends, to God the all-powerful Father that he will pour out the Holy Spirit on the newly-baptised, to strengthen him/her/them with his abundant gifts, and anoint him/her/them to be more like Christ, his Son.
The celebrant lays his hands on the candidate(s) as he says:

All-powerful God, Father of Our Lord Jesus Christ, by water and the Holy Spirit, you freed your son(s)/daughter(s) from sin and gave him/her/them new life. Send your Holy Spirit upon him/her/them to be his/her/their Helper and Guide. Give him/her/them the Spirit of wisdom and understanding, the Spirit of right judgement and courage, the Spirit of knowledge and reverence. Fill him/her/them with the Spirit of wonder and awe in your presence. We ask this through Christ Our Lord. Amen.

The celebrant anoints the candidate with chrism on the forehead in the form of a cross.

Celebrant: NN, be sealed with the gift of the Holy Spirit.
Candidate: Amen.
Celebrant: Peace be with you.
Candidate: Amen.

The essential of the sacrament of confirmation in the Latin Rite, is laid down by Pope Paul VI as: 'The sacrament of confirmation is conferred through the anointing with chrism on the forehead, which is done by the laying on of the hand, and through the words: "Be sealed with the gift of the Holy Spirit."'

The sign of peace that concludes the rite of the sacrament signifies and demonstrates ecclesial communion with the bishop and with all the faithful. (*Catechism*, No. 1300–1301)

The effects of confirmation

Confirmation brings an increase and deepening of baptismal grace but it is a separate sacrament from baptism.

1. It makes us more deeply children of God. Romans 8:14–17: 'Everybody moved by the Spirit is a child of God. The Spirit you received is not the spirit of slaves bringing fear into your lives again; it is the spirit of children, and it makes us cry out "Abba", Father! The Spirit and our spirit bear witness that we are children of God. And if we are children we are heirs as well; heirs of God and coheirs with Christ, sharing his sufferings so as to share his glory.'

2. It unites us more firmly with Christ.

3. It increases the gifts of the Holy Spirit within us.

4. It makes our bond with the church more perfect. The Vatican II *Constitution on the Church*, No. 11, tells us: 'The sacred nature and organic structure of the priestly community is brought into operation through the sacraments, and the exercise of virtues. Incorporated into the church by baptism, the faithful are appointed by their baptismal character to Christian religious worship; reborn as children of God, they must profess before men the faith they have received from God through the church. By the sacrament of confirmation, they strengthen their bound to the church, and are endowed with the special strength of the Holy Spirit. Hence they are, as true witnesses of Christ, more strictly bound to spread the faith by word and deed. Taking part in the eucharistic sacrifice, the source and summit of the Christian life, they offer the Divine Victim to God, and themselves along with it. And so it is that, both in the offering and in Holy Communion, each in his own way, though not of course indiscriminately, has their own part to play in the liturgical action. Then strengthened by the body of Christ in the eucharistic communion, they manifest in a concrete way the unity of the People of God which his holy sacrament aptly signifies and admirably realises.'

5. It gives us a special strength of the Holy Spirit to spread and defend the faith by word and action as true witnesses of Christ, to confess the name of Christ boldly, and never to be ashamed of the Cross of Jesus.

6. Confirmation gives us a 'seal' or 'character' or 'indelible spiritual mark'. This means that Jesus Christ has marked a Christian with the seal of his

Spirit by clothing that person with power from on high so that he/she may be his witness. This 'character' or 'seal' perfects the priesthood of the faithful received in baptism, and as St Thomas Aquinas says the 'the confirmed person receives the power to profess Christ publicly, and as it were officially.' Because of this 'seal' a person may only receive baptism or confirmation once.

St Ambrose says: 'Recall then that you have received the spiritual seal, the seal of wisdom and understanding, the spirit of right judgement and courage, the spirit of knowledge and reverence, the spirit of holy fear in God's presence. Guard what you have received. God the Father has marked you with his sign; Christ the Lord confirmed you and has placed his pledge, the Spirit in your hearts.' (cf. *Catechism*, Nos 1303–1305)

Final Prayer

Come Holy Spirit, Creator, come,
from thy bright heavenly throne,
come take possession of our souls,
and make them all thy own.

Thou who are called the Paraclete,
best gift of God above,
the living spring, the living fire,
sweet unction and true love.

Thou who are sevenfold in thy grace,
finger of God's right hand;
his promise, teaching little ones
to speak and understand.

O guide our minds with thy blest light,
with love our hearts inflame;
and with thy strength, which ne'er decays,
confirm our mortal frame.

All glory to the Father be,
with his co-equal Son;
the same to thee, great Paraclete,
while endless ages run. Amen.

All: All-powerful Father, pour out the Holy Spirit upon us,
to strengthen us with its abundant gifts,
and make us more like Christ.
All-powerful God, Father of Our lord Jesus Christ,
by water and the Holy Spirit, you freed us from sin,
and gave us new life.

Send your Spirit once more upon us, to
be our Helper and our Guide.
Give us the Spirit of wisdom and understanding,
the Spirit of right judgement and courage,
the Spirit of knowledge and reverence.
Fill us with the Spirit of wonder and awe in your presence.
Let us be sealed with the gift of the Holy Spirit.
Let us be filled with the peace of Christ.
We ask this through Christ Our Lord. Amen.

Reflection
A Reading from the *Constitution on the Church*, Nos 4 & 12.
When the work which the Father gave the Son to do on earth was accomplished, the Holy Spirit was sent on the day of Pentecost in order that he might continually sanctify the church, and that consequently, those who believe might have access through Christ in one Spirit to the Father. He is the Spirit of life, the fountain of water springing up to eternal life. To people, dead in sin, the Father gives life through him, until the day when, in Christ, he raises to life their mortal bodies. The Spirit dwells in the church and in the hearts of the faithful, as in a temple. In them he prays and bears witness to their adoptive children status. Guiding the church in the way of all truth, and unifying her in communion and in the works of ministry, he bestows upon her varied hierarchic and charismatic gifts, and in this way directs her; and he adorns her with his fruits. By the power of the gospel he permits the church to keep the freshness of youth. Constantly he renews her and leads her to perfect union with her Spouse. For the Spirit and the Bride both say to Jesus, the Lord: 'Come'.

Hence the universal church is seen to be 'a people brought into unity, from the unity of the Father, the Son, and the Holy Spirit.' (SS. Cyprian and Augustine)

The whole body of the faithful who have an anointing that comes from the Holy One cannot err in matters of belief. This characteristic is shown in the supernatural appreciation of the faith of the whole people, when 'from the bishops to the last of the faithful' they manifest a universal consent in matters of faith and morals. By this appreciation of the faith, aroused and sustained by the Spirit of truth, the People of God, guided by the sacred teaching authority (magisterium), and obeying it, receives not the mere word of men, but truly the word of God, the faith once and for all delivered to the saints. The people unfailingly adhere to this faith, penetrate it more deeply with right judgement, and apply it fully in daily life.

It is not only through the sacraments and the ministrations of the church that the Holy Spirit makes holy the people, leads them and enriches them with his virtues. Allotting his gifts according as he wills, he also distributes special graces among the faithful of every rank. By these gifts he makes them fit and ready to undertake various tasks and offices for the renewal and building up of the church, as it is written, 'the manifestation of the Spirit is given to everybody for profit.' (1 Corinthians 12:7) Whether these charisms be very remarkable or more simple and widely diffused, they are to be received with thanksgiving and consolation since they are fitting and useful for the needs of the church.

1 Corinthians 3:16: 'Do you not realise that your body is the Temple of the Holy Spirit, who is in you and whom you received from God?'

Homework
Readings from the Acts of the Apostles

Day	1	2	3	4	5	6	7
Chapter	21	21	22	22	23	23	24
Verses	1–26	27–40	1–21	22–29	1–22	23–35	1–27

SESSION NINE

The Sacrament of Reconciliation: Part I

Many people worry too much about sin and we need to start by having a better understanding of what sin really is, and how it is an offence against God. The account of sin starts in the Old Testament in Genesis 3:1–7 where we have an account of the sin of Adam and Eve against the authority of God. 'No! You will not die! God knows in fact that on the day you eat it your eyes will be opened, and you will be like gods, knowing good and evil.' (The temptation in Genesis 3:5) This cannot be taken in isolation as the following chapters in Genesis up to the end of chapter 11 tell us about the spread of sin, in the form of jealousy and murder and so on. In Genesis chapter 12 God calls Abraham to be the father of a new people, and later in chapter 17 makes a Covenant with him. The fight against sin has started. Not everything needs to be taken literally, but this was a simple way to tell our ancestors how our present situation came about. However the Fall is historical. (Genesis 3)

The biblical concept of sin is expressed in four different words:

1. *Hatta't* – Missing the mark. One who sins fails to meet what is expected of him in relation to another person. Also means the rebellion a subject against his lord.
2. *Awon* – means a twisted or distorted condition. One who sins is deformed in some way, he deviates from standard behaviour.
3. *Pe'sa'* – means rebellion. When used in regard to interpersonal relations it designates the violation of the rights of others. In regard to Israel itself, it meant infidelity in regard to the Covenant.
4. *Ma'al* – means infidelity in regard to the Covenant, the breaking of an obligation freely undertaken. Sin is a lie, an act of folly because the course of action chosen can only lead to disaster. Elsewhere the prophet Hosea said that sin – especially idolatry – was regarded as adultery by Israel.

In the Old Testament era there is often linkage between sin and the Old Testament Covenant. Moreover, sin was regarded as fairly common, and the result of evil inclinations in people. The removal of sin and guilt is a matter of vital concern in the religion of the Old Testament. Sometimes we are told of punishments which are seen to be coming from God as punishment for particular sins. For instance the child of the unlawful liaison of King David and Bathsheba died despite the prayers of David. (2 Samuel 11 &12) For forgiveness, conversion or a change of heart was necessary. We also read of people doing penance by fasting, and wearing sackcloth and ashes.

As we read in Leviticus 16:18–20, sacrifices for sin were common. Again in the same chapter of Leviticus verses 1–34 we read of a great Day of Atonement. The High Priest as the representative of the people before God, entered the sanctuary … 'He is to receive two goats for a sacrifice for sin and a ram for a holocaust from the community of the people of Israel. After offering the bull as a sacrifice for his own sins and performing the rite of atonement for himself and his family … he is to draw lots for the two goats and allot one to Yahweh and one to Azazel (A demon of some kind thought to live in the desert). The goat whose lot was marked "For Azazel" shall be set before Yahweh, still alive, to perform the rite of atonement over it, sending it into the desert of Azazel … Aaron must lay his hands on its head and confess all the faults of the children of Israel, all their transgressions and sins, and lay them to its charge. Having laid them on the goat's head, he shall send it out into the desert … and the goat shall bear all their faults away with it into the desert place.' (*Jerome Biblical Commentary* 77:125–135)

In the Old Testament there was always hope of forgiveness, and we read of many cases of the Israelites getting involved in idolatry, but later coming back to God and getting forgiveness. In Isaiah 1:18 we read: 'Come now, let us talk this over, says Yahweh. Though your sins are scarlet, they shall be as white as snow; though they are red as crimson, they shall be like wool.'

Jesus Reveals the Loving Mercy of God

In the New Testament Jesus does not speak much about sin, but rather about the love and mercy of God the Father. He did not just speak about God's way of thinking, but also practised it by meeting with, talking to and eating with sinners despite the fact that he was condemned for doing these things. He used parables to put forward this teaching of the mercy and love of God, and showed it by action in his treatment of other people. In Luke 15:1–7 we have the parable of the Lost Sheep and how the shepherd left the other ninety-nine and went and searched for the missing sheep until he found it, and then returned rejoicing. Again in Luke 15:8–10 we have the parable of the woman searching for the lost drachma until she found it, and then rejoicing. Probably the greatest story of all is that of the Prodigal Son or better called the All-Forgiving Father (Lk 15:11–32). Luke also gives us the story of Zacchaeus who climbed the tree to see Jesus, and was then invited down by Jesus who wished to eat in his house. (Lk 19:1–10). John gives us the story of the woman caught in adultery and how Jesus treated her very kindly. (Jn 8:1–11) There are other stories and incidents but I think that it is all well summed up in the words of Luke 5:31–32 when Jesus was challenged for associating with sinners and he said: 'It is not those who are well who need a doctor, but the sick. I have not come to call the virtuous, but sinners to repentance.'

Some other parts that you might like to read are: Mark 2:1–12 about the man let down from the roof and how Jesus forgave his sins before curing him; Luke

7:36–50 about the woman who was a sinner but anointed his feet in the Pharisee's house; John chapter 9 about the miracle of the man born blind – the Pharisees had the idea that his sickness and sin were linked together, but Jesus said that was not true. There may be other incidents or teachings that appeal to you like Mark 2:23–28 and the attitude/teaching of Jesus about the Sabbath.

An interesting question is what did Jesus teach people about how to get to heaven. Let us look at three answers from Jesus.

1. Mark 10:17–22: 'He was setting out on a journey when a man ran up, knelt before him and put this question to him. "Good Master what must I do to inherit eternal life?" Jesus said to him, "Why do you call me good? No one is good but God alone. You know the commandments: You must not kill; You must not commit adultery; You must not steal; You must not bring false witness; Honour your father and your mother." And he said to him, "Master, I have kept all these from my earliest days." Jesus looked steadily at him, and loved him, and he said, "There is one thing that you lack. Go sell everything you own and give the money to the poor, and you will have treasure in heaven; then come follow me." But his face fell at these words, and he went away sad, for he was a man of great wealth.' The scribes and Pharisees had taken the Ten Commandments of Moses and multiplied them into 613 precepts, but Jesus was not interested in their 613 precepts, but he was prepared to challenge this young man – obviously a good person – to greater things.

2. Mark 12:28–34: 'One of the scribes who had listened to them debating, and had observed how well Jesus had answered them, now came and put a question to him. "Which is the first of all the commandments?" Jesus replied; "This is the first: Listen, Israel, the Lord our God is the one Lord, and you must love the Lord your God with all your heart, with all your soul, with all your might and with all your strength. The second is this: You must love your neighbour as yourself. There is no other commandment than these." When the scribe agreed and said that this was more important than any sacrifice, Jesus told him: "You are not far from the kingdom of God."' Two commandments instead of 613 precepts would be much simpler. These two commandments are positive and challenging whereas more than half of the 613 precepts were negative.

3. The third time that Jesus set forth his way of getting to heaven for us was at the Last Supper and it was short, simple and challenging. John 15:12: 'This is my commandment: love one another, as I have loved you.'

There is a progression among these three statements of Jesus, but they are also fundamentally linked together. Whichever you pick for yourself it should be liberating and freeing. If we let ourselves worry about the 613 precepts of old or their modern equivalent, we will live in fear and not in love. Better to know the love and mercy of God, that to be an expert in making catalogues of sins for yourself and others that are often not sins at all but imperfections and scruples, and based on the pride of getting to heaven by your own efforts of keeping many rules. Heaven is a gift of God and we get there with the help of God, and there is a new freedom and joy and peace of mind in handing things over to him. We may fail at times but he is always there to help and forgive us, and we should never allow ourselves to get depressed.

The Fundamental Option

When Jesus started to preach he was dealing with a situation where the Ten Commandments of God had been expanded to 613 precepts – all binding under sin. A large number of people would fall into the category of sinners because of this – including the shepherds who went to see him at the nativity at Bethlehem. As they wandered from place to place with their sheep they could not keep all these precepts. A simple story in Mark 2:23–28 tells us of the attitude of Jesus to many of these laws. 'One Sabbath day he happened to be taking a walk through the cornfields, and his disciples began to pick corn as they went along. (This was considered by the Pharisees to be work and so forbidden on the Sabbath) And the Pharisees said to him, "Look, why are your disciples doing something on the Sabbath that is forbidden?" And he replied, "Did you never read what David did in his time of need when he and his followers were hungry – how he went into the house of God when Abiathar was High Priest, and ate the loaves of offering which only the priests are allowed to eat, and how he also gave some to the men with him?" And he said to them, "The Sabbath was made for man, not man for the Sabbath."'

Sin in the New Testament is seen as relational to God. In the early church, every vestige of the taboo notion of sin in the Old Testament, together with the legalistic and impersonal notion has disappeared. Sin is usually presented in the context of forgiveness. Sin is seen as slavery and death as well as an offence against God. Christ's life and mission was to destroy Satan's reign of slavery and death, and replace it with freedom and life in the Father's house.

In Romans 5:18–22 we read:

1. As one man's fall brought condemnation on everybody, so the good act of one man brings everybody life and makes them justified.
2. As by one man's disobedience many were made sinners, so by one man's obedience many will be made righteous.
3. When law came, it was to multiply the opportunities of falling, but however great the number of sins committed grace was even greater;
4. And so, just as sin reigned wherever there was death, so grace will reign to bring eternal life thanks to the righteousness that comes through Christ Our Lord. (Numbering added)

In the early church they were mainly concerned with graver sins, for example, idolatry, murder or adultery, and if one was guilty of these sins one had to confess them publicly and do public penance. 'During the seventh century Irish missionaries inspired by the Eastern monastic tradition took to continental Europe the "private" practice of penance, which does not require public and prolonged completion of penitential works before reconciliation with the church. From that time onwards, the sacrament has been performed between penitent and priest. In its main lines this is the form of penance that the Church has practised down to our day.' (*Catechism*, No. 1447)

We have seen how Jesus spoke more of the love and mercy of God and the forgiveness of sins rather than condemnation. The early church was also more concerned about living a good Christian Life in the Spirit rather than worrying about sin. The Council of Trent (1545–1563) did many great things but it mentioned confessing sins numerically and generically. After that we had a multiplication of sins and all kinds of imperfections were added to them. The scientific age tended to divide and sub-divide all kind of things. You could commit several sins saying Mass by not observing the rubrics! Even small children could commit mortal sins!

Is it possible that a good living person can suddenly commit a mortal sin? Or again has a child the maturity to commit a mortal sin? Most moral theologians would say *no* in both cases. With the help of the psychological sciences, and the contribution of behavioural sciences, some theologians speak of the fundamental option, which when misunderstood is questioned by church authorities. It does not mean that it is possible to commit a deliberate mortal sin and then continue to say that one has a fundamental option for God. Jesus said: 'He who is not with me is against me, and he who does not gather with me scatters' (Mt 12:30). The fundamental option for God differs from person to person, and it needs to be cultivated and strengthened.

The fundamental option is based on the fundamental freedom of the individual, and needs a profound knowledge of what is good. It brings forth a great spontaneity in individual ethical decisions. It starts with our knowledge of God, and as our knowledge of God grows, our fundamental or basic option for God grows. As Häring CSsR says: 'A simple peasant saint with loving knowledge of God and of good is closer to divine wisdom and freedom, than the greatest scientist and most learned theologian, if these are lacking the same kind of existential knowledge or do not reach the same level of depth or wholeness.' (*Free and Faithful in Christ*, Vol. 1, p. 181)

We make several fundamental or basic options in our life in regard to work, state in life and so on. However, the most important option that we make is for God. It is not something static, and it can grow or weaken. Sometimes it is two steps forward and one step backwards. We are sinners and will continue to commit all kinds of small sins, but that does not mean that our fundamental option is not for God but for sin.

God is not just concerned with external deeds – God wants our hearts and our commitment to him in our fundamental option to Him. God wants a new heart in us as Jesus said in Matthew 6:21: 'Where your treasure is, there will your heart be also.' In the Old Testament the prophet Ezekiel in 36:25 speaking about New Testament times said: 'I shall give you a new heart, and put a new spirit in you; I shall remove the heart of stone from your bodies and give you a new heart of flesh instead. I shall put my spirit in you, and make you keep my laws and sincerely respect my observances.'

At the beginning of Mark, in 1:15, we have a summary of the teaching of Jesus: 'The time has come,' he said, 'and the kingdom of God is at hand. Repent, and believe the Good News.' Repent means to have a change of heart, and a new spirit. In doing that we have a change of heart and a new spirit that will not be suddenly taken away from us. St Augustine treats of grateful memory and the heart of a person. He calls for a firm and wholehearted commitment of self, and is convinced that freedom of action is then guaranteed. 'Change your heart and your work will then be changed.'(Augustine, *De Civitate Dei*, lib 14, c.7PL 41, 410) We cannot say that we have made a fundamental option or commitment for God if our actions are evil. Jesus said: 'You will know them by their fruits.'(Mt 7:16) Fr David Rohr explains how a loving relationship with God (traditionally the state of grace) may be reversed. (David Rohr OMI, *Catholic Moral Teaching*, p. 213) It could be through one serious mortal sin or a series of so-called venial sins, leading to a mortal sin. There are several rightly called commitments that direct a person in a definite way of life, e.g. to become a Christian or a criminal, and these commitments do entail mind stances on the part of the person, for Christ or against him, for good or for evil, to love or to hate and so on.

To make a fundamental option for God, we need experience of life, reflection on our life, knowledge of God, and freedom to act. 'From all this it becomes clear that freedom in its "basic depth" is not just a matter of saying "Yes" or "No" to a specific decision; it is the power to mould and create ourselves, to become what we truly are. The fundamental option decides one's "heart", which can overflow with love and goodness, but can also harbour deeply rooted selfishness. Self-realisation is openness towards others – love is the true moral commitment of a person's basic freedom. Withdrawal into oneself is the negative self-commitment.' (Häring, *Free and Faithful in Christ* Vol. 1, p. 188)

'Life's great decisions will release the energies of creative freedom and fidelity to the extent that one has reached the level of responsibility to oneself, and is able to mould and create and, at the same time, to commit oneself in a covenant for the common good in the sight of God. In these great decisions that relate to our fundamental option, and affirm and strengthen it, we must be keenly aware that they are not once-and-forever; they have to be nurtured.' (Häring, *Free and Faithful in Christ*, Vol. 1, p. 192)

Many good people are over worried about sin in their lives. They often worry about things that are not sins at all. This worry about sin can lead to scruples. A person's life can become sin-centred instead of life-centred, meaning that a person is continually worried about avoiding sin. After his resurrection the usual greeting of Jesus to his disciples was, 'Peace be with you.' The word that Jesus used meant a totality of peace – body, mind and soul. If we want that peace of Jesus then it is important to make our fundamental option for Jesus, his teaching and his church. His church is for sinners and we can relax there as Jesus liked to relax with sinners during his Life on earth. His grace and help are always greater than our weakness.

1 Thessalonians 5:9–10: 'God never meant us to experience the retribution, but to win salvation through Our Lord Jesus Christ, who died for us so that, alive or dead, we should live united to him.'

John 10:10: 'I have come so that they may have life and have it to the full.'

John 8:31–32: 'If you make my word your home, you will indeed be my disciples, you will learn the truth, and the truth will make you free.'

Fr Häring CSsR once said: 'Do not allow anyone to propose an ethics of prohibitions and controls to you, instead of an ethics of creative liberty and fidelity and love.'

Final Prayer
General Prayers of Intercession.

Reflection
Since many people may not be familiar with the idea of the fundamental option I will make a brief summary of it. At the time of Jesus the Ten Commandments had been expanded into 613 precepts which made living in relationship with God very difficult for most people. Jesus was more interested in the spirit of the law rather than in the letter of the law. He spoke of two commandments of love and finally at the Last Supper just told his disciples to love others as he had loved them.

In the early church sin is presented in the same way as Jesus had done it – in the context of forgiveness and the mercy of God. The taboo notion and the various purification ceremonies have disappeared. Sin is seen as slavery and death, as well as an offence against God, and they are only concerned with a few of the graver sins. Christ's life and mission destroyed Satan's reign of slavery and death, and replaced it with freedom and life in his Father's house.

We make many options or choices in life that are intended to last for a long time. When we make our fundamental option or choice for God it is a commitment to God. That commitment for God is not going to suddenly disappear. We may sin at times, but those sins are not going to suddenly destroy our commitment and relationship with God. We always have the mercy and forgiveness and grace of God in the sacrament of reconciliation. St Thomas Aquinas says that habitual grace gives so strong a basic inclination to the good, that one act cannot easily destroy it. However, he also acknowledges that it is through one act that the friendship of God can be finally lost. God is not just concerned with

external deeds – God wants our hearts, our commitment to him – our fundamental option. To make the fundamental option for God, we need experience,
reflection, knowledge and freedom = maturity.

Some people are so worried about sin that their lives become orientated to
avoiding sin and unfortunately many of these so-called sins are not sins at all.
People like this can become so worried about sin and imperfections and feelings
that they can lose the peace of mind that Jesus promised.

Peace I bequeath to you,
My own peace I give to you,
A peace that the world cannot give,
this is my gift to you. (Jn 14:27)

Homework
Readings from the Acts of the Apostles

Day	1	2	3	4	5	6	7
Chapter	25	25	26	26	27	27	28
Verses	1–12	13–27	1–23	24–32	1–25	26–44	1–16

SESSION TEN

The Sacrament of Reconciliation: Part II

What is sin? Sin, in its fully malicious sense, is a turning away from God, and it destroys the fundamental option for the good self-commitment to the service of God, and for love of neighbour. Sin it its most serious form is choosing death over life. As we grow in grace and virtue, our fundamental option or choice of God will also grow in strength and depth. Fr Häring CSsR states his opinion: 'It is my conviction that there can be no mortal sin without a fundamental option or intention that turns one's basic freedom towards evil.' (*Free And Faithful in Christ*, Vol. 1, p. 215) Some good people have an unconscious idea that God is some kind of cruel ruler who is just waiting for them to get out of line so that he can punish them. This kind of thinking is very different from the Abba Daddy God that Jesus spoke about, and also very different from the way that Jesus treated people of all kinds – especially sinners. It does not make sense that someone could commit several mortal sins, get them forgiven, be in a state of grace for a short while and then repeat the process again after a short break. It would be like being on a roundabout with no exit.

According to *The Catechism of the Catholic Church*, Nos 1849–1851, sin is described and defined as follows: it can be any or all of these. I break it up into sections to make it clearer.

1. Sin is an offence against reason, truth and right conscience.
2. It is a failure in genuine love for God and neighbour, caused by a perverse attachment to certain goods.
3. It wounds the nature of individuals and injures human solidarity.
4. It has been defined by St Augustine as an 'utterance, a deed or a desire contrary to the eternal law.'
5. Sin is an offence against God: 'Against you, you alone, have I sinned, and done what is evil in your sight.'(Psalm 51:4)
6. Sin sets itself against God's love for us, and turns our hearts away from it.
7. Like the first sin (of Adam), it is disobedience, a revolt against God, through the will to become 'like gods', (Gen 3:5) knowing and determining good and evil.
8. Sin is thus 'love of self even to contempt of God'. (St Augustine)
9. In this proud exaltation, sin is diametrically opposed to the obedience of Jesus, which achieves our salvation.
10. It is precisely in the passion, when the mercy of Christ is about to vanquish it, that sin most clearly manifests its violence and its many forms: unbelief, murderous hatred, shunning and mockery by the leaders and the people, Pilate's cowardice and the cruelty of the soldiers, Judas' betrayal so bitter to Jesus, Peter's denial and the disciples' flight.

Previously, theologians spoke of two kinds of sin, and most still do – including the *Catechism* – namely, mortal and venial. Nowadays some theologians speak of venial, serious and mortal. Moreover, the *Catechism* in No. 1863 tells us: 'Deliberate and unrepented venial sin disposes us little by little to commit a mortal sin.' There are venial sins that are more serious than other venial sins, and when they are repeated they are more likely to predispose us to commit a mortal sin. The more serious they are, the more likely they are to cause carelessness, and a hardening attitude within us to the love of God, to our neighbour and so on, disposing us more and more to the danger of committing a mortal sin. A mortal sin involves cutting off our relationship with God, and three conditions are necessary:

1. Grave matter as defined by God or the community. The seriousness of the sin and to whom it is directed must be considered. Murder would be a grave matter, and if it was directed at one's parents it would be graver.
2. Full knowledge. The sinner must know that it is wrong and a sin and is a serious matter.
3. Full consent. The sinner must fully agree to the grave matter, be fully aware of the gravity, and be free to commit or not commit the sin.

With the knowledge that we now have from the behavioural sciences, and from psychology, we know that it not likely that mortal sin will occur very often in the normal practising Christian's life. However, we do know that if there is carelessness about sin – venial or serious – it can lead to vice and to mortal sin. For a variety of reasons a person can also make an option for evil, instead of for good and for God. To understand this all we need to do is to look at the evil in the world around us, or throughout history. A good way to examine your conscience is to look at your relationships. This is a better and more positive way than looking at lists or catalogues of sins.

1. Relationship with yourself. To become addicted to alcohol or drugs or gambling or sex is to damage your relationship with yourself. To become addicted to work at the expense of other things is also wrong. Ambition and hard work are good and praiseworthy, but if they hinder or inhibit your growth as a human being then they are wrong for you. You need time for yourself, and for others – especially those who are close to you – also for God, and if anything interferes with that, then it is wrong for you, no matter how attractive it may seem. Of course the opposite could be a problem in the case of laziness, or putting things off too much. These matters may not be sins in themselves, but could lead to sins if they are neglected or ignored. For the sacrament of reconciliation it would be a good thing to pick out some aspect of your personal relationship with yourself that you need to work on.

2. Relationship with others. This is the great test as Jesus told us in John 15:12: 'This is my commandment, love one another, as I have loved you.' We need to start with those who are close to us – those we live with, or meet with on a regular daily basis. This is where most problems occur. On the other hand it is important to remember that we react to different people in different ways:

a) Person A, we like from the beginning and hence no problems there.

b) Person B we do not like at the beginning, but gradually as we get to know them we begin to like them. It is interesting that when we get to know people better, and the burdens that they may have, that we very often develop sympathy and a liking for them. A solution in many interpersonal relationships is to get to know a person better.

c) Person C is when we feel a strong negative reaction to somebody. We feel a tightening of the stomach muscles or wish to avoid them or run away from them. This is a reaction in our feelings, and there is never a sin in our feelings because they arise spontaneously, and we cannot stop them. What we can do is make sure that our feelings do not lead us into committing evil against that person. Do not worry about sin but try to be kind, or patient or tolerant towards that person. A good way is to recognise your feelings and to pray for the particular person. What irritates us most in others is our own faults.

In Luke 6:31 Jesus said: 'Treat others as you would like them to treat you.' This has wide implications for many of our relationships with others – both close and distant. It means to do a good day's work for our pay, and also to pay a just wage for work. Something else that may not be a direct sin, but is a challenge to us as Christians, are the social problems of the country and the world. In Luke 16:19–31 we have the story of the rich man and Lazarus. What was the sin of the rich man? He lacked compassion for the poor, hungry and sick man at his gate. It is often easier to ignore problems rather than to get involved in trying to solve them. We need to look at sins of omission as well as sins of commission. What we need to do from time to time is ask ourselves: 'What would Jesus do in my place?'

3. *Relationship with God.* This is the foundation stone of everything that is important in our lives. Without God our lives do not have much meaning. We need to make time for God in our lives – to get to know him in prayer. If we do not get to know him how can we expect him to be our friend and helper or to have a close relationship with us? We read in the life of Jesus of how at regular times or before important decisions he went off by himself to pray in some lonely place. For us the Eucharist is the most important prayer in our lives, and the source of the spiritual nourishment that keeps us going. Doing things for God and others are important, but we have to make private time for God in our lives. It may be prayer, meditation, reading the scriptures or visits to the Blessed Sacrament.

To examine one's conscience in regard to these three relationships is a simple and practical approach for the sacrament of reconciliation. It is also the basis for making a few good resolutions for the future. There is an obligation to confess all mortal sins – other sins are optional. There is no need for a kind of laundry list of sins for God. People can sometimes be worried by sins that they forget about, but God knows about them and he will forgive them. God's forgiveness is often much easier to get than that of others or even to forgive ourselves. God also forgives sins – especially venial ones but even mortal ones with perfect contrition – when we ask him in prayer for forgiveness, or attend the Eucharist, or engage in good works.

It is no good concentrating on all the many things we could do in regard to resolutions for our future life, but much better to concentrate on one or two resolutions in regard to the three basic relationships in our lives – to self, to others and to God. This is a positive and practical approach, and not only does it help us to develop virtues and help them grow, but it wipes out the corresponding vices or sins. You do not just prepare ground for planting, but you also plant the seeds or flowers that you hope to harvest. For many Christians who are trying to make an effort to live as Christians, there is a great danger of wasting time and energy in worrying about things that are not sins. On the other hand the murderous bedlam in the world today results because many people seem to have lost a sense of sin. Despite that if we try to build up virtues, and walk the path of love, sin will not be a problem in our lives. Romans 8:14–15: 'The spirit you received is not the spirit of slaves bringing fear into your lives again; it is the spirit of children, and it makes us cry out, "Abba, Father!" The Spirit himself and our spirit bear witness that we are children of God.'

The main roots of sin, traditionally known as the seven deadly sins are: Pride, Covetousness, Lust, Anger, Gluttony, Envy and Sloth. Evil tendencies in these directions exist in all of us. We read St Paul's words in Romans 7:15: 'I cannot understand my own behaviour. I fail to carry out the things that I want to do, and I find myself doing the very things I hate.' No wonder Jesus taught us to pray in the Our Father: 'Lead us not into temptation ...' We Christians know that we are sinners, but we also know that we are saved and forgiven by the passion-death-resurrection of Jesus. We have risen into a new life through our baptism. We need to protect this life within us from sickness and death, and Jesus has given us the means to do so through the sacrament of reconciliation.

Jesus entrusts the power to forgive sins to his church
We already have seen how Jesus forgave sins here on earth at times. Some of his listeners considered this to be blasphemy, and this caused them to hate him and seek his death. In *The Catechism of the Catholic Church* No. 1443 is written: 'During his public life Jesus not only forgave sins, but also made plain the effect of that forgiveness: he reinstated forgiven sinners into the community of the People of God from which sin had alienated them or even excluded them. A remarkable sign of this is the fact that Jesus receives sinners at his table, a gesture that expresses in an astonishing way both God's forgiveness, and the return to the bosom of the People of God.' (This practice is continued in the Mass at Holy Communion.)

Jesus promised the power to forgive sins to his church when he said to Peter in Matthew 16:18–19: 'So I now say to you: You are Peter and on this rock I will build my church. And the gates of the underground can never hold out against it. I will give you the keys of the kingdom of heaven: whatever you bind on earth shall be considered bound in heaven; whatever you loose on earth shall be considered loosed in heaven.' The Vatican II *Constitution on the Church* No. 22 #2 tells us that the office of binding and loosing on earth which was given to Peter was also assigned to the college of apostles united to its head. Moreover, 'the words *bind* and *loose* mean: whomever you exclude from your communion, will be excluded from communion with God; whomever you receive anew into your communion, God will welcome back into his. Reconciliation with the church is inseparable from reconciliation with God.' (*Catechism* No. 1445)

Jesus entrusted the power to forgive sins when he appeared to his apostles on the day of his resurrection: 'As the Father sent me, so I am sending you.' After saying this he breathed on them and said; 'Receive the Holy Spirit. For those whose sins you forgive, they are forgiven; for those whose sins you retain, they are retained.' (Jn 20:21–23)

Only God can forgive sins but he gives this power to bishops and priests, as *The Catechism of the Catholic Church* No. 1461 tells us: 'Christ entrusted to his apostles the ministry of reconciliation. Bishops who are their successors, and priests, the bishops' collaborators, continue to exercise this ministry. Indeed bishops, and priests by virtue of the sacrament of orders, have the power to forgive sins "in the name of the Father, and of the Son, and of the Holy Spirit".' The confessor is not the master of God's forgiveness, but its servant. We also need to be reconciled with the church through the priest, because we have injured the church and the community by our sins. The *Catechism* No. 1465 tells us: 'When he celebrates the sacrament of penance the priest is fulfilling the ministry of the Good Shepherd, who seeks the lost sheep, of the Good Samaritan who binds up wounds, of the Father who awaits the Prodigal Son and welcomes him on his return, and of the just and impartial judge whose judgement is both just and merciful. The priest is the sign and instrument of God's merciful love for the sinner.'

The Sacrament of Reconciliation
If the sacrament is carried out formally it will have the following elements:

1. The priest welcomes you and blesses you.
2. Scripture reading.
3. Confession of sins.
4. Act of Contrition.
5. Absolution. Time normally does not allow for all of these elements.

Justice may demand another element in the form of restitution if money or goods were stolen or some person's good name was damaged.

There are three forms of the sacrament:

1. 'Private' confession facing the priest or behind a screen.
2. Common preparation and common penance with private confessing of sins and private absolution.
3. General absolution in times of necessity.

I have found that putting on the sacrament during Mass and using the first part of the Mass as preparation was a very helpful way of doing it. It would mean using the second form.

Postscript

Catechism No. 1863: 'Deliberate and unrepented venial sin disposes us little by little to commit mortal sin.' This is what some modern theologians mean by slipping into mortal sin. The same article quoting St Augustine says: 'While he is in the flesh, man cannot help but at least have some light sins. But do not despise these sins we call "light": if you take them for light when you weigh them, tremble when you count them. A number of light objects make a great mass; a number of drops fill a river, a number of grains make a heap. What then is our hope? Above all Confession …'

The *Catechism* in No. 1864 also tells us that not all mortal sins are the same. Jesus said: 'And anyone who says a word against the Son of Man will be forgiven; but let anybody speak against the Holy Spirit and he will not be forgiven either in this world or in the next.' (Mt 12:32; cf. Mk 3:29 and Lk 12:10) It explains what this means: 'There are no limits to the mercy of God, but anybody who deliberately refuses to accept his mercy by repenting, rejects the forgiveness of his sins and the salvation offered by the Holy Spirit. Such hardness of heart can lead to final impenitence and eternal loss.' My *Jerome Biblical Commentary* explains speaking against the Holy Spirit as blasphemy by attributing the works of the Holy Spirit to demonic powers.

The above words of Jesus in regard to some sins being forgiven after death would also support the practice of praying for the dead in the church. Of course it is mentioned in 2 Maccabees 12:38–45. It was also the practice of the church and is mentioned in the Councils of Florence (AD 1439) and Trent (AD 1563). Tradition of the church speaks of a cleansing fire. (1 Corinthians 3:15 and 1 Peter 1:7) See also *The Catechism of the Catholic Church* Nos 1030–1032.

Reflection

David Bohr, in his book *Catholic Moral Tradition*, dealing with sin on pp. 198–199 writes: 'A decade ago, an eminent psychologist, Karl Menniger, wrote a book entitled *Whatever Became of Sin?* While making full allowance for the limits placed on freedom by the influence of heredity, environment, intellectual drives, and subconscious motives, he insisted that there was still such a thing as moral responsibility. He further maintained from his professional standpoint that the world would be a healthier place if we showed more concern for repentance and conversion. The loss of the sense of sin in modern times can be attributed to several factors.

1. The scientific achievements and philosophical currents of the nineteenth century espoused an overly optimistic view of evolution and human progress that allowed no room for human failure.
2. Ethics has been shaped, in many instances, by historical relativism.
3. The advance of secularism lessened the sense of God and promoted a world-wide decline for authority.
4. Certain schools of psychology confused sin with neurotic feelings of guilt, and frequently stressed the role of psychic determinism at the expense of moral responsibility.
5. Conscience has been frequently equated with subjective feelings.
6. An overemphasis has been placed on collective responsibility for sinful social structures downgrading personal guilt.
7. And among members of some Christian churches there has been a reaction against the overemphasis on sexual sins, as well as against a legalistic, for-malistic and juridical notion of sin and morality. (Numbering added)

In regard to No. 7 we had the effects of the Jansenist heresy in the Catholic Church and of Puritanism in the Protestant churches. Nowadays there also seems to an overemphasis on personal freedom even when it infringes on the rights of others. For instance, you will hear it said that a woman has a right over what she does with her body even when it means killing her unborn child.

St Paul says in 2 Corinthians 5:17–19: 'And for anyone who is in Christ, there is a new creation; the old creation has gone, and now the new one is here. It is all God's work. It was God who reconciled us to himself through Christ and gave us the work of handing on this reconciliation. In other words, God in Christ was reconciling the world to himself, not holding people's faults against them, and he has entrusted to us the news that they are reconciled.'

Homework
Readings from the Acts of the Apostles & First Letter of Peter

Day	1	2	3	4	5	6	7
Chapter	28	1	1	2	2	3	3
Verses	17–31	1–12	13–25	1–12	13–25	1–12	13–22

There is a gap at the end of Acts as it is recognised that Paul was freed from prison after the normal two years, and that he probably travelled to some of his former missionary places and maybe even to Spain before he was rearrested and put to death.

The Sacrament of Anointing the Sick

James 5:13–16: 'If anyone is in trouble, he should pray; if anyone is feeling happy, he should sing a psalm. If one of you is ill, he should send for the elders of the church, and they must anoint him with oil in the name of the Lord, and pray over him. The prayer of faith will save the sick man, and the Lord will raise him up again; and if he has committed any sins, he will be forgiven.'

The sacrament of the sick was formerly known as Extreme Unction or the Last Rites and these names caused people to have a negative attitude towards it. In the mid-seventies, I was asked by a woman in Japan to visit her husband who was dying in hospital. I got into the Intensive Care Unit, heard his confession and gave him communion. When I suggested the sacrament of the sick he got excited and said he was not that bad. I dropped the matter as his heart was the problem and I did not want him to get excited. He died the next day. 'In the liturgical tradition of both East and West it was, at first, used widely, but with the passage of time it was conferred more and more exclusively to those at the point of death.' (*Catechism*, No. 1512 synopsis) Also in the *Catechism* No. 1499 we read: 'By the sacred anointing of the sick, and the prayer of the priests, the whole church commends those who are ill to the suffering and glorified Lord, that he may raise them up and save them. And indeed, she exhorts them to contribute to the good of the People of God by freely uniting themselves to the passion and death of Christ.'

In the book of Isaiah 29:18–19 and 35:5–6 and 61:1, we read oracles alluding to signs of healing when the Messiah would come. Matthew 11:2–5 quotes Jesus that healing of the sick was one of the signs of the arrival of the Messiah: 'Now John in his prison had heard what Christ was doing and he sent his disciples to ask him, "Are you the One who is to come, or have we got to wait for someone else?" Jesus answered, "Go back and tell John what you hear and see; the blind see again, and the lame walk, lepers are cleansed, and the deaf hear, and happy the person who does not lose faith in me."' Another relevant matter is that in the case of the man born blind in John 9:1–41. Jesus makes it clear that his blindness is not related to sin in any way but 'so that the works of God might be displayed in him.' (Verse 3)

Sickness can result from ageing, disease, the misuse of drugs, alcohol, tobacco or through psychological factors. If we allow our hearts to be taken over by hatred or envy, the end result can often be mental and/or physical sickness, and we need to remember that the mind often needs to be healed as much as the body. Going back many centuries we read in the Book of Job 5:2: 'Resentment kills the senseless, and anger brings death to the fool.'

Sickness is something that affects most of us at some time in our lives, and there is a profound psychological and spiritual dimension to it. In *The Catechism of the Catholic Church* Nos 1500–1501: 'Illness and suffering have always been among the gravest problems confronted in human life. In illness, we experience our powerlessness, our limitations and our boundaries. Every sickness can make us glimpse death. Illness can lead to anguish, self-absorption, sometimes even despair and revolt against God. It can also make a person more mature, helping that person discern in life what is not essential so that person can turn to what is really important. Very often sickness provokes a search for God and a return to him.' This happened to St Ignatius of Loyola. As he was recuperating from his wounds as a soldier, he started his journey back to God and to founding the Jesuit order.

For some people sickness is a purifying and growing experience, for others it is a destroying experience. Sickness brings us face to face with ourselves in a basic naked way which other misfortunes can rarely do. The big question is how do we cope with sickness, how do we react. Some years ago an American woman called Dr Kübler-Ross wrote a book called *Death and Dying*. She was working in a hospital dealing with many terminally ill patients. As a result of her studies and research she found that terminally ill people passed through five stages in their sickness. Some people passed from Stage One to Stage Five very quickly, and others might revert to a stage that they had already passed through. It is not as clearcut as some people might wish, but I have found it very helpful in understanding sick people and their moods. I have also found that healthy people dealing with a loved one who is seriously ill seem to pass through the same stages.

1. Stage One – Denial – Isolation. Some mistake – it cannot be true – check further.
2. Stage Two – Anger – Resentment. It's not fair – why me? People are very difficult at this stage as they are always complaining about many things and never satisfied.
3. Stage Three – Bargaining – Attempt to postpone. If I get better I will be a much better person and/or a better Christian.
4. Stage Four – Depression – Sense of loss. They go in on themselves – silent – morose – nothing is right – not interested in talking.
5. Acceptance. This brings peace of mind and brings the person closer to God. A way to remember these stages is the mnemonic – DABDA.

Exercise: Take these five stages and apply them to some crisis in your life, or in the life of someone close to you.

Sickness and the Ceremony of Anointing

The Jerome Biblical Commentary tells us, on pages 376–377 (Nos 35–36) the following in regard to James 5:13–16: 'If anyone is in trouble he should pray, if anyone is happy, he should sing a psalm. If one of you is ill, he should send for the elders of the church, and they must anoint him with oil in the name of the Lord and pray over him. The prayer of faith will save the sick man and the Lord will raise him up again; and if he has committed any sins, he will be forgiven. So confess your sins to one another, and pray for one another, and this will cure you; the heartfelt prayer of a good man works very powerfully.'

* In the Early Christian Communities the 'elders' were the priests.
* The Anointing with Oil is not a mere medical treatment, but it symbolises the healing presence and the power of God.
* The Prayer of Faith saving the sick man refers to saving both body and soul, but the emphasis here is on restoration to health.
* The Anointing of the Sick in the church for James is a sacrament that was already in use at that time, and performed by the priests of the church.
* It is not just a charismatic ritual as mentioned in 1 Corinthians 12:9, 28 and 30.
* The mention of confessing sins to one another is not clear, and is not directly linked to the sacrament of anointing the sick, but perhaps James is reminding the community of the normal way of obtaining forgiveness for their sins.
* The Council of Trent defined the anointing of the sick to be 'truly and properly a sacrament instituted by Christ and promulgated by James the apostle.' (Session XIV)

Discussion points
1. If you were terminally ill would you wish to be told?
2. Have you ever been present when someone was dying? What were your feelings?
3. Do you think that it is good to tell terminally ill people about their state? Dr Kübler-Ross says that people instinctively know their true state and should be told delicately. You could start by saying that the doctors are worried about you, and then respond as the patient responds. There is a need to be sensitive about how much the patient wishes to talk about the matter. Stop if the patient seems not to want to talk about it.

The Christian View of Death
Death is the one thing certain in our lives, and yet it is very easy to ignore it or deny it – it is something that happens to other people. Not everybody who receives the sacrament of the sick recovers. It is often a preparation for death. The sacrament will help the dying person to die at peace. There is often a *denial* of death in our modern society with dead people being done up to give the impression that they are still alive. Formerly people died in their own homes, but nowadays it is often in the cold antiseptic atmosphere of some hospital. Many people end their journey in life peacefully. Death can be a great relief for many people. Death to some extent is a jump into the unknown, but if we analyse our feelings about it, we find that very often what we are most worried about

is pain, isolation or helplessness. Modern medicine combined with hospice care can take care of most of these problems.

The resurrection of Jesus is the most important fact in our lives. It gives us hope and confidence in the face of death. The resurrection of Jesus is the cornerstone of our faith. Jesus told us in John 12:24: 'I tell you, most solemnly, unless a wheat grain falls on the ground and dies, it remains only a single grain; but if it dies, it yields a rich harvest.' We go through death to new abundant life and eternal life. Just as death was not the end for Jesus, our death is not the end for us but the beginning. Death was not defeat for Jesus but victory. For us death is the end of a limited life with all kinds of problems of sickness, work and unhappiness, and the beginning of an eternal life of happiness, joy and love with God. We all seek the eternal and not the transient, because God has made us that way. Death is the doorway to eternal life and happiness. Jesus says in John 11:25-26: 'I am the resurrection. If anyone believes in me, even though he dies he will live, and whoever lives and believes in me will never die.'

The resurrection of Jesus himself is the proof that he has conquered death for himself and for us. Jesus promised us in regard to Holy Communion in John 6:54: 'Anyone who does eat my flesh and drink my blood has eternal life, and I shall raise him up on the last day.' The promises of Jesus are the basis of our hope. The strength of a promise depends on who makes it, and in this case it is the Son of God – the God-Man. The resurrection of Jesus is the all-important proof that he has conquered death and also his enemies. Look at how it transformed the apostles and disciples – of how with the help of the Holy Spirit they went out to preach Jesus resurrected and set out to change the world. They lost their fear of suffering and death and instead died for the truth of what they preached.

Death is fearful and sad. But for the Christian there is hope. Death is not just black and empty despair, but a doorway leading to an encounter with Jesus and to everlasting life. Jesus at the Last Supper in John 14:1–3 said: 'Do not let your hearts be troubled. Trust in God still, and trust in me. There are many rooms in my Father's house; I am going now to prepare a place for you, and after I have gone and prepared you a place, I shall return to take you with me, so that where I am you may be too.'

St Paul speaks of death and resurrection as follows in 1 Corinthians 15:

*   Verse 42: 'The thing that is sown is perishable, but what is raised is glorious.'
*   Verses 54–57: 'When this perishable nature has put on imperishability, and when this mortal nature has put on immortality, then the words of scripture will come true: Death is swallowed up in victory. Death where is your sting? Now the sting of death is sin, and sin gets its power from the law. So let us thank God for giving us the victory through Our Lord Jesus Christ.'

It is our hope in the resurrection of Jesus, and in life after death which gives meaning and colour to our present lives. Without such a hope for the future there is no real meaning in the present life, and no one could live a full and meaningful life. As long as we live here on earth we need hope and meaning in our lives. Christianity brings a message full of hope and meaning to our lives. Jesus Christ tells us that God our Father – our Abba – created us for this eternal life, and eternal destiny. Our death is the passage way to our eternal destiny. We wait now in this world for the actualisation of the fulfilment of the Father's love and tender care as we put out trust in the words of Jesus in John 6:40: 'Yes, it is my Father's will that whoever sees the Son and believes in him shall have eternal life, and I will raise him up on the Last Day.'

Judgement

In *The Catechism of the Catholic Church* we read in No. 1022: 'Each person receives their eternal retribution in their immortal soul at the very moment of death, in a particular judgement that refers his/her life to Christ: either entrance into the blessedness of heaven – through a purification or immediately – or immediate and everlasting damnation.' The Council of Lyons 11 (1274), Council of Florence (1439) and the Council of Trent (1563) all affirm that for some people some purification is necessary. In Matthew 25:31–46 Jesus speaks also of a general judgement at the end of the world. 'When the Son of Man comes in his glory, escorted by all the angels, then he will take his seat on the throne of glory. All the nations will be assembled before him, and He will separate one from another as the shepherd separates sheep from goats, He will place the sheep on his right hand, and the goats on his left. Then the King will say to those on his right hand, "Come, you whom my Father has blessed, take for your heritage the kingdom prepared for you since the foundation of the world. For I was hungry and you gave me food; I was thirsty and you gave me drink; I was a stranger and you made me welcome; naked and you clothed me, sick and you visited me, in prison and you came to see me." Then the virtuous will say to him in reply, "Lord, when did we see you hungry and feed you; or thirsty and give you drink? When did we see you as a stranger and make you welcome; naked and clothe you; or sick or in prison and visit you?" And the King will answer, "I tell you solemnly, in so far as you did this to one of the least of these brothers of mine, you did it to me ..."' Here we see what God wants from us in this life, and also the standards by which he will judge us. St John of the Cross said: 'At the evening of our lives we will be judged on our love.'

It has always been the tradition and practice of the church to pray for the dead that they may attain the Beatific Vision of God in heaven. 'From the beginning the church has honoured the memory of the dead, and offered prayers in suffrage for them, above all the eucharistic sacrifice, so that, thus purified, they may attain the Beatific Vision of God. The church also commends almsgiving, indulgences and works of penance undertaken on behalf of the dead.' (*The Catechism of the Catholic Church*, No. 1032) We do not know how exactly these dead people will be purified, or the process of purification but we call it purgatory. The practice of the church is that we on earth can help those going through the process of purification. As a matter of consolation the opinion of many theologians is that the majority of people get to heaven. We should also think of heaven as a *state* of eternal life, love, happiness and joy rather than a place.

Reflection

Lead Kindly Light

Lead, kindly light, amid the encircling gloom,
Lead thou me on;
The night is dark, and I am far from home,
Lead thou me on.

I was not ever thus, nor prayed that thou
Should lead me on;
I loved to choose and see my path; but now
Lead thou me on.
I loved the garish day, and, spite of fears,
Pride ruled my will: remember not past years.

So long Thy power hath blest me, sure it still
Will lead me on
O'er moor and fen, o'er crag and torrent, till
The night is gone,
And with the morn those angel faces smile,
Which I have loved long since and lost awhile.
Cardinal J. H. Newman, 1801–1890.

Homework
Readings from First Letter of Peter and Second Letter of Peter

Day	1	2	3	4	5	6	7
Chapter	4	5	1	1	2	2	3
Verses	1–19	1–14	1–11	12–21	1–10	11–18	1–22

Afterword

1. It would be nice to have the sacrament of the sick for the group if there is a priest available. Besides sicknesses of various kinds we all need healing from memories of past hurts that we may have forgotten but which still affect us in various ways.

2. One of the articles of the Apostles' Creed is the communion of saints. 'Since all the faithful form one body, the good of each is communicated to the others ... We must therefore believe that there exists a communion of goods in the church. But the most important member is Christ, since he is the head

... Therefore, the riches of Christ are communicated to all the members, through the sacraments. As the church is governed by one and the same Spirit, all the goods she has received necessarily become a common fund.' (*Catechism*, No. 947)

The communion of saints means that there is a link between the church members on earth, the saints in heaven, and the souls in purgatory, and that they can help one another. It means that death does not sever the links between us. For a detailed account it is worth reading *The Catechism of the Catholic Church* on the communion of saints in Nos 946–962. Pope Paul VI in No. 962 sums it all up very well: 'We believe in *the communion of all the faithful of Christ*, those who are pilgrims on earth, the dead who are being purified, and the blessed in heaven, *all together forming one church*; and we believe that in this communion, the merciful love of God and his saints is always attentive to our prayers.' (Emphasis added)

Holy Orders

'Two other sacraments, holy orders and matrimony, are directed towards the salvation of others; if they contribute as well to personal salvation, it is through service to others that they do so. They confer a particular mission in the church, and serve to build up the People of God. Through these sacraments those already consecrated by baptism and confirmation for the common priesthood of all the faithful can receive particular consecrations. Those who receive the sacrament of holy orders are consecrated in Christ's name 'to feed the church by the word and grace of God'. On their part, 'Christian spouses are fortified and, as it were, consecrated for the duties and dignity of their state by a special sacrament.' (*The Catechism of the Catholic Church*, Nos 1534–5. Quotations are from Vatican II, *Dogmatic Constitution on the Church*, Nos 10–11) These sacraments are aimed at building up the community of the faithful in the church. They are sacraments of service or mission in the church.

In regard to priests Michael Quoist, in *Prayers* (New York, Sheed and Ward, 1963, p. 64), writes: 'People ask a great deal of their priests, and they should. But they should also understand that it is not easy to be a priest. He has given himself in all the ardour of youth, yet he still remains a man, and every day the man in him tries to take back what he has surrendered. It is a continual struggle to remain completely at the service of Christ and others.' Quoist brings out both the reality and the ideal. The Catholic Church has always put forward high ideals for its priests. The Second Vatican Council reiterated the same ideals for priests. The Council maintained that within the People of God – the community of Christ, the church – the priest is chosen specially by Christ for special work. But this 'being chosen' is not to be understood in the meaning of being separated from, or apart from the People of God, but rather *chosen for* the community or the People of God by Christ. Living in the world, and for the world, but untainted by the world. The Council quotes Hebrews 5:1–2: 'Every high priest has been taken out of humankind, and is appointed to act for people in their relations with God, to offer gifts and sacrifices for sins; and so he can sympathise with those who are ignorant or uncertain because he too lives in the limitations of weakness.' It is much easier to criticise bishops and priests – and we often deserve it – than to pray for them.

Priesthood in the Old Covenant
In the history of religions we find that in most there is something like priesthood and also priests of some kind. We find the same in the history of the

Jewish people. 'The Chosen People was constituted by God as a kingdom of priests and a holy nation.' (Exodus 19:6) But within the People of Israel, God chose one of the twelve tribes, that of Levi, and set it apart for liturgical service; God himself is its inheritance. (Num 1:48–53) Moreover the Levites received no part of the land of Israel. They were dependent on offerings from the other tribes for their priestly work. A special rite consecrated the beginnings of the priesthood of the Old Covenant. The priests are 'appointed to act on behalf of the people in relation to God, to offer gifts and sacrifices for sins.' (Heb 5:1; Ex 29: 1–30; Lev 8)

Instituted to proclaim the Word of God and to restore communion with God by sacrifices and prayer, *this priesthood nevertheless remains powerless to bring about salvation*, needing to repeat its sacrifices ceaselessly and being unable to achieve a definitive sanctification, which only the sacrifice of Christ would accomplish.' (*The Catechism of the Catholic Church* No. 1539–1540 – Emphasis added). Hebrews 7:26–27 tells us: 'To suit us the ideal high priest would have to be holy, innocent and uncontaminated, beyond the influence of sinners, and raised up above the heavens; one who would not need to offer sacrifices every day, as the other high priests do for their own sins, and then for those of the people, because he has done this once and for all by offering himself.'

For the very ancient Israelites the patriarch of the family served as priest, but during the Exodus, God ordered Moses to ordain Aaron, and his descendants as priests of Israel. (Ex 28:1–43) From that time onwards, the People of God offered their sacrifices to God through the hands of Aaron and his family. Aaron was the High Priest, his sons the ordinary priests. When Moses received the revelation from God, he anointed Aaron with oil as a sign of his elevation to the office of priest. By this ceremony Aaron was entrusted with the special function of officiating at the worship of God. He was consecrated for this work. The office and the consecration were passed on to his sons. (Lev 8:1–36)

Scripture memo
Hebrews was not written by St Paul but by someone else. It was written for Jews who had become Christians, but still had a longing and nostalgia for the ceremonies of the Temple and its sacrifices. Some of them may have been priests in the Temple. It emphasises the greatness of Jesus as High Priest, and the limitless and eternal value of his sacrifice versus the many sacrifices of old.

The One Priesthood of Christ
The Catechism of the Catholic Church tells us about the one priesthood of Christ in No. 1544. 'Everything that the priesthood of the Old Testament prefigured finds its fulfilment in Christ Jesus, the "one mediator between God and humankind".'(1 Tim 2:5) The Christian tradition considers Melchizedek, 'priest of God most high', (Gen 14:18 & Heb 5:10, 6:20) as a prefiguration of the

priesthood of Christ, the unique 'high priest after the order of Melchizedek' (Heb 5:10), 'holy, blameless, unstained' (Heb 7:26), 'by a single sacrifice he has perfected for all time those who are sanctified' (Heb 10:14). That is the unique sacrifice of the Cross at Calvary.

According to Hebrews 5:10, Jesus 'was acclaimed by God with the title of high priest of the order of Melchizedek'. What this means is that Jesus is not a priest because of Aaron, or because he is a descendant of Aaron. Another kind of priesthood is involved, a priesthood from the time of Abraham – linked with that of Melchizedek. Genesis 14:17–20 tells us: 'When Abram came back after the defeat of Chedor-laomer ... Melchizedek king of Salem brought bread and wine; he was a priest of God most high. He pronounced this blessing: "Blessed be Abram by God Most High, creator of heaven and earth, and blessed be God Most High for handing over your enemies to you." And Abram gave him a tithe of everything.' (Abram was later named Abraham.)

Melchizedek's origins are not mentioned. He is King and Priest of Salem which is considered to be Jerusalem. He blesses the father of Israel, namely, Abram. He receives tithes as a priest from the father of Israel, namely, Abram. His offerings are bread and wine. He meets the father of Israel, Abram in the Valley of the King which is said to have been within a short distance of Jerusalem. Psalm 110, verse 4 represents him as a figure of the Messiah:

> Yahweh has sworn an oath which he will never retract,
> You are a priest of the order of Melchizedek, and for ever.

The application is worked out in Hebrews 7:1–8: 'You remember that Melchizedek, king of Salem, a priest of God Most High, went to meet Abraham who was on his way back after defeating the kings, and blessed him; and also that it was to him that Abraham gave a tenth of all that he had. By the interpretation of his name, he is first, "king of righteousness" and also king of Salem, that is, "king of peace"; he has no father, mother or ancestry, and his life has no beginning or end: he is like the Son of God. He remains a priest for ever.'

'Now think how great this man must have been, if the patriarch Abraham paid him a tenth of all the treasure he had captured. We know that any of the descendants of Levi who are admitted to the priesthood are obliged by the law to take tithes from the people, and this is taking them from their own brothers, although they too are descended from Abraham. *But this man, who was not of the same descent, took his tenth from Abraham, and he gave his blessing to the holder of the promise.* Now it is indisputable that a blessing is given by a superior to an inferior. Further, in the one case it is ordinary mortal men who receive the tithes, and in the other, someone who is declared to be still alive.' (Emphasis added) We should consider the role and symbolism of Melchizedek.

In No. 1545 the *Catechism* goes on to develop the uniqueness of the one priesthood of Christ: '*The redemptive sacrifice of Christ is unique, accomplished once for all; yet it is made present in the eucharistic sacrifice of the church. The same is true of the one priesthood of Christ; it is made present through the ministerial priesthood* without diminishing the uniqueness of Christ's priesthood.' St Thomas Aquinas writing on Hebrews 8:4 states: 'Only Christ is the true priest, the others being only his ministers.' (Emphasis added)

All baptised people from their baptism and confirmation share and participate in the priesthood of Christ. The ministerial priesthood is different. 'While the common priesthood of the faithful is exercised by the unfolding of baptismal grace – a life of faith, hope and charity, a life according to the Spirit, the ministerial priesthood is at the service of the common priesthood. (Common = common to all baptised) It is directed at the unfolding of the baptismal grace of all Christians. The ministerial priesthood is a means by which Christ builds up and leads his church. For this reason it is transmitted by its own sacrament, the sacrament of holy orders.' (*Catechism* No. 1547, emphasis added)

'Catholic doctrine, expressed in the liturgy, the magisterium and the constant practice of the church, recognises that there are two degrees of ministerial participation in the priesthood of Christ: the episcopacy and the presbyterate. The diaconate is intended to help and serve them. For this reason the term "sacerdos" in current usage denotes bishops and priests but not deacons. Yet Catholic doctrine teaches that the degrees of participation (episcopacy and presbyterate) and the degree of service (diaconate) are all three conferred by a sacramental act called "ordination", that is, by the sacrament of holy orders.' (*Catechism* No. 1554)

We might wonder why there is not much more written about the sacraments in scripture, but they were so taken for granted in the early church that there was never any urgency or inclination to do so. However, let us look briefly at a few things that are said:

Baptism: 'All authority in heaven and on earth has been given to me. Go, therefore, make disciples of all the nations; baptise them in the Name of the Father and of the Son and of the Holy Spirit, and teach them to observe all the commands that I gave you. And know that I am with you always; yes to the end of time.' (Mt 28:18–20)

Confirmation: 'When the apostles in Jerusalem heard that Samaria had accepted the word of God, they sent Peter and John to them, and they went down there, and prayed for the Samaritans to receive the Holy Spirit, for as yet he had not come down on any of them: they had only been baptised in the name of Jesus. Then they laid hands on them and they received the Holy Spirit' (Acts 8:14–17).

Eucharist: 'On the night that he was betrayed, the Lord Jesus took some bread, and thanked God for it, and he said, "This is my body, which is for you, do this as a memorial for me." In the same way he took the cup after supper and said, "This cup is the New Covenant in my blood. Whenever you drink it, do this as a memorial for me." Until the Lord comes therefore, every time you eat this bread and drink this cup, you are proclaiming his death.' (St Paul in 1 Cor 11:23–27) cf. Chapter 6 of John's gospel and also accounts of the Last Supper – Mt 26:26–29, Mk 14:22–25, Lk 22:14–20. We read of what happened in practice in the early church: 'They remained faithful to the teaching of the apostles, to the brotherhood, to the breaking of the bread, and to the prayers.' (Acts 2:42) Breaking of the bread = the Mass.

Reconciliation: 'He breathed on them and said, "Receive the Holy Spirit. For those whose sins you forgive, they are forgiven; for those whose sins you retain, they are retained."'(Jn 20:22–23)

Anointing of the Sick: 'If one of you is ill, he should send for the elders of the church, and they must anoint him with oil in the name of the Lord, and pray over him. The prayer of faith will save the sick man, and the Lord will raise him up again; and if he has committed any sins, they will be forgiven him.' (Jas 5:14–15)

Holy Orders: We read in both the Old and New Testaments of the laying on of hands and/or anointing with oil of those who were appointed to the office of priesthood on behalf of the people. In relation to the sacraments, like in the case of Baptism, Jesus gave orders to carry them out. Paul wrote to his disciple Timothy: 'This is why I am reminding you now to fan into a flame the gift that God gave you when I laid hands on you.' (2 Tim 1:6)

Matrimony: Matrimony is mentioned at the beginning of Genesis after the creation of Adam and Eve. 'God blessed them, saying to them, "Be fruitful, multiply, fill the earth and conquer it."' (Gen 1:28) 'In the same way, husbands must love their wives as they love their own bodies; for a man to love his wife is for him to love himself.' Again, 'For this reason, a man must leave his father and mother and be joined to his wife, and the two will become one body. This mystery has many implications, but I am saying it applies to Christ and the church.' (Eph 5:28, 31–32) Here marriage is compared to the union of Christ and his church. Both Canon Law 1055 #1 & #2 and the Vatican II document *Pastoral Constitution on the Church in the World* 48 #1 state that matrimony is a sacrament. The *Catechism* No. 1623 has an interesting paragraph: 'In the Latin church, it is ordinarily understood that the spouses, as ministers of Christ's grace confer upon each other the sacrament of matrimony by expressing their consent before the Church. In the Eastern liturgies the minister of this sacrament (which is usually called 'crowning') is the priest or bishop who, after receiving the mutual consent of the spouses, successively crowns the bridegroom and the bride as a sign of the marriage covenant.'

There are many more statements in scripture, Canon Law and church writings about the sacraments. It is worth noting that anybody in a case of necessity can confer baptism, and that it is the spouses who confer the sacrament of matrimony on one another.

In holy orders the Pope has a special position. He is the head of the church, the Vicar of Christ on earth and the successor of St Peter. Christ said to Peter in Matthew 16:18–19: 'So I now say to you: You are Peter and on this rock I will build my church. And the gates of the underworld can never hold out against it. I will give you the keys of the kingdom of heaven: whatever you bind on earth shall be considered bound in heaven; whatever you loose on earth shall be considered loosed in heaven.' The Pope is the successor of St Peter and the bishops are the successors of the apostles. The Pope is chosen as Bishop of Rome in the conclave and that means automatically that he is Pope. A bishop is responsible for the diocese to which he is appointed as its head. He is the sign of unity in the diocese, and its unity with the whole church of Christ.

The Catechism of the Catholic Church in No. 881 tells us: 'The Lord made Simon alone, whom he named Peter, the "rock" of his church. He gave him the keys of his church, and instituted him shepherd of the whole flock. The office of binding and loosing which was given to Peter, was also assigned to the college of apostles *united to its head.* This pastoral office of Peter and the other apostles belongs to the church's very foundation, and is continued by the bishops under the primacy of the Pope.' (Emphasis added) cf. *Catechism* Nos 882–886 for relationship between the Pope and other bishops.

The sacrament of orders does not change the character or personality of the priest to that of an angel or something else miraculously. The personality is the same. It is open to growth and change and the grace of God is always available from the sacrament of orders to follow his calling. The weakness of the priest is always supported and blessed by Christ. The weakness or sinfulness of a priest does not affect the sacred value of the Mass or the sacraments.

Pope, bishop, priest and deacon are to serve people – to pastor, to lead, to guide and to comfort. Matthew 20:26–28: 'Anyone who wants to be great among you must be your servant, and anyone who wants to be first among you must be your slave, just as the Son of Man came not to be served but to serve, and to give his Life as a ransom for many.'

Reflection
Qualities of Love
'This is my commandment, that you love one another as I have loved you.' (John 15:12)

What is love? Take a look at a rose. Is it possible for the rose to say, 'I shall offer my fragrance to good people and withhold it from bad people?' Or can you imagine a lamp that withholds its rays from a wicked person who seeks to walk in its light? It could only do that by ceasing to be a lamp.

And observe how helplessly and indiscriminately a tree gives its shade to everybody, good and bad, young and old, high and low; to animals and humans and every living creature – even to the one who seeks to cut it down!

1. *This is the first quality of love: its indiscriminate character.* This is why we are exhorted to be like God 'who causes his sun to rise on bad men as well as good, and his rain to fall on honest and dishonest alike ... so you must be perfect as your heavenly Father is perfect.'(Mt 5:45–48)

a) Contemplate in astonishment the sheer goodness of the rose, the lamp, the tree, for there you have an image of what love is all about. How does one attain this quality of love? Anything you do will only make it forced, cultivated and therefore phony, for love cannot be forced. There is nothing you can do. But there is something that you can drop.

b) Observe the marvellous change that comes over you the moment that you stop seeing people as good or bad, as saints and sinners, and begin to see them as unaware and ignorant.

  You must drop your false belief that people can sin in awareness. No one can sin in the light of awareness. Sin occurs, not as we think in malice, but often in ignorance. 'Father, forgive them for they do not know what they are doing.'(Lk 23:34) To see this is to acquire the indiscriminate quality one so admires in the rose, the lamp and the tree.

2. *And here is the second quality of love – its gratuitousness.* Like the tree, the rose, the lamp, it gives and asks for nothing in return. How we despise the man whose choice of his wife is determined not by any quality she may have, but by the amount of money she will bring as dowry. Such a man, we rightly say, loves not the woman but the financial benefit she brings him. But is your own love any different when you seek the company of those who will bring you emotional gratification, and avoid those who don't; when you are positively disposed towards people who give you what you want and live up to your expectations, and are negative or indifferent towards those who don't?

  Here too there is only one thing that you need to do to acquire this quality of gratuitousness that characterises love. You can open your eyes and see. Just seeing, just exposing your so-called love for what it is, a camouflage for selfishness and greed, is a major step towards arriving at this second quality of love.

3. *The third quality of love is its unself-consciousness.* Love so enjoys the loving that it is blissfully unaware of itself. The way the lamp is busy shining with no thought of whether it is benefitting others or not. The way a rose gives out its fragrance simply because there is nothing else it can do, whether there is somebody to enjoy the fragrance or not. The way the tree offers its shade. The light, the fragrance and the shade are not produced at the approach of persons and turned off when there is no one there. These things, like love, exist independently of persons. Love simply *is*, it has no object. They simply are, regardless of whether someone will benefit from them or not. So they have no consciousness of any merit or of doing good. Their left hand has no consciousness of what their right hand does. 'Lord when did we see you hungry and feed you; or thirsty and give you drink?' (Mt 25:38)

4. *The fourth quality of love is its freedom.* The moment coercion or control or conflict enter, love dies. Think how the rose, the lamp, the tree leave you completely free. The tree will make no effort to drag you into its shade if you are in danger of a sunstroke. The lamp will not force its light on you lest you stumble in the dark.

a) Think for a while of all the coercion and control that you submit to on the part of others, when you so anxiously live up to their expectations in order to buy their love and approval or because you are afraid you will lose them. Each time you submit to this control and this coercion you destroy the capacity to love which is of your very nature, for you cannot but do to others what you allow others to do to you.

b) Contemplate, then, all the control and coercion in your life, and hopefully this contemplation alone will cause them to drop. The moment they drop, freedom will arise. And freedom is just another word for love.

(Anthony de Mello SJ, *Call to Love Meditations*, No. 18, pp. 67–70)

Homework

Readings from First Letter of John

Day	1	2	3	4	5	6	7
Chapter	1	1–2	2	2	2	3	3
Verses	1–4	5–2	3–11	12–17	18–29	1–9	10–24

SESSION THIRTEEN

Sacrament of Matrimony

In modern times talking about sex was taboo until around the 1960s. It was as if sex did not exist. It was not a socially acceptable topic of conversation. Now the pendulum has swung in the opposite direction, and it sometimes seems that sex is the only topic, and the only problem. Somebody said that 'sex' – in the form of a bikini clad lady – is used to sell refrigerators to Eskimos.

We seem to be placing more emphasis on sex than in previous times in history. Many of the former customs and taboos are gone but what is in their place? There is pornography available in many places. Explicit scenes in films and on television to which children have access are fairly common. Has all this so-called liberation brought happiness? We continually hear of unwanted pregnancies, abortions, sexual diseases, sexual assaults, dropping out of school or university, work, suicide and so on. Many parents do not have the confidence or knowledge to give their children proper sexual education. In the so-called agony columns of newspapers you can read about many problems in the area of sex, marriage, communication etc. Everything seems to be acceptable and that includes young women – many from overseas – being exploited in a form of sex slavery. Rarely is sex and marriage related to God in any way or placed in a religious setting.

At the beginning of Genesis, God said: 'Be fruitful, multiply fill the earth and conquer it … God saw all that he had made, and indeed it was very good.' (Gen 1:28–31) Sex is good and beautiful because it is part of God's plan for humankind, but God is seldom mentioned in regard to sex or marriage even though it is all part of his plan for us. Nowadays the emphasis in sexual matters is placed not on love but on technique. The mutual love of two people, the deepening of mutual relations, mutual understanding, growth as human beings have been ignored while the mechanics and possibilities of sexual activity are studied and propagated in clinical detail. It is proposed that sex is love rather than more correctly to say that sex is one expression of love.

We have seen that sex and marriage are part of God's plan for humankind as mentioned at the beginning of the book of Genesis. God could have achieved his plans for humankind in millions of other ways. However this is the way that he has chosen, and that makes it sacred and holy and fitting for human beings. Marriage means two human beings – a man and a woman – working closely with God in a way that builds up their mutual love, companionship and mutual support.

Now let us look at what the church has to say on this matter: 'The intimate community of life and love which constitutes the married state has been established by the Creator and endowed by him with its own proper laws ... God himself is the author of marriage.' (*Pastoral Constitution on the Church in the Modern World*, 48 #1) The vocation to marriage is written in the very nature of man and woman as they came from the hand of the Creator. Marriage is not a purely human institution despite the many variations it may have undergone through the centuries in different cultures, social structures and spiritual attitudes. These differences should not cause us to forget its common and particular characteristics. Although the dignity of this institution is not transparent everywhere with the same clarity (*Church in the Modern World*, 47 #2), some sense of the greatness of the matrimonial union exists in all cultures. 'The well-being of the individual person and of both human and Christian society is closely bound up with the healthy state of conjugal and family life.' (*Church in the Modern World*, 47 #1)

God who created man out of love also calls him to love – the fundamental and innate vocation of every human being. For man (or woman) is created in the image and likeness of God who is himself love. (Gen 1:27) Since God created them man and woman, their mutual love becomes an image of the absolute and unfailing love with which God loves humankind. It is good, very good, in the Creator's eyes. And this love which God blesses is intended to be fruitful and to be realised in the common work of watching over creation: '*And God blessed them, and God said to them: "Be fruitful and multiply, and fill the earth and subdue it."*' (Gen 1:28) (*Catechism of the Catholic Church*, Nos 1603–1604 – Emphasis added)

Sex is the expression of a complete, and exclusive personal relationship between a husband and a wife bound together in a life-time bond. The Christian teaching on human sexuality insists that sexuality is beautiful – part of God's plan, and that it builds up emotional union between human partners, and helps preserve and deepen their mutual love and bonds. There are four elements necessary for responsible love and sex and they are: consideration, responsibility, respect and knowledge.

The miracle of my birth and existence is something that I can take for granted. My parents, time and place of birth and so on are all variables. All of these circumstances could have been so different. I am the kind of person that I am because I was born at a particular time and to particular parents, and in a particular place. They did not have any choice about it as the most they could have hoped for was a child. The only person who wished for, foresaw, and brought about my existence in my particular case was God himself. God called me and he has a plan for me and my parents cooperated with his plan. My challenge is to cooperate with God's plan at the present time. From God's point of view he could have chosen someone else from unlimited possibilities.

Modern Dangers for Christian Marriage

There were always dangers facing marriage, but they have increased in our modern age despite the prosperity that we enjoy. Our age is more complex, more difficult to understand, and more lonely than for those who lived in the simpler, less complex times of the past. The expectations and hopes of people are greater than in the past. Also we now hear of pre-nuptial agreements which almost seem to mean that the couple are already planning for failure and divorce.

1. *Economics:* Young couples must save a considerable amount of money to pay for a plot of land, a house, furniture etc. The standard of living has risen a great deal – and thank God for that – but the efforts to support that standard of living are considerable and onerous. Previously a mortgage was calculated on the basis of the husband's salary, but now it is normally based on the salaries of both husband and wife.

One result of economic pressure is the rise in the number of working wives. To repay loans, to maintain living standards, the income of the wife has become necessary in many cases. When there are young infants and young children, the fees for day nurseries and child care centres must also be included. This has affected the traditional pattern of family life. Parents are tired when they want to give some quality time to their children. Sometimes they do not have time for the children or for one another, as they must prepare meals, clean the house, do laundry and even prepare for work on the following day. There is no substitute for the education and moral value system that a child gets in the home from its parents, but how do we achieve this? Where this is lacking society ends up with juvenile crime and mindless vandalism. If a mother or father stayed at home to bring up the children – especially when they are small – could she/he be paid in some way by the state? It might well pay for itself in the long run.

2. *Nuclear families:* Nuclear families are families where there are only husband and wife and children. Formerly, under the extended family system, a young couple married into a home that might have one or more grandparents. There are drawbacks in this system as the many mother-in-law jokes tell us, but at the same time, when there were clear demarcation lines, it meant that there was support, comfort, advice and help close at hand. The young wife-mother had somebody nearby that she could consult in regard to child-rearing, child-sickness and so on. In Japan there is a custom that very often a mother-to-be goes back to her mother's place to have her baby, and after the birth will stay with her mother for some time. After the birth of the baby she will usually stay in the hospital for several days while she gets used to handling the baby.

Urbanisation has added to the pressure on young couples, with problems of loneliness and alienation. Unless the young couple are mature and adaptable, the stress on their married life can be very severe, and can lead to marriage breakdown, and much suffering for them and their children. People living in an urban neighbourhood work in many different places, and lack the bonds of common work interests which were part of the former rural community.

3. Science and technology: Science and technology are the proud boast of our modern society, yet the defects and dangers of material progress are often ignored. Problems with pollution – including noise pollution – plus stress and overwork plague individuals and the whole fabric of society. The family unit – or the little church – are not valued as important in themselves. Even children find it hard to play unless they have video games! The marriage bond is taken for granted and the option of divorce is considered normal. Television and radio are obstacles to communication. These are often on during meals when the family should be communicating. Moreover people do not talk about how they are feeling but only about how they are thinking.

The family, particularly the husband and wife suffer from these internal and external dangers and pressures. When mutual excitement fades, some immediately begin to think of separation or divorce. Formerly responsibility for the home and the children was a shared responsibility of husband and wife. Responsibilities, expectations and hopes were shared. Nowadays often much of the responsibility falls on the mother. The father is often missing from meals because of his work. Parents and children all miss out on building a home based on love, acceptance and tolerance. The members of the nuclear family can live in the same house, but do not have adequate opportunities for talking and sharing and communicating. There can be much frustration. They know that they are missing something important, but are not sure what it is or how to go about getting it. It is easier to have the television on during meals than to talk to one another. We are allowing others to take over our thinking for us and our communicating. People feel uneasy if there is not noise about the place – music or otherwise. Radios are on all day and people seem afraid of silence. Even when people are exercising – walking or running – they often have earphones on and are not listening to nature all around them.

Nowadays there is much emphasis on personal growth and self-identity. In the past, people got it from the community that they lived in. They had a definite role in that community, and they also had the support and understanding of the community. There was shared work at times and common interests. The place of work and the place in which one lived were often close together but not anymore. There were no 'bed towns'. Nowadays it is much more difficult to have friends and a meaningful life, whether one is married or not. The whole pace of life is much faster. How does one find time for wife/husband, family, friends and especially oneself?

It is very important to know yourself. If you do not know yourself how can you give yourself to another person? What are you giving? And to accept the other he/she must be knowable, must know himself/herself. Otherwise there is no real giving or communication. To avoid real communication about feelings it is easy to end up discussing only work or the children's education or some similar topic. If the wife is focused solely on the education of children and the husband on his work, communication is very difficult. The pressure of work and of developing interpersonal relations at work can be very tiring. Many divorces in Japan occur in people who are over fifty-five years of age, and are initiated by the wives. By that time the children are grown up and have left the home, and husband and wife find that they are strangers to one another but living in the same house. Unanswered questions can abound in such a situation: 'Why is he so passive? What does he really want? Why is she so cold? Why has he/she no interest in sex? Why do we not talk anymore? Am I just a cook? Are the children more important in our lives than me?'

In Japan and other places in the Orient people are very good at non-verbal communication. Non-verbal communication is very important in any marriage. To look at one's spouse, and to be able to sense his/her mood, and to react accordingly is very important. Married people need to do things together as a couple, as well as doing things with their children. The danger is that a couple may have the same address, but do not live together in any real sense. This would be a disaster for them, their children, if they have any, for society in general and for the church.

Marriage in God's plan
The (1) *Catechism of the Catholic Church* No. 1601 quoting (2) Canon Law No. 1055 which is based on the (3) Vatican II *Pastoral Constitution on the Church in the Modern World*, No. 48 reads: 'The matrimonial covenant, by which a man and a woman establish between themselves a partnership of the whole of life, is by its nature ordered toward the good (well-being) of the spouses, and the procreation and education of offspring; this covenant between persons has been raised by Christ the Lord to the dignity of a sacrament.' Before Vatican II procreation would have been listed as the primary reason by theologians, and the rest as secondary reasons. David Bohr in his book *Catholic Moral Tradition*, page 243 says, in regard to Vatican II: 'The Council fathers, however, refused to say whether the love-making or the life-giving aspect was the most important.' This is a very important point as it refers to the purpose or ends of marriage. To refer to marriage as 'covenant' is a much better word than a contract. It also says that it is primarily for 'the good or well-being of the spouses' but of course the good of any children involved must also be considered. *The Catechism of the Catholic Church* No. 1617 says: 'The entire Christian life bears the mark of the spousal love of Christ and his church. Already baptism, the entry into the People of God, is a nuptial mystery: it is so to speak the nuptial bath, which precedes the wedding feast, the Eucharist. Christian marriage in its turn becomes an efficacious sign, the sacrament of the covenant of Christ and his church. Since it signifies and communicates grace, marriage between baptised persons is a true sacrament of the New Covenant.' Every home, to some extent, is a manifestation of the Covenant between God and his people.

Sacred scripture begins with the creation of man and woman in the likeness of God (Gen 1:27–28), and concludes with the 'wedding feast of the Lamb' in the Book of Revelation 19:7–9. At the beginning, Genesis tells us in 1:27–28: 'God created man in the image of himself, in the image of God he created him, male and female he created them. God blessed them, saying to them, "Be fruitful, multiply, fill the earth and conquer it." It is important to remember this at all times, as it is very easy for people to have all kinds of complexes about their sexuality, and all kinds of wrong notions of associating sin with sexuality.

As the Book of Genesis starts with an account of marriage between Adam and Eve, the Scripture ends with the Book of Revelation where there is an account of marriage between Christ and his church. Revelation 19:6–9: 'The reign of the Lord our God Almighty has begun: let us be glad and joyful and give praise to God, because this is the time for the marriage of the Lamb. His bride is ready, and she has been able to dress herself in dazzling white linen, because her linen is made of the good deeds of the saints.' Here St John says that at the end of the world the church will go to Christ – the Lamb of God – as a bride. We need to remember the Jewish custom by which a woman when her marriage was arranged – at the betrothal – was considered to be a wife, even before she went in procession as a bride to her husband.

The first miracle of Jesus that is recorded is at the marriage feast of Cana in John 2:1–10. It was at the request of his mother that Jesus performed this first miracle even though he said to her: 'My hour has not come yet.' (Verse 4) The *Catechism* in No. 1613 says 'the church attaches great importance to Jesus' presence at the marriage at Cana. She sees in it the confirmation of the goodness of marriage, and the proclamation that thenceforth marriage will be an efficacious sign of God's presence.' Jesus, moreover in many places liked to describe heaven as a great marriage banquet.

We also read in the *Catechism* No. 1614: 'In his preaching Jesus unequivocally taught the original meaning of the union of man and woman as the Creator willed it from the beginning: permission given by Moses to divorce one's wife was a concession to their hardness of heart. (Matthew 19:8) The matrimonial union of man and woman is indissoluble: God himself has determined it: 'what God has joined together let no man put asunder.' (cf. Mt 19:6) Jesus by his passion, death and resurrection has made available to spouses the graces necessary to live out their married life, and has also shown that all things are possible. Marriage needs to be worked at but a happy married life is worth the effort. We must emphasise that church teaching on human sexuality insists that sexuality is good and beautiful, that it builds up emotional union between married partners, that it preserves and deepens their bonds. If sex is devalued and regarded as a short-term fix or merely a physical thrill, it becomes dangerous, irresponsible and destructive, both personally and socially. Sexuality and sexual intercourse are worthy of the deepest respect, and are strong forces leading to a rich and rewarding life. In a world in which the power and mystery of sex are often unknown or ignored, the church has a special responsibility to continue to promote the loving and life-giving values of sex. The bonds of marriage are sacred and are not to be broken. In marriage a man and a woman give themselves to one another totally and completely. There is no more sacred bond than this. (cf. John Paul II: 'Theology of the Body')

The institution of marriage is under attack, and weakening in many ways. Marriage is the basic unit of society. Just as the health, strength and development of a body depends on the health of the individual cells in the body, the health of society depends on the health of marriage and family life. Many young people find it difficult to make a permanent commitment to work or marriage or anything else as they seem to be maturing later. The following words of Christ should be treasured in hearts and homes: 'This is why I am telling you not to worry about your life and what you are to eat, nor about your body and how you are to cloth it. For life means more than food, and the body more than clothing. Think of the ravens. They do not sow or reap; they have no storehouses and no barns; yet God feeds them. And how much more are you worth than the birds! Can any of you, for all his worrying, add a single cubit to his span of life? If the smallest things, therefore, are outside your control, why worry about the rest? Think of the flowers; they never have to spin or weave; yet I assure you, not even Solomon in all his regalia was robed like one of these. Now if that is how God clothes the grass in the field which is there today and thrown into the furnace tomorrow, how much more will He look after you, you people of little faith! But you, you must not set your hearts on things to eat and things to drink; you must not worry. It is the pagans of this world who set their hearts on all these things. Your Father well knows that you need them. No, set your hearts on his kingdom, and these other things will be given you as well. There is no need to be afraid, little flock, for it has pleased your Father to give you the kingdom.' (Lk 12:22–32)

A good marriage and a happy family life are wonderful, but they need hard work and commitment and an awareness of God's plan and purpose and help. St Augustine: 'Put love where there is no love, and you will find love.' We may all have scars but we are all capable of loving and being loved.

Afterword

There is much talk nowadays about sex education. It is a good thing and very necessary but why is there no talk about moral education? Why are God and his plans ignored? Condoms are put forward as a solution to many problems. People are told 'use a condom and you are safe'. What is not mentioned is that they have a twenty per cent failure rate in the prevention of the transmission of HIV–AIDS and sexual diseases. This failure rate is very high and there has been a huge increase in the transmission of sexual diseases. People are not told the true story because there is big money involved and the bottom line is profit.

Reflection

The Common Good

Because of the closer bonds of human interdependence, and their spread over the whole world, we are today witnessing a widening of the role of the common good, which is the sum of the social conditions which allow people, either as groups or as individuals, to reach their fulfilment more fully and more easily. The whole human race is consequently involved with regard to the rights and obligations which result. Every group must take into account the needs and legitimate aspirations of every other group, and still more of the human family as a whole.

At the same time, however, there is a growing awareness of the sublime dignity of the human person, who stands above all things and whose rights and duties are universal and inviolable. He ought, therefore, to have ready access to all that is necessary for living a genuinely human life: for example, food, clothing, housing, the right freely to choose his state of life and set up a family, the right to education, work, to his good name, to respect, to proper knowledge, the right to act according to the dictates of his conscience and to safeguard his privacy, and rightful freedom even in matters of religion.

The social order and its development must constantly yield to the good of the person, since the order of things must be subordinate to the order of persons and not the other way around, as the Lord suggested when he said that the Sabbath was made for man and not man for the Sabbath. (Mark 2:27) The social order requires constant improvement: it must be founded in truth, built on justice, and enlivened by love: it should grow in freedom towards a more humane equilibrium. (John XXIII, encyclical *Pacem in Terris*, *AAS* 55, 1963, p. 226) If these objectives are to be attained there will first have to be a renewal of attitudes and far-reaching social changes.

> The Spirit of God, who, with wondrous providence, directs the course of time and renews the face of the earth, assists at this development. The ferment of the gospel has aroused and continues to arouse in the hearts of people an unquenchable thirst for human dignity. (Vatican II: *The Church in the Modern World*, No. 26)

Homework

Readings from First, Second and Third Letters of John

Day	1	2	3	4	5	6	7
Chapter	4–1st	4	5	5	5	1–2nd	1–3rd
Verses	1–6	7–21	1–4	5–13	14–21	1–13	1–15

SESSION FOURTEEN

The Church in the World Today: Part I

Did Jesus found a Church?

The answer might seem to be obvious by just looking at the church. Yet there are only two pieces of scripture in the gospels where the word church is mentioned. On the other hand the words kingdom of God or their equivalent are mentioned 92 times in the gospels. It would be reasonable to say that Jesus wanted to put a great deal of emphasis on the kingdom of God. The two times that Jesus mentioned church are in Matthew's gospel and are as follows: Mt 16:18–19: 'So I now say to you: You are Peter and on this rock I will build my church. And the gates of hell can never hold out against it. I will give you the keys of the kingdom of heaven: whatever you bind on earth shall be considered bound in heaven; and whatever you loose on earth shall be considered loosed in heaven.' Again in Mt 18:17: 'But if he refuses to listen to these, report it to the community (church), and if he refuses to listen to the community, treat him like a pagan or a tax collector.' We also have to keep in mind that something may be so well accepted, and so well known that it may not be worth mentioning. Some scripture scholars would consider that these texts may have been formulated by the evangelists and put into the mouth of Jesus to express the faith and understanding of the early church. We also need to remember that Jesus as a prophet would have seen his work as calling the People of Israel (People of God) to repentance and renewal.

In regard to the word 'church' there is a big change when we read the Acts of the Apostles and the rest of the New Testament. The word *ecclesia* – meaning whole church, local churches and house churches – appears 108 times in this part of the New Testament. Jesus may have only left the foundation of a church but it took form and shape very rapidly after his resurrection. Joseph Ratzinger – Pope Benedict XV1 – wrote in *Kirke* (Church) that the early Christian community, universal as well as local, called themselves different names, like Followers of the Way, *Koinonia* (Community), or simply Christians. However, the most important and lasting name for the Christian community was church. The word church may not appear often in the words of Jesus, nevertheless, the concept of the messianic community, intrinsically bound up with the kingdom, implies what is meant by the word church. We can describe the kingdom as the vision of reality, creation, God and humankind that Jesus came to communicate. The seed and beginning of the kingdom was the 'little flock' whom Jesus came to gather around him, the flock whose shepherd he was/is. Luke 12:32: 'There is no need to be afraid, little flock, for it has pleased your

Father to give you the kingdom.' The church will cease at the end of time but the kingdom will last for eternity.

In the *Catechism* No. 766 we read: 'The church is born primarily of Christ's total self-giving for our salvation, anticipated in the institution of the Eucharist and fulfilled on the Cross.' Joachim Gnilka wrote in *Jesus of Nazareth*, page 198: 'The church originated from the death and resurrection of Jesus, through the work of the Spirit. It remains a provisional entity. What is ultimate is the kingdom. The better the church understands its provisional status, and is determined by the ultimate (the kingdom), the more it will be able to correspond with Jesus' ministry.' The church is revealed, guided and energised by the Holy Spirit. 'The Advocate, the Holy Spirit, whom the Father will send in my name, will teach you everything, and remind you of all that I have said to you.' (Jn 14:26) Again in Jn 15:26–27: 'When the Advocate comes, whom I will send from the Father, he will be my witness. And you will be my witnesses, because you were with me from the beginning.'

Fr Fuellenbach in his excellent book *Church Community for the Kingdom* makes an excellent and interesting point about the church on page 24. He says that 'for some scripture exegetes the question of whether or not Jesus founded a church is superfluous. Jesus did not have to found a church; it had existed for centuries as the People of Israel … The early Christian community understood itself in the context of Israel and had no intention of separating itself from the Covenant people. Only the resistance and rejection of the Jewish people forced the followers of Jesus to go to the pagans in the power of the Risen One's Spirit.' It is clear that the early Christians expected that other Jews would follow them in accepting Jesus and his message. They maintained their links with the Jewish religion. 'They went as a body to the Temple every day but met in their houses for the breaking of bread.' (Acts 2:46) The early converts were all Jews and it was to the Jews that they first preached. It was only when they were rejected by the Jews and persecuted that under the inspiration of the Spirit they turned to the Gentiles. We see it in the case of St Paul who started by preaching to Jews, but when he was rejected by them he turned to the Gentiles more and more. We often fail to realise how difficult it was for the Jewish Christians to accept Gentiles who did not follow the Law of Moses. Some years ago I read of a group of Jewish Christians somewhere in the Near East who were in communion with Rome but followed the Law of Moses as well.

Stages of Growth of the Church
We need to remember that the church has changed over the centuries, and most of all is still continuing to change. Look at the changes since Vatican II, and those changes are ongoing. It has learned to adapt to different cultures and this is still happening – barely started in many cases. The coming in of Gentiles into the early church brought many changes especially after the Council of

Jerusalem in AD 49, as after that Gentiles (and Jews if they wished) were no longer bound by Jewish laws or customs. The church never was and is not at present a static entity. It must always adapt to living in the world around it. This may be the cause of friction at times. These changes took time and it is not easy to be specific in regard to the time it took for specific changes.

1. *The First Epoch: Jewish Christianity*
    The disciples of Jesus did not move outside Israel. They saw themselves as Jews first and foremost and we see them in Acts 2:46 going to the Temple for prayers each day. A few characteristics of this early church were baptism, by which one entered it, communal prayer, the 'breaking of the bread' ceremony, their own leaders and the fellowship of love. They followed the Jewish Law to a large extent, and it was only after the Council of Jerusalem AD 49 that they allowed – especially the non-Jews – to break away from Jewish ceremonial Law and Tradition.

2. *The Second Epoch: The Gentile Christian Community Freed from Jewish ceremonial Law*
    As more and more Gentiles entered the church the question had to be faced in regard to how much Jewish Law bound them. The early Christians were slow to move outside the Jewish people to the gentiles, and especially to treat them as equals. It was against all their history and religion and culture. It was only when the Holy Spirit descended visibly on the centurion Cornelius and his family that Peter was convinced that they should be baptised, despite the fact that they were gentiles. (Acts 11:1–18) Paul was very influential in this change of thinking because in his preaching he was emphasising freedom from the Jewish Law in Christ Jesus, and that salvation came from faith in Jesus, and not from the Law. As mentioned previously the Council of Jerusalem was the turning point around AD 49. With the peace of Constantine in AD 313 the church also adopted the bureaucracy of the Roman Empire. The church also took on the culture of Europe as that was where it was primarily based. It was generally a European enculturated church that was spread around the world because the missionaries bringing it were mainly European or of European ancestry.

    During the centuries the church also grew in power and wealth which was not good for it, but there was also the foundation and spread of many religious orders. It has never been good for the church to be too closely associated with any state or civil power. There was the threat from Islam for Europe, the break with the Eastern Orthodox Church followed by the break with the Protestant churches. We would need another book to deal with all these challenges and changes and history. There was the development of nation states, many wars, the drive to go to the ends of the earth. Where the merchants went, the missionaries also went. The important thing is that the church grew and was responsible for many changes for the better in society. There were also great Councils, like Trent, which did much to reform and bring changes in the church, the education of priests, and its ruling bodies. The church was at the centre of much development in education, medicine, art etc. It was during this period that the church and society moved from an agricultural base to an industrialised base. With the coming of the printing press we also moved into the beginning of the era of mass communication.

3. *The Third Epoch: Transition from a Western Church to a World Church.*
This happened and is still happening since Vatican II. Vatican II was a gathering of the world episcopate. In Vatican I there was not one native-born bishop from the Third World present during its deliberations. At Vatican II the various languages of the world were accepted, and the values in non-European cultures were recognised. There was also for the first time a positive evaluation of the great religions of the world. Dialogue and enculturation became key words in expressing the mission of the church in the present age.

The Church of Today
The church is influenced by the society in which it lives. In *The Episcopacy and the Primacy*, Rahner and Ratzinger in 1963, we read: 'After decades of concentration on "Roman" which followed the First Vatican Council, the church has again directed more attention to the other side "Catholic".' 'Catholic' implies the diversity of the church throughout the world. We now talk of unity in diversity and diversity in unity and apply it to the church. For instance, Asia needs an Asian church rooted in Asian culture and not one rooted in European culture. It is sometimes difficult to get Rome to agree to these changes. Some years ago the Japanese bishops asked Rome to allow them to make a special liturgy for New Year's Day, but Rome insisted that they keep on the feast of Our Lady on January 1st. In Japan, Korea, China and some other countries New Year's Day has a very different, special, and important meaning but unfortunately Roman centralisation could not recognise that fact.

Since Vatican II there has been the emergence of 'Liberation Theology' in South America which tries to help people with the difficult economic circumstances of their lives. In Africa and Asia similar groups have emerged, but have concentrated more on enculturation. It is from Asia and Africa that most of the great religions of the world have emerged. It is important to remember that about seventy per cent of the Catholics of the world live in these three continents, but that fact is not reflected in the Roman bureaucracy. When this happens it will bring further changes and a new emphasis in various matters. I would venture to say that it will bring new colour, vibrancy, music and joy into the liturgy and other fields. Some years ago the bishops of Japan decided to take the Buddhist ceremonies for wakes and funerals and adapt them with Christian prayers and hymns and it was most successful. (Most people are buried with Buddhist rites in Japan.)

It is generally accepted that the kingdom of God is wider than the church. In 1991 the Asian bishops after a meeting in Thailand wrote: 'The Kingdom of God is therefore universally present and at work. Wherever men and women open themselves to the transcendent divine mystery which impinges upon them, and go out of themselves in love and service of fellow humans, there the reign of God is at work ... Where God is accepted, where the gospels values are lived, where the human being is accepted ... there is the kingdom. In all such cases people respond to God's offer of grace through Christ in the Spirit and enter into the kingdom through an act of faith ... This goes to show that the reign of God is an universal reality, extending far beyond the boundaries of the church. It is the reality of salvation in Jesus Christ, in which Christians and others share in different ways together; it is the fundamental "mystery of unity" which unites us more deeply than differences in religious allegiances are able to keep us apart.'

Megatrends Affecting the Church Today
The church is basically people and whatever affects those people affects the church. It is not churches or hospital or schools etc. – no matter how good they are but people who believe in Jesus Christ. Fr Fuellenbach, SVD says that there are two simultaneous evolving realities that affect the church. First, the ever more felt importance of the local cultures concerning the church's mission. Secondly, contrasting with the emphasis on the local culture, the emergence of a global culture that affects all cultures.

1. *Resurgence of Cultural Traditions:* Among all peoples of the world there is a resurgence of their cultural identity. It is a way by which nations can discover their identity. It is a bit like the individual searching for his/her 'roots'. Enculturation is the process by which the gospel enters a culture.
2. *Globalisation:* Globalisation is a double-edged sword. It can bring people together and break down barriers, but on the economic front it can be a form of neo-colonialism.
3. *Revival of Religious Experience:* People are longing for a religious experience: a hunger for the divine. The Pentecostal churches are the ones making most progress in the world as they strive to meet peoples' *felt needs*.
4. *Basic Ecclesial Communities:* With the support and encouragement of a small group, people find their way to God, and God finds a way to the people. The basic unit of the church, the parish, seems to fall short in this regard in many parts of the world and for many people.
5. *Problems in Ministerial Structures:* Peoples' needs are no longer being fully met in the present structures of ministry. The church has to develop different ministries and new styles of ministry. There has been a dramatic increase in non-traditional pastoral workers.

6. *The Western Church in Crisis:* It is in crisis because it is western, because it has modified the universality of its nature and has defined itself in terms that may have been relevant to westerners in the past, but are irrelevant to them at the present, and certainly irrelevant to non-westerners. Many trends towards a global church have been developed not in the west but in the mission churches: liturgical renewal, ecumenism, interfaith dialogue, movements of enculturation, being true to one's identity, and new understandings of ministry.

7. *The Poor as Evangelisers:* The poor are again at the centre of our understanding of God's plan for humanity. Once more, God has chosen the poor to evangelise the world, and to bring a new understanding of the gospel and gospel values, of the real value of life, of the true value of community, and the joy of sharing.

8. *New Presence and Significance of Women:* There is a new awareness of the presence of women in the life of the church. Theology, spirituality, and ministry take on new dimensions when women enter the field. This will start a new era of evangelisation and mission. What are asked for are equality, partnership, and co-responsibility.

9. *New Frontiers of Mission:* There is a rapid increase in the number of people who have not been exposed to the Christ event. The percentage of Christians in the world is decreasing.

10. *Co-partnership with the Earth:* The earth is the first sacrament of God's love for its inhabitants. It is the womb that gives life and nurtures, it is a partner in the journey of humanity towards the kingdom. To abuse the earth is to commit suicide, to misuse the earth is to threaten life, to respect the earth and to treasure it as one of God's greatest gifts is to ensure life. We need to develop a renewed theology of the earth and to promote ecology in all its aspects.
(Above ten points abbreviated from Fuellenbach, SVD, *The Church Community for the Kingdom*, pp. 100–104.)

I would like to add a few points of my own:

11. *The Proliferation of the Mass Media:* It has a huge effect on the way that people think or don't think. It often has some kind of hidden agenda, and it is hard to know who is in charge. It is very easy to be selective in what is put forward, and it must be admitted that it is difficult to be balanced and objective even with the best of intentions. From morning to night there is so much information thrown at us that it is very difficult to sort it all out. Many peoples' opinions are formed by the mass media, and one always needs to ask oneself about the particular slant that it has. The mass media has the power to bring down governments and greatly influence many events. Coming back from Japan after many years I found the mass media in many cases in Ireland to be often anti-church and anti-religion, and at times the church seemed to be cowed by it.

12. *Secularisation:* It is very seldom that God is publicly mentioned except perhaps to attack the notion of God. If there is a social problem to be faced one seldom hears about the possible contribution of religion to the solution. The suicide of young people is not going to be solved by increasing the number of social workers or drop-in centres – which can help – but by a return to God and his church. Abortion and gay marriage are put forward as 'human rights'. Religion is said to be something that should be confined within the church building for those who want it and are interested in it. There is no place for God in the world he made. Politicians and other experts can solve all the problems of society!

Finally two pastoral priorities seem to be emerging in the church today: contextualisation and solidarity with the poor. Contextualisation or Enculturation has a particular urgency in Asia, with its great cultural and religious traditions. This is also true of Africa. Solidarity with the poor has emerged from South America with liberation theology and is also related to enculturation.

The *Pastoral Constitution of the Church in the Modern World* from Vatican II says in Article One: 'The joy and hope, the grief and anguish of the people of our time, especially of those who are poor or afflicted in any way, are the joy and hope, the grief and anguish of the followers of Christ as well. Nothing that is genuinely human fails to find an echo in their hearts. For theirs is a community composed of people, people who, united in Christ and guided by the Holy Spirit, press onwards towards the kingdom of the Father, and are bearers of a message of salvation for all people. That is why Christians cherish a feeling of deep solidarity with the human race and its history.'

Over the centuries the church has changed in many ways. After the peace of Constantine in AD 313, the church had freedom and was able to build places of worship. It also took on some of the bureaucracy of the Roman Empire to cope with the larger number of believers scattered over a wide area. Nowadays it has over a billion members scattered all over the world. Moreover, our world has become much more complicated and the mass media has enormous influence. Little wonder that Vatican II in its various documents mentions the word church almost 2,000 times.

Vatican II emphasized three images for the Church:
1. The Church as the New People of God.
2. The Church as the Body of Christ.
3. The Church as the Temple of the Holy Spirit.

1. The Church as the New People of God
St Paul liked very much this image of the Church as the new People of God or Israel. It also provides a link with the Old Testament and the Old Covenant. Johann Auer and Joseph Ratzinger wrote in 1993: 'Although the church, as a community founded by Jesus Christ, appears only in the New Testament, it can

be understood only in connection with the history of the People of God in the Old Testament.' (*The Church: The Universal Sacrament of Salvation*, Vol. 8 of *Dogmatic Theology*, Washington DC, Catholic University of America Press, 1993) Fuellenbach writes: 'The metaphor People of God sees the church as a pilgrim people, a people on the road towards its final goal, the fullness of the kingdom to come. *The church is only the sacrament of the kingdom*, which accounts for its preliminary character, because a sacrament is never the full reality to which it points, and which it wants to open up to people in the here and now. By using this image for the church, the Council further wanted to stress that the church has to be seen as a growing community involved in history, one affected by the weaknesses and infidelities of its members, who constantly stand in need of God's mercy and forgiveness.' (Fuellenbach, *Church – Community for the Kingdom*, p. 45)

2. The Church as the Body of Christ

This refers back to the encyclical of Pope Pius XII, *Mystici Corporis* of 1943. The Body of Christ expresses the intimate union of the church with the risen and glorified Lord as his continuing presence in the world. It reveals the innermost heart of the church, namely, dependence and union with Christ and with one another. For St Paul the concept of the body was based on the Hebrew idea of *basar*, which sees the body first and foremost as a means of relating to and rendering service to others. From this understanding, Paul developed three basic aspects regarding the concept of body:

a) The total dependence of the church on Christ based on the corporate personality metaphor of the Old Testament. The Jew did not see himself as an individual Jew, but as a member of the People of God.

b) Also taken from the Hebrew background, the idea of bodily service for others in the footsteps and in union with the Lord.

c) The idea of unity and harmony of the whole body based on the Greek understanding of the term *soma*. (*Soma* = physical body) 'Just as a human body, though it is made up of many parts, is a single unit because all these parts, though many, make up one body, so it is with Christ. In the one Spirit we were all baptised, Jews as well as Greeks, slaves as well as citizens, and one Spirit was given to us all to drink.' (1 Cor 12:12–13)

3. The Church as the Temple of the Holy Spirit.

With this concept the Second Vatican Council wanted to stress the church as a creation of the Holy Spirit. We saw earlier the apostles and disciples had done nothing about spreading the Good News until after the coming of the Holy Spirit at Pentecost. St Irenaeus spoke of the Son and the Spirit as the two hands of God that always work together. The church is both eucharistic and at the same time pentecostal. Jean Zizoula, an Orthodox theologian, in his book *Les Eglises* said 'Christ institutes and the Holy Spirit constitutes the church'. The realisation and understanding of the message of Jesus for believers in the early church community came through the help of the Holy Spirit who was the gift of the Risen Lord. The church perceived as a creation of the Holy Spirit, opens a new way of seeing itself as a charismatic community in which each member has a function to fulfil.

4. Another Point is to View the Church as Communion

The church is viewed as sacramentally expressing here and now the mystery of the communion of the Holy Trinity. Walter Kasper in *The Church as Communio* writes: 'The mystery of the church consists in the access we have to the Father in the Holy Spirit through Jesus Christ, so that we may share in God's divine nature. The communion of the church is made possible and sustained through the Trinitarian communion of Father, Son and Holy Spirit. Finally, the church as communion, as Vatican II said following up what the martyr Bishop Cyprian said, is participation in the Trinitarian communion itself. The church is in the same way the icon of the community of Father, Son and Holy Spirit.' (Kasper, *The Church as Communio*, New Blackfriars, 1993, p. 235)

The church looks after us from birth to death. It also helps us to share in the life of God by making us children of God. The church gives us the Mass which is the only way that we give God the worship that is His due. By it we have many brothers and sisters in the new People of God.

Reflection

    Bend in the Road
    Sometimes we come to life's crossroads,
    And view what we think is the end.
    But God has a much wider vision,
    And he knows that it is only a bend.

    The road will go on and get smoother,
    And after we have stopped for a rest,
    The path that lies hidden beyond us,
    Is often the path that is best.

    So rest and relax and get stronger,
    Let go and let God share your load,
    Have faith in a brighter tomorrow,
    You've just come to a bend in the road.
    (Columban Fathers, New Zealand)

Homework
Readings from St Paul to the Romans

Day	1	2	3	4	5	6	7
Chapter	1	1	2	2	3	3	4
Verses	1–15	16–32	1–11	12–29	1–20	21–31	1–15

The Church in the World Today: Part II

People are the church and hence to understand the church today we need to look at the people of today and the world that they live in, and especially I want to look at the church in Ireland. How are the various developments of the world affecting the lives and thinking of people in the world and Ireland today with the spread of a global culture? Today the human race is going through a crisis of change but where will it all end? Power can be used for good or abused for evil. Human experience is extremely polarised – rich and poor, left and right, us and them.

With more knowledge – greater uncertainty.
With more wealth – more hunger and poverty.
With more communications – more loneliness.
With more freedom – social and psychological loneliness.
With more unity – more conflicts, divisions, wars, ethnic cleansing …
With a search for a better world – no spiritual advancement.

One of the greatest problems people have to face is loneliness. With the improvements in communications people can have many acquaintances, but few real friends that they can turn to when they have a personal problem or crisis. Moreover if they do not have God and the church who can they turn to? Hence the need of 'drop-in' centres where someone will listen. I am all in favour of such places but they can only go so far in helping someone.

Science and technology are changing the world, but not all of it for the good of humankind. People are dominated by the mass media which controls information, and seeks to mould people's thinking and behaviour in advertising, politics, religion and so on. PR people play a very important role in our modern society. They tell us what we need to know and how to be happy. Traditional social groups – families, clans, villages – are changing and not always for the better. Industrial and urban living is increasing, and community support and help are decreasing. People are lonely and frustrated and lacking meaning in their lives. If you do not have product XYZ you cannot be happy they are told. It is so easy for people – especially young people – to turn to alcohol, drugs or even suicide. A small number of people are dropping out of our modern society and seeking friendship and meaning for their lives in small groups or communes – in simpler lifestyles. We need to be aware of the dignity of each person as a child of God – starting with ourselves – and respect that dignity.

A person is made 'in the image of God', and is a body and soul with particular needs, hopes and desires which need to be catered for if that person is going to be happy and fulfilled. While utterly rejecting atheism, the church believes that all people – believers and non-believers alike – ought to work with all people of goodwill for the betterment of the world. The church believes in dialogue with the world, and is prepared to engage in dialogue with all peoples and at all times. The church recognises the good elements found in today's social movements, especially the movements towards unity and cooperation in civic and economic fields, the protection of the environment and the search for peace. Christians must avoid a split between their professional and social activities, and their religious lives. Their religious life should be a source of strength for them to carry out the duties of their professional and civic lives. They need to draw from the wellsprings of prayer, the sacraments and especially the Eucharist.

Looking at the situation here in Ireland, the country has become very prosperous, but not any happier than it was in the past. Of course the recession is making things even more difficult. Many people are suffering from an identity crisis, and the old supports of community life are getting weaker – especially in urban settings. There are very serious problems in the matter of a drink culture, drugs, irresponsible sexual activity – which results in over one third of births being out of wedlock. Children lack the security of a stable marriage. Crimes against people seem to be on the increase, and many people do not feel safe walking the streets after dark. People living on their own can often be living in fear. There is a continuous litany of mindless vandalism. Materialism seems to be rampant, and if you have money it does not seem to matter where or how you got it.

The Irish Church of the Future: Similarly for most European or Western Churches
I have worked mainly in Japan but I also have limited experience of working in Ireland, England and the USA.

a) The great missionary movement of the Irish church that started in 1916 is over, and it might be said that Ireland itself needs to be evangelised.

b) The number of vocations for priests, nuns and brothers have almost dried up, and this means that the influence of the church and Christian teaching will diminish in schools, hospitals and other charitable institutions.

c) The number of people attending Mass on Sundays has gone down and the age profile of those attending is older.

d) The age profile of priests working in parishes is increasing every year and there is a serious shortage of vocations for this work. Up to now some of the vacancies have been covered by priests coming back from abroad. In the near future it will mean priest-less parishes or at least a non-resident priest. Even now, at times, one priest is put in charge of more than one parish, but an older priest will not be able to do this for very long. A team of priests looking after several parishes will only put off the inevitable for a short time. There will be no priest automatically available for people in the future. What can be done? I was once in a parish in the mountains of Japan with another priest and we had six churches to look after. With the rough terrain there was no way we could get around all of them at the weekend. Our solution was to celebrate Sunday on a Thursday night in one place, in another place on Friday night, and then we could take care of the other four places at the weekend.

e) Everybody says train the laity to do much of the work now done by the priest. Everybody agrees but not much is being done by non-paid staff. From much experience I know that the laity can run a parish in most things except to say Mass and administer the sacraments, if they are given the opportunity to do so. I doubt that paid staff are feasible in most cases as the income of many priests is not very high, and there are plenty of competent parishioners if they are given the chance. It is very easy to train people to do a Liturgy of the Word. I used either members of the pastoral council or eucharistic ministers. I always put them in pairs and in that way they could split the work and support one another. After going through things with them and explaining how to do things I went ahead with a practice during Sunday Mass. At the beginning of Mass I just sat down until the Offertory, and let the two people alternate on different parts up to the Offertory when I took over. In regard to the homily one of them read a homily from a book written by a Japanese bishop. There is the same kind of book here in Ireland written by the former archbishop of Tuam, Joseph Cassidy, called *These Might Help* … There is also material on the internet. I did the part of the Mass from the Offertory to the end of the Canon, and then continued in a low voice up to the time I had finished my own communion. Meanwhile the pair took over from the Our Father up to the end of Mass. Having two people working together gives them mutual support and confidence. I never found it necessary but in some parishes they had people trained to do wakes and funerals.

f) There is a need for active pastoral councils. Japan has a history of them going back to the 1880s. If they are going to be effective then they have to have power and responsibility. They were only set up in the West with the New Canon Law of 1983. In Japan and other Far East Asian countries that I am familiar with, pastoral councils are always headed by a lay person – man or woman. I have never been the head of the pastoral council and have let the pastoral council make the decisions. Very often I was late going into the meetings as they would normally be at the end of the last Mass on a Sunday morning, which would be about 10.30 a.m., and there would be people who wanted to talk to me about various things. I did try to spend as much time as I could at the meetings. In regard to money it was in my name as that was the instruction from the bishop. We had a rebuilding fund and that was completely under my control and responsibility. The financial councillors of the pastoral council paid whatever money came in for it into the account each week/month. As for the rest of the money the account was in my name in the bank, but it was the financial councillors who paid in money and took it out using a plastic card. They even paid me my wages each month, and paid the deductions from the wages to the appropriate authorities. Pastoral councils if given authority and responsibility are great but otherwise a waste of time. They have worked successfully in Japan for over a hundred years. Comparisons may be odious but the following are some things that I have learned over the years.

1. I found a four-year term worked well using a junior member (four years) and a senior member (two years). This meant that half the pastoral council carried on when new members came in. I liked to have two people with responsibility for any particular work aspect.

2. There was also a panel behind these two people to help them in their work. People were encouraged to voluntarily join one of the panels which helped the two councillors in their work, and also nominated others when members had finished their term. Councillors had to stand down for at least two years after they had finished their term.

3. Some specific functions for pastoral councils were: (i) president and vice-president who were responsible for communication in producing any kind of newsletter, chairing meetings etc. (ii) There were also two people responsible for finance. Naturally they needed other people on their panel to count money or maybe put it into a bank on a weekday and so forth. They were also responsible for the maintenance of buildings, trees etc. (iii) Another pair were the liturgical councillors who planned liturgical matters. In Japan there is normally a MC at Mass and he/she leads the celebration by announcing hymns, when to stand up or sit down and make announcements. (iv) Two more councillors to cover education of both children and adults. We would have both Saturday and Sunday schools for religious education. (v) Evangelisation would need two more and (vi) then there could be some special project in a parish that would require two more. The heads of the women's society, the men's society and the youth society were also members. Active pastoral councils are the great need for the Irish church at present but they will need priests to give up power and responsibility, and for lay people to take on that power and responsibility.

4. How does the Irish church incorporate migrants from abroad with different cultural backgrounds and different liturgical expectations? They could breathe life and energy into the church and the liturgy.

5. One thing that I find very depressing at Masses in Ireland is the lack of music and singing. Even at weddings and funerals a professional singer and musician is engaged. I would not mind what musical instrument is used at Mass. I am used to Masses in Japan that last about an hour because of the amount

of singing. If Protestant churches can get the people to sing in Ireland, why is it so rare in Catholic churches? Even recorded music would add to the atmosphere. This would be a challenge to the liturgical councillors on the pastoral council and the panel supporting them. In a fully functioning pastoral council I would consider the liturgical councillors as very important. This is probably because of my own incompetency in music matters.

6. Many priests in Ireland feel under attack and on the defensive because of clerical scandals. They need the active support and encouragement of the laity. They are lonely and isolated and need human support. Previously they were considered as knowing everything, but now they are considered to know nothing, and to be out of date in their thinking, and irrelevant to the world around them. They are under continual attack. In regard to the pae-dophile problem, the Iona Institute published an interesting survey recently, it found that because of all the adverse publicity many people thought that there were large numbers of priests involved whereas the actual number is quite small. (An American survey found, some years ago, that the number of Catholic priests involved was smaller than other professions.) Using the Mass to announce a priest is going on a leave of absence seems inappropri-ate and also makes him seem guilty, especially if a bishop appears on the scene. Should there not be an investigation beforehand to see if there is any substance to the allegation?

There is no doubt that some bishops and superiors made very poor judgements but many could be excused. They were acting on both medical and professional legal advice and some of the medical advice was unbeliev-ably bad. I have been told that in the medical field it is only about three years ago that they developed a test that would show if a person is a pae-dophile. There was ignorance on all sides. It would be very hard for a bishop or a superior in authority to go against legal and medical advice. One of the problems that I see in dealing with paedophiles is the question of whether they are sick or criminally guilty. If the former, should they be sent to prison or hospital? The church is often judged and blamed by standards of today for work that was done in the past when the standards were different, e.g. corporal punishment. Reading the newspapers about the work and failures of the HSE with its trained staff dealing with troubled youngsters, one be-comes quickly aware of the bias in the media. 196 children in state-care died between 2000 and 2010; imagine the outcry if church people were involved!

7. Various groups exist within the church, like the St Vincent de Paul, Legion of Mary, prayer groups and charismatic groups amongst others, and they need to be encouraged. It is in small groups that many people find God and his church.

Various kinds of prayer appeal to different people, and there should be something to suit the tastes of different people. Bible and study groups are good, and pilgrimages both near and far are to be encouraged. Pilgrimage is part of all the great religions. There is talk of Celtic spirituality, and that basically is folk and nature related spirituality, and it appeals to the emotions and the feelings more than to the intellect and is to be encouraged. The beauty of nature can move us to think about God, feel his presence and lead us to prayer. Prayer is both intellectual and emotional and should fill the religious needs of the whole person. Christianity took over and adapted the old folk religions of Europe and places of pilgrimage and Christianised them.

8. As somebody used to early Masses all my life I wonder if the late Masses here in Ireland really appeal to people. By the time some of the late Masses are over the day is limited for other normal activity. I do not know the answer but I think that it is a question that needs to be discussed.

9. Recently on the radio, I heard an Anglican bishop from England discussing what he called the 'eighth sacrament'. He went on to say that it was the basement of the church where people gathered for a cup of tea and fellowship after worship. We often had it in the parish hall after the last Mass on Sunday and at the back of the church on Saturday evening. Of course it is easy to come up with Japanese green tea as you do not need sugar or milk.

10. I would like to see some festivals celebrated in the church. The Protestant churches often have a harvest festival on some Sunday in the autumn. When I was young there were often 'may trees' to be seen. Could that custom be revived with something inside the church? Halloween also had a religious significance but nowadays it has turned into almost a pagan festival that is a serious worry to the emergency services and hospitals.

I write down these ideas in no particular order but I would regard active pastoral councils, with real power, as the most important factor for the future. In the pastoral council the liturgical group can be very helpful. Finally, I regard the local church as the concern of the people and for that reason I would try to use unpaid volunteers as much as possible rather than paid staff. I think that the future will depend on pastoral councils and a well educated laity. The time to establish good pastoral councils and also a well educated and confident laity is fast running out. A recent report by Archbishop Martin of Dublin about the decline of the number of priests that will be available for parish work in the archdiocese over the next few years is frightening. Even if they started studies now it would be too late.

Reflection

I think that there is much in the above points to think about and discuss. I see them as points of discussions to start a dialogue and not as definite conclusions. As Japan adapted ideas coming from abroad so also Ireland needs to adapt proposals coming from Japan or any other country. We all need a point to start at and it is in that way that I ask people to look at the situation in Ireland and come up with proposals. There will have to be big changes within five to ten years at the longest as the shortage of priests happens and is felt. *After all the church is your church.*

Homework
Continue with short daily readings from St Paul and the other epistles or go back to one of the gospels, and the gospels are great material for prayer. Another way is to take the daily readings from the Mass.

My final word is a poem by another Columban priest Fr Patrick O'Connor called:

For a City
Visit, O Lord, the city,
Mansion and street and mart,
For the walls of the city moulder,
And moulders the people's heart.

Thy Truth is told to the people,
Is told but they have not heard,
And he would be strange to the city
Who would take thy Son at his word.

Thy Friends are seen in the city,
But no one can understand;
The monk and the nun and the poor man
Are here in an alien land.

And if Francis rode from Assisi
To be Christ's Fool once more,
They would bid him go from their fine streets
To knock at the madhouse door.

Death is a word unspoken,
We turn our eyes from a tomb,
And life is a cheap piano,
Strummed in a stifling room.

Oh, blameless are we, the pious,
Never a crime is seen
Safely blameless and pious,
But O! how shallow and mean!

Nor was it the public sinner,
Whose name would taint the breath,
But the easeful ones, and the blameless,
That put the Christ to death.

To see thy wide horizons,
Who in the city strives?
The sides of a grill-room table
Are boundaries to our lives.

O visit, great God, the city-
Come with thy flaming host,
In thunder and splendid tempest,
In the winds of Pentecost.

So, hearing thy Voice majestic,
The people may turn to thee,
And, purged by thy awful lightings,
Their eyes at last may see.

Books

I am only going to suggest a few books, but there were several other books that I quoted from in the text that you might like to use.

1. You need a Bible. I use the *Jerusalem Bible* because I have always used it and I like the notes in it. It is good to have explanations and also have an overview of a particular book in the Bible. Use whichever Bible you have or like.

2. *The Catechism of the Catholic Church*. The index will enable you to look up items and it is an excellent reference book.

3. *Church: Community for the Kingdom* by Fr John Fuellenbach, SVD. Fr Fuellenbach is one of the top theologians of our time but much of what he has written is out of print. Another very good book of his is *Throw Fire* if you can get it.

4. *Sadhana: A Way to God* by Anthony de Mello SJ. It is a very good book on how to pray and meditate using the method that I introduced in the early chapters of the first book. Fr de Mello was an Indian Jesuit, and he has written many excellent books that give material for prayer. He died young on a visit to New York.

5. *Jesus of Nazareth* by Pope Benedict XVI, the first of three books. The second is now published, dealing with the last week in the life of Jesus. It is also called *Jesus of Nazareth*. The third book is due for publication in 2013.